THIS HAUNTED ISLE

The Ghosts and Legends of Britain's Historic Buildings

PETER UNDERWOOD

President of The Ghost Club (1960-1993)

For

Cathy Turner

friend and kindred spirit

with love

CONTENTS

Acknowledgments

9

Preface

11

Geographical Index

15

This Haunted Isle (A-Z)

19

ACKNOWLEDGMENTS

The author gratefully acknowledges the encouragement and help that he has received from Andrew Hewson of John Johnson: Authors' Agents and also the generous co-operation of the directors, administrators, custodians, tenants and occupants of the properties included. He is also deeply grateful for all the help he has received from many other people and would like to especially mention: Geoffrey Abbott, Mrs Margaret Bagueley, Dennis Bardens, the Duke and Duchess of Bedford, Major R.J.G. Berkeley, Michael Bingham, Sir Reginald Blacker, Hector Bolitho, Michael Brett, Ninian Brodie of Brodie, Tony Broughall, E.W. 'Teddy' Butler, Lord Croft, Tom Corbett, James Wentworth Day, Philomena, Lady de Hoghton, Mrs A.H. Evans, Lady Jean Fforde, Leslie Finch, Michael Garside, Godfrey Goolden, Affleck Gray, G. Howard Heaton, Dr Peter Hilton-Rowe, John Howden, Air Commodore R.C. Jonas, Freda and Steuart Kiernander, Fred Knowles, Laurie Lee, Dame Flora MacLeod of MacLeod, Angus Macnaghten, Eric Maple, Harry Martindale, Denis Mead, John Mitchell, Major and Mrs James More-Molyneux, Major W.D. Morris-Barker, Patricia Moxey, David F. Musson, Carey Newson, Bob Parsons, Grace and Arthur Peters, Donald Ross, Brian Rowland, Margaret Royal and Abson Books, Adrian Sansom, Cecilia, Lady Sempill, Mrs Ann Strickland, Lord St Leven, Lord Strathmore, Denys Sutton, John and Pauline Thompson, Mrs Diana Uhlman, Andrew Usher, Dr David Walker, Michael Williams and Alistair J. Wilson.

To his wife, Joyce Elizabeth, who has accompanied him on his journeys to these haunted properties, he acknowledges not only much understanding and help in many ways but also recognition and gratitude for having the idea for this book in the first place.

PREFACE

The subject of this book is ghosts: ghosts that have been seen, heard, felt or sensed in historic properties and places in Britain. Ghosts?

They are no longer creatures of the darkness that strike terror into the hearts of those who see them; rather they are gentle shades who return for a variety of reasons, to a variety of places, at a variety of times, and are seen by a variety of people and affect those who see them in a variety of ways. Ghosts have become respectable.

My intention is not to add a sensational element to any of the houses or places included in this book but simply to present in a sober manner some of the legends, ghostly experiences and little-known facts concerning some of the most beautiful and interesting houses in the land.

I have collected the facts carefully and then attempted to sort the wheat from the chaff. It should be emphasized that the accounts included are stories that are or have been associated with these properties; it is not suggested that all these places are still haunted, although some of them certainly are and perhaps most of them to people who are sensitive to such things.

It is an interesting fact that some people can live for years in a haunted house without seeing or hearing or sensing anything unusual; my own grandmother lived for years in a house well known to be haunted, where many people had reportedly seen the ghost of a man in one bedroom and where it became so troublesome at one period that attempts were made to exorcise it; yet my grandmother always said she had never seen anything there — worse than herself!

It may be that just as some people seem to promote the presence of ghosts, others may actually prevent their activities; the personality and interest and sympathy of the occupants of the haunted houses may well play a considerable part in the appearance or non-appearance of ghosts.

In a few instances I have been unable to include names and dates for particular incidents. This is due to respect for personal wishes, but all the names, dates and details that are included are factual and I have attempted to specify precisely where the ghosts have reportedly walked.

Of necessity the evidential value varies; occasionally a first-hand account is available, at other times it is second- or third-hand; sometimes it is only hearsay or legend but I have found all the people, the places and the stories interesting. I hope these accounts may even prove to be important, for subsequent discoveries and experiences have sometimes had a definite effect or bearing on the history and appearance of a ghost — as you will see.

If you are interested in other aspects of the historic properties of Britain — the furniture, the gardens, the pictures, the architecture — there are books dealing with all of them. This volume deals with the reported ghosts and I hope it will bring a new and absorbing interest to visitors to these places that are our national heritage, as are our ghosts.

We have not yet discovered a way to prove the existence of ghosts; therefore it is not a subject that one can be erudite about, such as architecture or history, for so much depends upon human testimony.

Nevertheless the wealth of varied testimony for ghosts in Britain's historic properties cannot but be impressive to any impartial reader. Needless to say I am always glad to hear of any ghost that may be encountered as visitors wander through these wonderful, lovingly cared for houses, castles and mansions where the atmosphere and environment of these unique properties can sometimes take us back in time.

Peter Underwood
The Savage Club
London
May, 1984

Geographical Index

(Each individual entry can be found alphabetically)

ENGLAND
Avon
Assembly Rooms, Bath
Horton Court, Chipping Sodbury
Leigh Woods, Bristol
Bedfordshire
Woburn Abbey, Woburn
Berkshire
Windsor Castle, Windsor
Buckinghamshire
Claydon House, Middle Claydon
Hughenden Manor, High Wycombe
West Wycombe
Cambridgeshire
Abbey House, Cambridge
Wicken Fen
Cheshire
Alderley Edge
Gawsworth Hall, Gawsworth, Macclesfield
Lyme Park
Tatton Park, near Knutsford
Cornwall
Antony House, Torpoint
Bedruthan
Cotehele, Calstock
Lanhydrock House, Bodmin
Pengersick Castle, Praa Sands
St. Michael's Mount
Tintagel
Trerice, Newquay
Zennor
Cumbria
Burnmoor Tarn, Eskdale
Cartmel Priory Gatehouse, Cartmel
Sizergh Castle, Kendal
Windermere

Derbyshire
Hardwick Hall, near Mansfield
The Winnats, Castleton
Devonshire
Buckland Abbey, near Tavistock
Lydford Gorge
Shute Barton, near Axminster
Dorset
Clouds Hill, near Bovington
Corfe Castle, Purbeck
Essex
Rainham Hall, Rainham
Ray Island
Gloucestershire
Berkeley Castle, Berkeley
Newark Park, Wotton-under-Edge
Snowshill Manor, near Broadway
Hampshire
Bramshill House, near Hartley Wintney
Selborne
Hereford and Worcester
Berrington Hall, Leominster
Croft Castle, near Leominster
Harvington Hall, near Kidderminster
Hertfordshire
Shaw's Corner, Ayot St Lawrence
Kent
Chartwell, near Westerham
Ightham Mote, Ightham, Sevenoaks
Leeds Castle, near Maidstone
Old Soar Manor, near Borough Green
Scotney Castle, Lamberhurst
Sissinghurst Castle, Sissinghurst
Lancashire
Chingle Hall, Goosnargh, Preston
Hoghton Tower, Hoghton, Preston
Rufford Hall, near Ormskirk
Lincolnshire
Gunby Hall, Burgh-le-Marsh
Greater London
Ham House, Petersham

Hampton Court Palace, Hampton Court
Osterley Park, Osterley
The Tower of London
Merseyside
Formby Coast
Speke Hall, Liverpool
Norfolk
Blickling Hall, Aylsham
Felbrigg Hall, Felbrigg, Norwich
Horsey Mere
Northumberland
Bellister Castle, Haltwhistle
Dunstanburgh Castle, Alnwick
Lindisfarne Castle, Holy Island
Wallington Hall, Cambo
Somerset
King John's Hunting Lodge, Axbridge
Priest's House, Muchelney
Suffolk
Dunwich Heath, Dunwich
Thorington Hall, Stoke-by-Nayland
Surrey
Clandon Park, West Clandon
Loseley House, near Godalming, Guildford
Polesden Lacey, Bookham
Sussex, East
Bateman's Burwash
Bodiam Castle
Sussex, West
Bramber Castle, Steyning
Uppark, South Harting
Tyne and Wear
Washington Old Hall, Washington
Warwickshire
Baddesley Clinton, Knowle, Solihull
Charlecote Park, Stratford-upon-Avon
Coughton Court, Alcester
Wiltshire
Cley Hill, Warminster
Lacock Abbey, near Chippenham
Stourhead, Stourton, Mere

Westwood Manor, Bradford-upon-Avon
Yorkshire, North
Treasurer's House, York
Yorkshire, West
East Riddlesden Hall, Keighley

NORTHERN IRELAND
Co. Londonderry
Springhill, Moneymore

SCOTLAND
Grampian
Brodie Castle, Forres, Morayshire
Craigievar Castle, Lumphanan, Aberdeenshire
Crathes Castle, Crathes, Kincardine
Leith Hall, by Kennethmont, Aberdeenshire
Highland
Ben MacDhui, The Cairngorms
Culloden, east of Inverness
Dunvegan Castle, Sligachan, Isle of Skye
Lothian
House of the Binns, Linlithgow
Strathclyde
Brodick Castle, Isle of Arran
Culzean Castle, Maybole, Ayrshire
Inveraray Castle, Inveraray, Argyllshire
Tayside
Glamis Castle, Glamis, Angus
Pass of Killiecrankie, Pitlochry, Perthshire

WALES
Dyfed
Ramsey Island, off St David's Head
Powys
Powis Castle, Welshpool

A

Abbey House, Cambridge, Cambridgeshire

It was at a Ghost Club dinner, years ago now, that Jimmy Wentworth Day, that renowned raconteur, author and collector of ghostly happenings, first told me about the many ghosts at the old Abbey House in Barnwell, a place he referred to as 'the most haunted house in all England'.

Perceiving the scepticism on my face he reeled off the reported manifestations: a ghostly squire, a grey lady, a phantom squirrel, a spectral hare, a disembodied head, a clanking chain and a poltergeist of preternatural strength...and I understandably sank back in my chair to hear more.

The Abbey House, in Abbey Road off the Newmarket Road, was built about 1580 from the remnants of Barnwell Priory, established in 1112 by Pain Peverel to house thirty Augustinian canons. Said to have had a church 200 feet long, the priory profoundly influenced life in Cambridgeshire during the Middle Ages. A house of Benedictine nuns was established in what is now Jesus Lane and the nuns of St Radegund built a large church which serves in part as the beautiful chapel of Jesus College. Barnwell Priory, the oldest and most wealthy of the religious houses in Cambridge, surrendered to the University and the King in 1538 when the houses of the friars were dissolved.

In 1714 Jacob 'Squire' Butler, a famous Cambridge character, inherited the abbey estate. Six feet four inches tall, a graduate who became a barrister and who engaged in numerous lawsuits, he called himself Old Briton' in his old age because of his many strenuous fights for what he considered to be his rights. Once, in an attempt to re-establish the ancient custom that decreed that anything still standing on the age-old fairground on 24 August could be trampled down by stall-holders and that booths not cleared away by Michaelmas Day could be demolished, he drove his carriage through piles of crockery. Among his other eccentricities, long before his death at the age of eighty-four in 1765, 'Squire' Butler had an enormous oak coffin made for himself, and at his funeral this coffin was lowered into a vault and a smaller, leaded coffin, containing his body, placed inside it. But all this does not seem to have prevented his ghost from walking.

Some years ago there were repeated reports of the appearance of the unmistakable form of 'Squire' Butler, who died in the house. Those who encountered the tall, fierce-looking figure, I learned from Jimmy Wentworth Day, always mentioned the dark-green wool coat with gold-braid edges, and from independent and separate but corroborating reports a picture has emerged of a lanky, overbearing figure in the green thigh-length coat with gold buttons and heavy cuffs, a satin embroidered waistcoat, green wool breeches and black leather shoes with metal buckles. On his head he wore a black felt tricorn hat with gold-braid edge and he sported a long, thin cane walking-stick. Such a figure was apparently encountered many times within the old gabled house he knew so well.

The grey lady ghost, sometimes referred to as a lady in a grey cloak, is believed to have been one of the nuns of St Radegund who came to the abbey to meet her lover, an Austin friar. Her ghost, a hesitant figure, was usually seen in the area of the tall iron gates set in the grey stone wall and on the age-old path at the back of the house, amid the mouldering stones of the vanished abbey. She was reportedly seen once in 1968 and twice in 1969.

The ghostly white lady may have a similar provenance; possibly her presence within the present part timber and part brick house stems from some long-forgotten errand of mercy or act of charity, for most often the white lady ghost used to be seen in one of the bedrooms. A typical example of the reported appearance of this presence has been provided by the children of Dr Grey of Emmanuel College who complained, after the clergy had exorcised the house, that they were no longer tucked-up in bed by the kind lady'.

Either or both of these poor ladies may have come to the house by means of an underground tunnel, from the old nunnery of St Radegund, now Jesus College, to meet with a monk who was also a lover of the ladies. Some evidence for such a tunnel is provided by the presence of a bricked-up archway in the cellar of the present house. It is said that at one time such a clandestine scheme was discovered and that the erring nun was walled-up alive — 'small wonder she haunts the place', Jimmy Wentworth Day added.

The phantom squirrel and the spectral hare have, it seems, been seen on the lawn at the front of the house; the squirrel, a red one, now extinct in Cambridgeshire, runs along the grey wall and drops to the ground. It always disappears when the person who sees it approaches and thinks that there is no escape for the handsome and seemingly well-fed animal. The hare, a large one with floppy ears, is also seen in the garden, often when snow is on the ground, and it sits watching whoever sees it and then suddenly it is no longer there, and there are no traces of any animal on the snow. No one has ever suggested why these ghostly animals appear at certain places but perhaps they are some kind of atmospheric photograph that recurs under certain climatic conditions and disappears when conditions alter by the close presence of a human being; who can tell?

The disembodied head and the eerie sound of a clanking chain are among the many manifestations reported some years ago. Professor FJ.M. Stratton, president of the Society for

Psychical Research from 1953 to 1955, rented the Abbey House for a month and invited there many people who, like himself, took ghosts seriously: a former Colonel of the Royal Engineers, with the D.S.O. and Legion of Honour to his credit, who was also a Deputy-Lieutenant of the County of Cambridgeshire, Director of the Solar Physics Observatory, former President of Caius College and a Fellow of the Royal Society. If he took the hauntings seriously, which he certainly did, as Jimmy Wentworth Day put it, you may be sure there was something in them.'

I also talked with Professor Stratton at an SPR gathering about the ghosts at Abbey House. The disturbances he and some of his guests experienced may have been less spectacular, but they were none the less inexplicable, and he told me of one incident when curious noises, including the sounds of muttering and singing, emanated from an empty room.

In 1968 Mr Young lived with his daughter in the largest part of the Abbey House and he told Jimmy Wentworth Day that when his daughter, a level-headed young lady in the County Health Service, came to the house, some eight years earlier, 'the place was undoubtedly haunted'. She heard strange noises, night after night; sensed unseen presences repeatedly and, perhaps what is even more significant, her dog would suddenly take to rushing to one corner of a panelled room, its hair on end, and bark furiously — for no apparent reason. 'Dogs', said Jimmy, 'I always regard as good witnesses.'

Mr Young said that the previous tenant had been a lady and she also saw and felt some very frightening presences. She was glad to leave the place.

Earlier still, in the 1920s, the occupant had been old Mr Ascham, a descendant of Roger Ascham, and he had welcomed

Jimmy Wentworth Day and half-a-dozen undergraduate friends to the house, regaled them with stories of his many weird and frightening experiences and allowed them to sit up one night in the old house, all by themselves. It was his wife who had been terrified almost out of her wits by the sudden and ghastly appearance at chest-level of the apparition of a woman's head. Deathly white, without any body or arms or legs, it hovered in mid-air at the foot of her bed. Once — well you might put such an experience down to a dream or hallucination, but Mrs Ascham saw the awful form on three occasions, always in the same room but in different positions; and even in mid-afternoon as she entered the bedroom to fetch something. The form always hovered for a few moments, swaying slightly, backwards and forwards and from side to side, as though it found difficulty in remaining in one position and then, with a curious dip that always caught Mrs Ascham by surprise, the frightful appearance disappeared.

Before the Aschams moved into the house, I was told, the two previous tenants both left the place in a great hurry, one of them at two o'clock in the morning. Neither ever returned to the haunted house.

More recently poltergeist-like phenomena were reported, with various occupants and visitors complaining of indistinct forms or presences moving about their bedrooms at night in the dark, of sheets and bedclothes being suddenly twitched off the beds, and of groans and raps and rustling noises that had no rational explanation and the undoubted movement of very heavy furniture. After three local clergymen visited the house and exorcised the place with holy water and prayers, most of the uninvited and unwelcome guests seemed to depart but still, especially when the autumn afternoons draw in and the shadows lengthen around the long front of the house, an odd shadow or movement is noticed somewhere within or outside this lovable, warm old house, and the heart of a watcher skips a beat. Are some of the ghosts of yesteryear returning again to their old haunts?

Alderley Edge, Cheshire

Some of the finest views in the whole of the county can be found looking down on the Cheshire plain from the Edge, once the site of a Neolithic settlement and of prehistoric copper-mining. It is a beautiful and peaceful place; but some visitors have found it vaguely disturbing and it may be that on rare occasions there is something here that cannot easily be explained.

There was the little girl who ran back to her parents with a story about a little man with a long beard and no clothes...a tale that may have had a perfectly logical explanation were it not for a couple who were lazily and quietly enjoying each other's company one balmy summer day when they both saw a similar figure emerge from the trees, pass close to where they lay and then suddenly disappear in front of their eyes.

There is the evidence too of a retired police officer and his wife who were having a picnic and became aware that they were being watched from some nearby bushes. With long years of police training behind him, the man idly got up off the ground and slowly walked away in the opposite direction and then circled round to come up behind the watcher or watchers. Sure enough he saw a short, long-haired man who appeared from the back to be naked. As he quietly approached the still figure, he suddenly found himself completely alone.

One moment the figure was a few yards in front of him, the next it had completely disappeared. For all his professional experience and keen policeman's eye, he was completely baffled as to any possible explanation. He and his wife now choose other picnic sites. A friend of mine who is psychic says there is an expectant atmosphere at Alderley Edge and she believes that, very occasionally, when all the necessary ingredients are present, it is possible for some people to see some of the inhabitants of this area who lived here long, long ago.

There is also a tradition that a pagan burial mound exists in the vicinity and that Alderley Edge is one of the places where the ghosts of King Arthur and his Knights have been seen.

Certainly Alderley Edge and its surrounding area has occult associations going back for centuries like that great cliff, Pendle Hill, where modem witchcraft practices have been reported At Alderley Edge a famous wizard is commemorated in the name of a local inn and in the inscription beside a well at the base of the sandstone outcrop:

*Drink of this and take thy fill
For the water falls by the wizard's will.*

The well water was renowned for promoting fertility and those who study such matters say a number of ley lines intersect here.

The story of a wizard and legends of King Arthur intermingle in an age-old story that is to be found at several places traditionally associated with the Arthurian legend. Here it is said that one day, 300 or more years ago, a farmer sold a white horse to a bearded stranger who conducted him through the woods to a large rock face which opened to reveal King Arthur and his Knights and their white steeds, all sleeping until the day that England would need them again. They were short of one horse and the farmer took the purse of gold, left the animal in exchange, and made a hasty escape, the cliff closing magically behind him.

An equally unlikely story tells of an enormous mere that once stretched from Alderley Edge to High Legh and of a mermaid who was repeatedly seen, left high and dry by the vanished waters; but oddly and inexplicably she only seems to have been seen at Easter-time.

Antony House, Torpoint, Cornwall

There are many mysteries at this grand and unaltered Queen Anne property. For a start no record has ever been found of the architect who designed the present house, erected in 1721. It is certain that the Carew family came to Antony much earlier, probably in the fifteenth century, but of that house and the tidal 'fishful' pond, why is there no trace? Sir Alexander Carew was hanged in December 1644, and his speech from the scaffold reveals a troubled mind; he wished for death. What is the story behind his portrait from the cellars being re-stitched into its frame? Perhaps the portrait was cut from the frame when the family were ardent Royalists and Alexander Carew supported Parliament, and when he died his family's sympathies were again with him and his portrait was re-stitched into the frame — who can say? The church that William Henry Pole-Carew built to commemorate the birth of his son (who laid the foundation stone when he was sixteen) was duly dedicated but it was never fully consecrated. Was the artist Edward Bower, whose portrait of Charles I dominates the Hall, a Westcountryman, a pupil of Van Dyck, and why would John Carew, one of the judges at the King's trial, have such a portrait prominently displayed in the house? What is the story behind the picture known as The Horse Thief and who was the artist? And, quite apart from such prosaic mysteries, there are the ghost stories.

One of the strangest of all ghost narratives is told of Antony House, for the ghost was that of a living person. In October 1880 Lady Helen Waldegrave visited Antony House taking with her Helen Alexander, her reserved Scottish maid. The shy girl did not go out of her way to make friends with the servants of the house, although she did mention to one or two of them that she had a sister to whom she would be writing while she and her mistress were in Cornwall. She does not appear to have mentioned the fact that her mother and father were also alive.

A few days after arriving at Antony House, Helen Alexander was taken ill. She quickly grew worse and a doctor diagnosed typhoid fever. A trained nurse was sought, and until one was found one of the housemaids, Frances Reddel, was detailed to look after the patient.

An unemotional and stolid girl, in no way imaginative or subject to nervous excitement, Frances was not in the least perturbed when, the patient seeming to go from bad to worse, she was asked to remain on duty at night. All was quiet and entirely normal in the bedroom where the patient was sleeping fitfully until four o'clock in the morning, when just as Frances Reddel was preparing a dose of medicine, due at that time for the sick girl, she heard a bell sound in the passage outside. Frances had noticed the same sound a few times previously followed by complete silence, and she assumed that the bell wires had become tangled.

Frances therefore continued with the preparation of medicine for her patient and was very surprised when an elderly and stout lady entered the bedroom without any preliminary knock. Even more surprising to the puzzled Frances was the fact that the woman was dressed in a long, red nightgown over a red flannel petticoat and she carried an unusually ornate brass candlestick.

The observant maidservant even noticed, with some disapproval, a definite hole in the petticoat, apparently caused by stay busks. She was not in any way alarmed by the unexpected appearance of the figure, only momentarily surprised; and then she reasoned Helen Alexander's mother must have been sent for and had hurried to be by her daughter's side.

Imposing Antony House in Cornwall - where Frances Reddell was surprised by a figure in red.

[Image previously spread across two pages]

She remained quietly observing the visitor for some moments. The rather odd figure crossed the room without speaking or even looking anywhere but straight ahead, and stopped when she reached the bedside of the sick girl. At this point Frances turned to resume her preparation of the medicine and when she turned back towards her patient she was amazed to see no trace of the visitor who, only seconds before, had crossed the room. In the two or three seconds that Frances' back had been turned it was obviously quite impossible for anyone to have turned, re-crossed the room and left; yet of the elderly woman she had so clearly seen, there was now no sign whatever.

What was obvious was the deterioration of the patient's condition. She had worsened considerably and the doctor was hurriedly called but to no avail; Helen Alexander was dead within two hours.

Two days later the dead girl's family arrived at Antony House from Scotland. When Frances Reddel saw Helen's mother she nearly fainted. In every physical respect this stout, elderly, motherly figure exactly resembled the 'apparition' she had seen the night Helen had died!

For a few days the incident was not mentioned to the grieving family but after the funeral the whole story was told to the dead girl's sister. She immediately revealed that her mother did possess a nightgown and a red flannel petticoat exactly as the bewildered Frances Reddel described them; furthermore the petticoat had a hole where the busks of her stays had worn through — as Frances had mentioned.

When asked about the unusually designed candlestick which Frances said had been carried by the figure she had seen, the puzzled girl mentioned a brass candlestick that her mother used. It was exactly as Frances described, even down to a small dent that she had noticed.

There was yet one more strange detail in this very strange story. Helen had persistently refused to write home about her illness, insisting that she would soon be well again and she did not want to worry her family. Yet, the evening before Helen died, her mother had suddenly remarked to her husband: 'I'm worried about Helen. I have a feeling that she is very ill.'

One theory advanced in an attempt to explain this remarkable psychic puzzle — and it should be noted that from what is known of the participants there is no reason to doubt the integrity of any of them — is that what Frances saw was a figure projected from the mind of the dying Helen. Yet, plausible as that may be, is it reasonable to assume that quiet and unimaginative Frances Reddel, described by all who knew her as completely down-to-earth, matter-of-fact and without any imagination and never given to flights of fancy, would be likely to pick up a thought or vision projected by a dying girl? It seems the only possible explanation.

There are several versions of what is, in essence, the same story. In 1982 the Administrator at Antony House, Mrs P.D. Isaac, told me that the apparition or thought-form was seen by Sir John Carew Pole's grandmother who entered the room of the dying girl and saw, sitting by the bedside, a little old lady with a finger to her lips, indicating silence. Some hours later a carriage arrived at the House bearing the said old lady, mother of the, by then, dead girl.'

When my old friend John Butler, Baker Street dentist and former amateur boxer, visited south Cornwall with a companion, they explored the lovely countryside west of Plymouth and came across an impressive house which they entered and explored with interest but without any guide book. In particular John always remembered the enormous stairway, which may have grown in his memory over the years, but he said it seemed so big that it might have taken five or six people abreast. They climbed the staircase, completely at ease and then suddenly, almost at the top, John came to a sudden stop and said he could not go on. He saw nothing but felt an overwhelming compulsion not to continue and not to explore the rooms upstairs. The feeling was so strong that he turned back and never did see the upper part of the house. Such an experience was quite alien to John Butler, a Master Mason, property owner and confidant of Special Branch officers, and it was an experience that he never forgot.

Once downstairs and outside he and his friend had tea and found the outside of Antony House and the garden utterly charming, but nothing would induce him to climb the staircase there again.

Years afterwards John Butler's secretary-cum-dental nurse acquired a history of Antony House and there discovered that some of the former inhabitants of the house had been named Butler. (In 1901 Reginald Pole-Carew married Lady Beatrice Butler, daughter of the third Marquess of Ormonde.) What had happened, perhaps to someone with the surname of Butler, that so affected my friend? It is one more mystery associated with Antony House.

Assembly Rooms, Bath, Avon

Bath, Aquae Sulis, so named from the British goddess of the waters, Sol a Sulis, has many ghosts, but unquestionably the best-documented ghost in Bath — perhaps in the county — is the 'Man in the Black Hat', whose spectral form has been repeatedly seen in the vicinity of the Assembly Rooms. These Rooms were built in 1771 by John Wood the younger but gutted by German fire bombs in 1942 and subsequently restored. Even the bombs could not destroy the mysterious 'Man in the Black Hat', it seems, for judging from his apparel, he would seem to date from about the time the Assembly Rooms were erected, possibly earlier.

In 1981 a party of Ghost Club members spent a day at Bath, where they sought out the haunted places and walked where ghosts have walked, under the benevolent guidance of Margaret Royal, a city guide who is a mine of information on the subject of ghosts in Bath and the surrounding area. She is the co-author of three collections of local ghost sightings.

Witnesses for the ghostly Man in a Black Hat go back many years and there are references to the unidentified figure in private documents of the eighteenth and nineteenth centuries; but one of the best descriptions comes from Mrs Cynthia Montefiore who saw the figure in 1950, a fact that was reported in the Bath and Wilts Evening Chronicle dated 16 March 1950.

During the course of her account of the experience Mrs Montefiore wrote: 'I was walking from Portland Place to George Street. When I reached the end of Saville Row a man approached me from the comer of Evans and Owens store. He wore a large black hat, rather resembling the old-fashioned Quaker hat. He crossed the road noiselessly and came abreast of me as I gained the end of Saville Row. There was no one else in sight and then I suddenly had the feeling that the person I was facing was odd and unearthly. I had that peculiar sinking feeling in the stomach, but I definitely did not feel frightened. I am much too interested in the occult to be afraid.

'As I passed I turned round: I turned immediately. I just had to. I wanted to see his back. But he had vanished completely. He certainly had no time to enter a doorway, as not two seconds had passed from the time he passed until I looked back. I had a distinct view of him. He was small, thin and walked with a stoop.'

The Assembly Rooms in Bath - where the 'Man in the Black Hat' has frequently been seen.

Mrs Montefiore provided a sketch of the figure she saw. This is one of the four sketches available that have been made independently by four different eyewitnesses who are all complete strangers to each other but have all seen the Man in the Black Hat. The other three were all sightings of the ghost in 1972 and were provided by three residents of Bath: Mrs Harrison, Mrs Jill Dixon and 'W.E.G.'. All depict a slightly stooping figure and the predominant feature in each case is a large black hat.

In May 1974, Mrs Eileen Parrish of Elderley, Wotton-under-Edge, wrote to say she too had seen the 'Man in the Black Hat'. She stated: 'I was trying to park my car opposite Evans and Owens and he came down Saville Row, stepped into the road, hesitated, turned back and began to walk towards the front of the Assembly Rooms.

'I took my eyes off him for a moment and when I looked again he had vanished although he could not possibly have got to the end of the road. He was dressed very much like Guy Fawkes and, as he turned, his black cloak swirled around him. He seemed to have black breeches and gaiters on. I must admit that I never thought of him as being a ghost, which is strange, as I have had many ghostly experiences in Africa where I normally live and I can always tell if a place is haunted.'

The same figure has been seen in different parts of the interior of the Assembly Rooms and one report comes from a particularly reliable witness, former Regimental Sergeant-Major Emmett, who was Caretaker at the building for many years. One day he was stoking the boiler in the boiler-room when he sensed that he was being watched. He turned at once and in the doorway stood a figure in a cloak and black hat. As he stared, astonished at the presence of such a person in the boiler-room, the figure slowly disappeared.

Among other witnesses for the ghostly Man in a Black Hat there is the woman who was standing near the Assembly Rooms watching a film being made when she noticed an oddly dressed man standing beside her. There was something unpleasant about the dark figure wearing a black hat and she suddenly felt very upset — and then suddenly, there was nobody standing beside her.

The original Assembly Rooms, an important part of Bath at its most fashionable period, is mentioned in Charles Dickens's Pickwick Papers and several times in the works of Jane Austen. It is interesting to speculate on the possibility that these literary giants and sensitive writers may have been aware of the psychic atmosphere of Bath's Assembly Rooms.

B

Baddesley Clinton, Knowle, Solihull, Warwickshire

Parts of this medieval moated manor house date back to 1300 and it is little changed since 1634. Baddesley Clinton, a gem of beauty set in perfect surroundings, has long held many grim secrets within its stone walls. Here there are clever improvisations to cope with ancient emergencies, including provision for spanning the moat other than by the drawbridge, several secret passages and hiding-places, and a 'devilish contrivance' for pitching unwanted visitors into the deep waters of the silent moat.

The house was probably built by one of the Catesbys and it passed from that family to one John Brome, a lawyer who flourished in the reign of Henry VI. Brome was killed in London in a dispute with a man named Herthill over a mortgage; a death that was avenged by Brome's son, Nicholas, three years later when he waylaid Herthill and attacked him so fiercely that he later died. Nicholas Brome was required to do penance for this act and he did that which was required of him. But his troubles were not over, for on his return home unexpectedly one day in 1485, he discovered his domestic chaplain in compromising circumstances with his wife and, being a man of hasty temper, Brome slew the priest on the spot; and so he was in serious trouble with the Church yet again. This time, by way of expiation, he had to embellish the parish church at Baddesley Clinton and erect a new steeple for the church at Packwood.

Nicholas Brome died in 1517, a man weary of this life, but whether it is his ghost or that of the priest he murdered — or possibly both — that haunts the old manor house is not known; but the haunting was sufficiently well authenticated at one time, or sufficiently well-known, to be included in Charles Harper's classic work on haunted houses, published in 1907.

There have been a number of reported manifestations in the house that support the idea that the place is indeed haunted; stories of the sound of muttered argument and disagreement between several men, emanating from an empty room; shadowy and silent forms in passages and rooms that are patently devoid of any human being; footsteps, stealthy and quick on occasions and at other times heavy and leisured, have been repeatedly heard from many deserted parts of this house where, tradition has it, Guy Fawkes once lived; and there has been unexplained movement of physical objects. On one occasion, at least, the atmosphere here has been completely overwhelming: one lady was so 'oppressed by the atmosphere' in the library that immediately she had to leave that room — a room that has long been known as the Ghost Room.

Nicholas Brome was the last of his line and the house passed to the Ferrers family who lived at Baddesley Clinton, generation succeeding generation, until it came into the possession of the National Trust a few years ago. Many strange incidents seem to have taken place here about a century ago and a diary, kept by a member of the Ferrers family, details some of these happenings and included signed statements by the percipients, as Meg Elizabeth Atkins recounts in her Haunted Warwickshire (1981).

There is the incident in 1884 when a lady visitor, sleeping in the Tapestry Room, woke suddenly and saw the figure of a fair-haired woman, dressed in black, glide past her bed and vanish through a closed door. Three years later this same lady visited Baddesley Clinton again and this time occupied the State Room. Again she had a disturbed night, finding herself suddenly awake and this time she saw the ghostly figure more clearly since the room was flooded with moonlight. She was certain that it was the same form she had seen in the Tapestry Room, for the overall appearance, hair and style of dress, were the same. The form was standing beside the writing desk in the room and she was facing the bed. Her features, the visitor thought, had a definite resemblance to those of the Ferrers family. After a moment the figure disappeared.

Other people also saw this figure, both employees and guests, and it seems that she always appeared in the upper part of the house, usually inside a bedroom but occasionally in one of the corridors. Once a visiting clergyman entered his room and found the ghost sitting in a chair; a moment later she was no longer there.

Major Thomas Ferrers died in an accident abroad, and seventy years after his death his ghost was seen and recognized from a portrait by a guest. On a second visit she saw him again, seemingly surrounded by a gilt frame — almost like a picture — and the whole appearance was superimposed on one of the pictures hanging in the room. A similar ghostly experience was reported some years later in the Blue Room by a visitor who had no knowledge of the history of the house or its reputed ghosts. An exorcism seems to have laid the ghost of Major Ferrers.

In the early 1900s yet another guest, Miss Henrietta Knight, spent an eventful and frightening night at Baddesley Clinton. She was awakened by the sound of footsteps on the staircase outside her room, footsteps that were of such variety and volume that she judged there must be at least four or five people involved. When these sounds ceased they were replaced by a rapping sound that seemed to emanate from the walls and flooring of the room; then she heard the noise of cloth being tom and finally the sound of breathing that seemed to be very close beside her. Again a service of exorcism was held at Baddesley Clinton.

The present Administrator has told me about two incidents and supplied me with the names and addresses of the people concerned. Some forty years ago the ghost of a priest was reportedly seen celebrating Mass in the chapel. This form was also seen to remove vestments or something from a box and deposit whatever it was on top of a box in the sacristy. No reason or historical fact has ever been discovered for this curious ghostly performance, but perhaps it has something to do with the murdered chaplain for he does seem to have left behind some psychic influence that is evident from the second incident. This concerned a visitor who was about to enter the solar but discovered that he was unable to do so because of an overwhelming feeling of an unseen presence in the immediate vicinity. This visitor was completely unaware of the murder here in 1485.

There is also a ghost story associated with the Red Room at Baddesley Clinton. This concerns a member of the family who owned the house at the time of Waterloo. He was a soldier, and being killed in battle apparently did not receive Christian burial and, perhaps for that reason, his ghost has appeared, I am reliably informed, on more than one occasion, to people sleeping in the Red Room. Following a special Mass, 'after entreating the Pope, his soul was comforted and he did not appear again'.

Mr G. Howard Heaton tells me that fifty years ago when he was a young man he spent a good deal of time at Baddesley and in those days the house was occasionally opened in aid of the Red Cross. He continues: 'I, who knew the place well, acted as guide to parties of the visiting public and on several occasions when we passed out of the chapel into the small closet adjoining, we would find a set of priests' vestments lying on the floor, as if they had been cast off in a hurry. Once, when I mentioned this to the then owner (this was before the property passed to the National Trust), she told me she had had a similar experience and added that she had been into the room in question that morning when everything had been in order. These vestments were kept in a large bow-fronted chest of drawers in the room, so that they could lie unfolded. The theory is that in the days of the persecution of the Catholics, if a priest was celebrating Mass when government troops or officials arrived, he would leave as quickly as possible: and in such a case of urgency he would discard his vestments and use a ladder in the passage under the room, leading to the passage on the ground floor and then he would flee across the moat through the secret opening in the wall. These passages are still open, I believe, and I have been inside them all in those far-off days.'

Bateman's, Burwash, East Sussex

This seventeenth-century house was the home of Rudyard Kipling from 1902 until his death in 1936. The great writer was always aware of the paranormal and indeed he had a psychic sister, Mrs Holland, who received many messages, through automatic writing, that seemed to emanate from the dead; messages that many people consider far more intelligent and thoughtful than the majority of such scripts. Some of the rooms at Bateman's, including the study, remain exactly as they were during Kipling's lifetime. He designed the garden that leads down to the mill on the Dudwell and it seems likely that reports of the house being quietly haunted by the presence of Kipling may well be true, especially his study and his garden. Antony Hippisley Coxe tells me that the house is haunted by the ghost of Kipling and that his ghost and that of his wife have been seen in the garden.

The whole place is full of atmosphere and it is easy to imagine Kipling's presence in many parts of the house and garden; where the Dudwell stream flows, for example, is the setting for the Puck of Pook's Hill stories and Rewards and Fairies, both books full of a strange enchantment.

In 1975 some members of the Ghost CLub visited Bateman's and John Harvey, a long-standing and practical member who did not usually see or experience anything of a psychic nature, encountered the unmistakable figure of the supreme story-teller and master of magic atmosphere, standing by his desk in the study, apparently looking out of the window.

As John Harvey stood quietly in the doorway, taking in the seemingly solid and vigorous figure who had often talked about 'inherited continuity', another member came along and attempted to pass into the room. John Harvey turned to point out the figure of the Nobel Prize winner who had always been so deeply interested in what he called 'haunted landscapes', and when he turned back the figure had completely disappeared and the room was empty.

Invisible 'presences' have also been experienced at Bateman's, both by official guides and by visitors. One witness described to me the unmistakable feeling of the presence of someone with 'enormous enthusiasm and energy' in various parts of the house but especially in the study at dusk; and I

Rudyard Kipling, whose presence has often been sensed at Bateman's, the house where he lived for over thirty years.

treasure the enigmatic sentence contained in a letter to me by the Administrator in 1975, to whom I had written on a mundane matter and then had casually asked about any ghosts. The sentence reads: 'As to whether Bateman's is haunted — that is another story.'

In 1982, the present Administrator, who had only been there a year, told me that on my behalf he had researched each of the past tenants of the house since Kipling — those alive that is — but none of them 'could give any details or recount any happenings'. The only comment was received from a Mrs Lees who lived at Bateman's in the 1940s and she said she had always felt uneasy in the room in which Mr and Mrs Kipling slept. Mr R.C. Taylor goes on to say that during the short time he and his wife have been there 'nothing untoward has occurred and in fact we find the whole house very friendly'. He does add, by way of a postscript, that 'a character nearby tells the tale of Mrs Kipling's ghost walking at night in the garden and carrying a basket (which she used to sit on)' — but Mr Taylor has doubts about this witness's sobriety!

Years ago, R. Thurston Hopkins, who wrote some fascinating books about ghosts and knew Kipling well during his latter years, told me that towards the end of his life the great man would often stand 'and fix his eyes, like some old eagle, on the "blunt, bow-headed, whale-backed Downs" and say "these hills are full of pure magic...the continuity of this moment is forever; this 'now' is everlasting".'

Nearby Glydwish Wood, now sadly all but disappeared, held a strange fascination for Kipling and he believed that it was full of 'a sense of ancient ferocity and evil'. He told Thurston Hopkins, who wrote a biography of Kipling: 'I have sometimes, while taking an evening walk through it, felt a secretive and menacing feeling all around me, holding me expectant and always on guard. In that evil wood everything is evil. There's a horrible suggestion of intelligence. It's not as

though the woods were lonely or anything. It's not empty —
there's too much life there: a kind of ill-natured and venomous
life. There is a spirit of some kind there for one evening
something suddenly gripped me and despite my attempts to
walk forward I was gradually forced back. I felt some unseen,
unknown power pushing against me and in the end I was
compelled to turn around and leave the wood....'

Some years later Thurston Hopkins organized a midnight
ghost hunt through the heart of Glydwish Wood and one of
the hunters encountered more than he had bargained for. He
had heard something scrambling with incredible swiftness
through the mud and bramble and then out of the
undergrowth blundered the shape of a man, a form that came
staggering towards him, coughing, choking and moaning as it
did so, its hands clutching at its throat. The startled ghost
hunter forced himself to look into the horrible eyes and flesh
of a face that was withered and decayed and he knew
instinctively that the man had been hanged and that he was
looking at someone who had been dead for many years. He
never knew how he got out of the wood and back among his
companions.

After lengthy research Thurston Hopkins discovered that
a man named David Leany had been hanged for a murder
committed in Glydwish Wood in 1928. After the execution had
been carried out fresh medical evidence showed that in fact
the victim had died of a heart attack. The condemned man had
protested his innocence to the end and his last words to the
chaplain were: 'I beg of you to believe me when I say I am
innocent and to prove it I shall return to haunt those people
who have hounded me to my death.'

Bedruthan, Cornwall

These sixty acres of National Trust cliff-top land
overlooking Bedruthan Beach and the rock formation known

as Bedruthan Steps include sites of ancient tin and iron mines and perhaps even a castle that may have been named after the red ironstone that abounds here and in other parts of Cornwall. Standing here, facing countless miles of ocean and completely alone it seems even when other people are in sight, it is not difficult to believe that there are many visitors who have reported hearing sounds they cannot explain: the heavy and weary tread of long-dead miners' boots and the click-click of the 'knockers' picks.

Although in the main the miners were afraid of these 'withered, dried-up creatures' the size of a two-year-old child, with large eyes and ugly heads, the knockers were usually only to be found in the vicinity of rich lodes of tin and so they were tolerated and endured. Indeed, according to the 1975 publication The Folklore of Cornwall, they are still feared in the far west of the county. Many are the stories of miners and others who have encountered, and not infrequently felt the power of, these little people.

When I was at Bedruthan in 1981 I met a local man who told me that here, where there were iron mines centuries ago, he has many times heard faint 'clicks' from the ground, sounds that he and others accept as being produced by knockers; for once he saw such a creature himself and fled for his life from the sight.

Bellister Castle, Haltwhistle, Northumberland

The vicinity of the border fortress, Bellister Castle, which is not open to the public apart from existing rights of way, has long been regarded as being haunted by a Grey Man. In folklore greyness is the symbol of grief, and perhaps the grief and remorse of some ancient lord of Bellister plays its part in the appearance of the ghost of the old and defenceless man whose death he caused.

Nearby Blenkinsopp Castle (where there are at least two ghosts) was the home of the de Blencansopp family for more than 200 years, before they moved to Bellister Castle in 1542. The tragic event that is said to have given rise to the haunting is preserved in an old ballad and the story goes than an old travelling minstrel was in the habit of calling at Bellister and providing entertainment in return for food and a night's lodging. He became a frequent and welcome visitor until one night the lord of Bellister became suspicious.

Those were troubled days, full of Border feuds with surprise Scottish raiding parties always a possibility, and that fateful night the lord of Bellister began to wonder whether the old man could really be a spy, an enemy agent who sought to lull the occupants of a Border castle into a sense of security before hastening across the Border with news of another castle ripe for the picking. The more he thought about it, the more the master of Bellister decided that he was probably right. After the old man had left, he roused his sleeping servants and retainers, told them to take fierce dogs with them, and hunt down the man he believed would betray them all.

The pursuit was quickly organized, horses were hastily saddled for the lord and his men and bloodhounds were released on the trail of the old musician. The dogs caught up with him on the banks of the Tyne where the hounds almost tore the defenceless old man to pieces before the arrival of the baron and his men. Too late they called off the savage dogs; the old man was dead. Thereafter the form of an old, grey man haunted the woods and lanes adjacent to the castle, a dreadful spectacle: the ancient features terribly gashed and torn and the blood running into the white beard. It was a terrifying sight for those who came face to face with the spectre and dreaded by all who dwelt in the neighbourhood for centuries after the story of the frightful death of the old man had spread far and wide.

Another version of the story has it that the old man was rescued before he had been killed by the dogs and was speedily hanged from the branch of an ancient tree in front of Bellister Castle, a tree known to this day as the Hanging Tree. Whatever the truth of the matter it seems possible that something like the traditional story of the death of an old man happened hereabouts and that subsequently the area was, and perhaps still is, haunted by a ghostly, old, grey man.

Ben MacDhui, The Cairngorms, Highland

This main peak of the Cairngorms, with its flat and bare summit, has long been associated with an unusual spectral presence known as the Big Grey Man of Ben MacDhui.

Over the years a considerable volume of evidence has been collected from various people to suggest that something very strange happens on this mountain from time to time. As long ago as 1891 Norman Collie, Professor of Organic Chemistry at the University of London and a Fellow of the Royal Society, stated that as he was returning from the cairn to the summit in a mist he heard footsteps following him but seeming to take steps that were three or four times the length of his own. He stopped several times but could see nothing. Eventually terror seized him and he took to his heels and ran blindly for several miles until he saw the Rothiemurchus Forest ahead and he realized that at last the mysterious footsteps were no longer following him.

In the summer of 1904 Hugh Welsh and his brother spent a fortnight camping near the summit, collecting alpine plants and studying the spiders there. The first night they were there they both heard soft footsteps following them about whenever they stirred. Later they heard more distinct footsteps in the daylight and they were both very conscious of 'something' near them, an eerie experience on an apparently deserted mountain. They never saw anything or discovered any explanation for the sounds.

In the early 1920s Tom Crowley, one-time President of the Moray Mountaineering Club, was descending Ben MacDhui when he suddenly heard footsteps behind him and looking over his shoulder he saw a huge grey figure — misty, undefined but with long legs...he turned and fled.

Dr A.M. Kellas, who died during the 1921-22 Mount Everest Reconnaissance Expedition, was a very experienced climber. One clear June night he was on the summit of Ben MacDhui with his brother. They were resting a little way apart from each other. Suddenly, much to his astonishment, Kellas saw a figure climbing up out of the Lairig Ghru pass. It walked round the cairn and then disappeared again into the pass. As far as Keller was aware he and his brother were the only people on the summit at that time, but most of all he was amazed at the enormous size of the figure he saw for it passed close to a ten-foot cairn and seemed to be about the same height!

George Duncan, a former High Sheriff of Aberdeen, saw a tall figure in a black robe as he drove along the Derry Road at dusk after coming off the mountain one evening in 1914. The figure appeared to be waving long arms in a menacing fashion and the veteran mountaineer felt a cold shiver run down his spine before he turned a corner and the figure was lost to view.

In 1982 Joan Grant was suddenly overwhelmed with terror as she and her husband were walking in brilliant sunshine in the Rothiemurchus Forest towards the Cairngorms. She turned and fled back the way they had come. She was utterly convinced that something malign, fourlegged and obscenely human and invisible yet solid — for she could hear the pounding of hooves — was trying to reach her. A year later a visiting professor described an almost identical experience in the same area and a correspondent in The Times claimed to have been pursued by 'something invisible'.

In 1941, Miss Wendy Wood, the well-known Scottish Nationalist, fled in terror from the Lairig Ghru pass. She said she had heard a voice 'of gigantic resonance' suddenly close beside her. Then she heard heavy footsteps which seemed to follow her and as she hurried away she had the impression that something was walking immediately behind her. She decided that the footsteps must be some kind of echo and then discovered, to add to her fear, that the heavy crunch-crunch behind her did not coincide with her own progress. She raced down the mountain, oblivious to the fact that she might fall and injure herself, until, near Whitwell, a barking dog drew her mind back to the world of reality and she realized that the footsteps were no longer following her.

In 1943 Alexander Tewnion, another experienced mountaineer and also a noted naturalist and photographer, was climbing alone on Ben MacDhui one October afternoon and as he reached the summit a dense mist spread across Lairig Ghru, enveloping the mountain. As the wind rose, Tewnion feared that a storm was imminent and he retreated down the Coire Etchachan path. As he did so he heard first one loud footstep, echoing through the wind, and then another and another, spaced out at long intervals. Tewnion carried a revolver and he turned and peered into the mist. Suddenly a huge shape loomed up, receded and then came towards him again. He fired three times at the figure but it still came on and Tewnion turned and ran away down the path without another backward glance. He always said he reached Glen Derry in a time he never bettered!

The Ben MacDhui
plateau - where
mysterious shapes and
sounds have been
reported over the years.

In 1942 veteran mountaineer Syd Scroggie was standing at the Shelter Stone of Ben MacDhui, alone at twilight, when he distinctly saw a tall human figure appear out of the blackness at one side of Loch Etchachan below and, clearly silhouetted against the water, walk with long and deliberate steps across the burns and disappear into the blackness at the other side of the loch. He quickly made his way to where the figure had appeared but he could find no footprints and there was now no sign of the mysterious figure. He shouted but there was no reply and as he became aware of approaching darkness and the silence of the brooding Cairngorms, he hurried back to the Shelter Stone.

These are but some of the strange experiences reported from Ben MacDhui; reports that have convinced many hardened mountaineers and other shrewd observers, including the naturalist Henry Tegner, that something out of the ordinary does, on occasions, take place in these haunted mountains.

Berkeley Castle, Berkeley, Gloucestershire

For more than 800 years the storms of history have washed over the impressive ramparts of Berkeley Castle and it seems likely that something of the turbulent past still lingers about this noble and historic building.

A deep well or dungeon still exists in the old keep where carcasses of animals — and probably troublesome humans — were thrown in days gone by, for any commoner or thief who incurred the displeasure of the Lord of Berkeley was summarily dispatched to the depths of the sinister well where there is still stagnant water.

Those of nobler birth who displeased the long line of Berkeleys were likely to find themselves imprisoned in a tiny windowless cell that once stood above the dungeon and there left to inhale the stench of the rotting corpses below.

King Edward's Room at
Berkeley Castle

Such is the treatment that King Edward II received after he had been hounded, captured and imprisoned at Berkeley by orders of Queen Isabelle who had become the lover of Roger Mortimer, Edward's usurper; for one Thomas, Lord of Berkeley, had married the daughter of Roger Mortimer. The Queen had no intention of allowing the King to leave Berkeley Castle alive, but after five months in the loathsome cell the robust King had not sickened and died and on the instructions of the Queen more drastic action was undertaken.

The men responsible for the King's captivity were Sir John Maltravers and Sir Thomas Gurney and they lost no time in acting on the Queen's orders, with an imagination that could have been used to better advantage. Edward II was a homosexual and his jailors thought the manner of his death should be seen to be appropriate. They seized the King on the night of 21 September 1327, pinioned him with legs spread and 'a kind of horn or funnel was thrust into his fundament through which a red-hot spit was run up his bowels'. Small wonder that the shrieks of the tortured King were said to have been heard far outside the castle walls and that there are those who say those dying screams can still be heard today.

I asked the present owner, Major R.J.G. Berkeley, whether he had any knowledge of the ghostly sounds but he told me that as far as he knows no one has heard them. I asked poet and writer Laurie Lee whether he had any information for I knew that his mother's forebears lived in Berkeley. He said he had no first-hand evidence but 'it is strong hearsay' and his mother often repeated the story to him although she did not claim herself to have heard the sounds. Sir Reginald Blacker quoted to me a couple of relevant lines of poetry:

Shrieks that through Berkeley's roof did ring,

Shrieks of an agonizing King...

He tells me he has made extensive inquiries but has never discovered the source of these lines or whether they pertain to the legend of the everlasting screams. Certainly the carving on the King's sepulchre, said to have been copied direct from a contemporary death-mask, shows a haunting look of twisted anguish. Tragic and violent happenings sometimes leave some kind of impression on the atmosphere that still registers for certain people years, even centuries, later.

Berrington Hall, Leominster, Hereford and Worcester

Designed by one of the leading architects of the day, Capability' Brown's son-in-law Henry Holland, and standing in a park laid out by Brown, this late-eighteenth-century house is something of a mystery. In fact practically nothing is known of the history of Berrington before Thomas Harley bought the estate about 1775, but there are traces of a medieval house about half a mile from the present one.

Harley's daughter Anne inherited the estate from her father and married the son and heir of Admiral Lord Rodney. Much of the house is scarcely altered since it was built, including the hall, library, drawingroom, boudoir and the staircase that is reputedly haunted.

I am told that in May 1981 a dark figure was seen walking in the south-east wing (used as a hospital during both World Wars). The figure was seen to emerge from the Upper Ward and then it turned as if intending to go down the stairs. Who the figure is and why it walks has yet to be discovered. Perhaps it is associated with some part of the history of the house that we know nothing about.

Blickling Hall, Aylsham, Norfolk

The winding lane takes you from Aylsham and, once you are past the church, suddenly without warning, across an expanse of lawn bordered by dark yew hedges, the pinnacled, rose-red Blickling Hall comes into view - romantic, symmetrical and laden with history and legend.

Here, guarded by stone bulls, we enter the house that probably harbours the ghost of Anne Boleyn, although there does not appear to be any authentic evidence that she was ever at Blickling. Perhaps she lived for a time in an earlier house here as a little girl; this must at least be likely. What is certain is that the manor of Blickling is recorded in Domesday Book as having belonged to Harold, King of England, and to William the Conqueror. Later another warrior, Sir Thomas Erpingham, veteran hero of Agincourt, held Blickling and indeed sold it to the rich knight Sir John Fastolf (the Falstaff immortalized by Shakespeare); later still this lovely place saw King Charles II and Queen Catherine, when the King knighted the son of Sir John Hobard, and here Henry VIII may have courted Anne Boleyn — so a local poet penned the lines:

Blickling two monarchs and two queens has seen.

One king fetched thence, another brought a queen.

Another owner, John, second Earl of Buckingham, died an unusual death. According to Horace Walpole: 'He suffered from gout in his foot, dipped it in cold water, and so killed himself.' About a century earlier the owner was Sir Henry Hobart, the fourth baronet, and he met his death in a duel on 21 August 1698, on Cawston Heath. Unlucky Sir Henry had chosen a left-handed man to fight, Oliver le Neve, and he quickly ran Sir Henry through the body. At nearby Cawston, at the crossroads, stands to this day the duelling stone, inscribed 'H.H.' on the spot where the affair took place. It has been reported that 'sounds of swordsplay' have been heard in the vicinity of this duelling stone, which belongs to the National Trust.

The ghost of Sir Henry is said to come back to Blickling on the anniversary of his death to re-visit the south-west turret bedroom where he died the day after the duel.

The present house was built between 1616 and 1624 by Sir Henry Hobart, Lord Chief Justice of England, and to do so he pulled down the manor house that had stood on the site for at least two centuries. This is the house where Anne Boleyn, or Bullen, probably spent many months of happy childhood and may even have been bom. When she became Queen of England and failed to bear Henry VIII a son, she was beheaded by a French swordsman on the block at the Tower of London. While imprisoned there she is reputed to have written a number of poems; some of the more poignant lines read:

A captive, I in this dread Tower, scenes of childhood recall

They comfort bring in this dark hour now gaiety hath flown

Through Blickling glades I fain would ride, soft green sward

Sequested shade, no cruel intrigues to deride my simple rustic day.

A child, I watched the timid fawn, gentle eyed, steal to the lake

With thirst to quench when mists of dawn had from cool waters fled

Strutting peacocks, shimmering blue, roseate arbour, scented walk

Gladly I left, 'tis strangely true, for pageantry at Court

False vanities my pride hath tricked, this place of dank and anguished stone

By sullen river surges licked, doth mock my hopeless lot

Oh, were I still a child in stature small

To tread the roselined paths of Blickling Hall

Beautiful Blickling Hall, haunted by the ghost of Anne Boleyn and, once a year, by the ghost of her father Sir Thomas Boleyn.

[Image previously spread across two pages]

Anne Boleyn

Anne was executed on 19 May 1536, and it is said that, on the anniversary of her death, she drives at midnight in a coach through the lanes and over the long-disused tracks of Norfolk, back to Blickling, headless horses drawing the coach which is driven by a headless coachman. Over the fields, down the main drive, the phantom coach reputedly races, to disappear through the main entrance to the hall.

Anne was not thirty when she died and the figure in the coach is that of a young woman but the slim body is headless and she carries the bloody head on her lap. Christina Hole, a prominent member of The Folklore Society, writing in 1940, says: 'The occupants of the house are so used to her annual appearance that they take no notice of it.' Some reports state that the coach itself, the horses drawing it and the coachman are dark, vague figures, but the form of Anne in a white dress is clearly visible, bathed in a reddish light, the whole spectral appearance pursued by an eerie blue light. Some say the coach is driven by Sir Thomas Boleyn, Anne's father cursed for a thousand years, for some unknown reason, to cross forty bridges in Norfolk on the anniversary of the night his daughter died.

This legend seems to have become confused with that of the ghostly George Boleyn, Lord Rochfort, Anne's brother, who, it is thought, spent his early years at old Blickling Hall with Anne and their elder sister Mary, who later became one of Henry VIII's mistresses. Anne was arrested when she failed to bear the King a son, and was charged with repeated adultery — Mark Smeaton, a young musician, admitted as much under torture. She was also charged with distributing her favours among three of the King's intimate friends and finally of committing incest with her brother, who was executed at the same time as Anne.

As news of the execution reached Blickling four headless horses were seen careering across the countryside, dragging a headless man behind them, his head secured under his arm. This is supposed to be the ghost of Lord Rochfort and the ghostly journey is allegedly repeated from time to time, the horses galloping across hedges and ditches, following by screaming devils, and finding no peace until they have crossed twelve bridges, which they must do before dawn.

Another version has it that the phantom coach carrying Anne's headless body is hotly pursued by her ghostly brother, who has crossed twelve bridges and ditches in a belated attempt to avenge his sister's death.

Anne's ghost has also been seen inside the hall and in the grounds, about the same time of the year. According to the author of Highways and Byways in East Anglia, 'many people' have seen the ghost of Anne gliding through the corridors of the house, and the present Custodian tells me that 'the likeness of Anne has been seen walking in the gardens by the lake. She has been described as being dressed in grey with a white mop cap. Sydney Hancock, the butler at Blickling in the late Lord Lothian's days, has been reported as declaring emphatically that this "woman" spoke to him. The actual conversation has never been made clear but appears to have been something like this: Sydney Hancock: "Excuse me m'am, can I inquire if you are looking for someone?" Anne Boleyn: "That for which I search is lost forever." '

Mr M. Denis Mead, the Custodian at Blickling, has collected quite a few stories, legends and fantasies about the hall and its ghostly history over the years. In his early days at Blickling there were some of the old servants still living nearby who had worked at the hall while it was still in private ownership and these old folk, alas all now dead, told many a tale of 'happenings' in and around Blickling.

They told Denis Mead of the old cook's cat which was lost in the attic rooms and could be heard mewing there for many years afterwards; also of a fight between two men servants in the long 'cross-attic' room over a buxom servant girl: both antagonists later died as an indirect result of their conflict 'and it is said that the sounds of their struggles can still be heard in the cross-attic room on nights of the full moon'.

A more recent and perhaps more convincing ghostly episode at Blickling Hall concerns some former tenants who had a high-spirited son who, on his twenty-first birthday, dressed himself in a suit of armour and clanked his way along a corridor to awaken his startled parents as dawn was breaking. The following year the son died in tragic circumstances. Some three years later the occupants of the same area of the hall were awakened at dawn by 'heavy, ponderous footsteps, like those that would be made by a man in armour' walking along the corridor. The date was the anniversary of the young son's birthday. No explanation was ever found and nobody has ever heard these sounds again.

But the most persistent stories of ghosts at Blickling concern the ill-fated Anne. 'Perhaps the peace of Blickling attracts her tortured spirit,' as one visitor expressed it. She may not have been born here but her father certainly owned Blickling and it is likely that she knew the place in happy childhood days and remembered it with longing at the end of her life. Small wonder then that her spirit broods heavily over this mellow and beautiful house.

Bodiam Castle, East Sussex

Interesting and romantic, sitting like a bird on the waters of her moat, Bodiam looks every inch a castle and indeed the walls and towers remain almost intact, but within the two-metres thick walls it is largely a ruin. A curtain-walled castle, built in 1386, it has been described as one of the best examples of medieval military architecture. A few years before Bodiam Castle was built the French had sacked Rye and Winchelsea, and with the River Rother navigable up to Bodiam Sir Edward Dalyngrigge was given royal licence to fortify his manor house 'in defence of the adjacent countryside and for resistance against our enemies'. Having amassed considerable wealth abroad, and weary of exile, the knight returned to England and established himself at his wife's native place of Bodiam.

Over the succeeding years Bodiam Castle changed hands many times and local tradition has it that it stood siege more than once, but on this point history is silent. It is referred to in accounts of the Wars of the Roses and it was lived in during the fifteenth and sixteenth centuries and probably suffered internal damage during the Civil War.

The present Custodian has been there for fifty-five years. Both he and his father before him say they have never heard of a ghost; but back in the 1920s Harry Price, the noted psychic researcher and investigator, gave a lecture at the Ghost Club, of which he was then chairman, on the subject of 'Haunted Sussex', and he included Bodiam.

Of Bodiam Castle he said he had traced stories of the sound of revelry at night, at certain times during the winter months, the sound emanating quite distinctly from within the shell of the castle. He went on: 'The clanking of drinking cups, songs in a foreign tongue, intermixed with strange oaths, have been heard over and over again by people passing the ruins late at night.

Another feature of this haunt is the music — faint but distinct — which, it is stated, can always be heard on Easter Sunday by those whose ears are attuned to "psychic music". The foreign-sounding songs and expressions might be accounted for by the fact that Sir Edward Dalyngrigge (or Dalyngruge) and his men must have acquired a considerable knowledge of French during their adventures across the Channel (he had campaigned in Normandy and Brittany and was regarded as the hero of Crecy and Poitiers) and perhaps some of his henchmen were French.

Edward B. D'Auvergne, in his exploration of English castles, suggests that Bodiam Castle may have had bitter memories for its owner and perhaps it had been the scene of former joys, too sweet to be recalled'. It is not impossible that something of the tragic and romantic happenings that once took place here have impinged themselves on the atmosphere at this beautiful place. Some hauntings, and in particular ghostly sounds, have been found to diminish over the years, almost like a battery running down, and perhaps those supernormal sounds, once so frequently and regularly heard at Bodiam, have now become quiescent. Sir Edward Dalyngrigge won his spurs fighting under the Black Prince and later and with more profit under the famous land-pirate Sir Robert Knollys.

Bramber Castle, Steyning, West Sussex

All that remains of the once-proud Norman castle surrounded by a deep moat are a few meagre stones where the pathetic ghosts of three starved children have been seen, usually in the month of December.

The castle ruins are situated on the north-east side of Bramber Street and the Saxon word of 'Brymmburh' (a fortified place) gave the place its name. At the time of Domesday Book (a general survey ordered by William the Conqueror) there is reference to the 'Baronial Castle of the Honour of Brember or Brembre' and it was then held by William de Braose, who subsequently died during a pilgrimage to the Holy Land. He was succeeded by his son, another

The ruins of Bramber Castle, Sussex, where the ghosts of the children of William de Braose have long been reported seen around Christmas-time.

William; he was likewise succeeded by a son named William who is said to have treacherously murdered many important people when he was invited to a feast at his castle at Abergavenny, including Sitsylt ap Dimswalld. He then proceeded to Sitsylt's dwelling, slew his surviving son in his mother's presence and set fire to the house. Later, appalled at his atrocious conduct, he built the church at New Shoreham and conferred large endowments on churches in Normandy and Abergavenny, by way of restitution.

This William de Braose had five children, three boys and two girls. Reginald the heir, some years older than the rest, lived in a castle in Ireland. The rest of the family lived amid much pomp and grandeur at Bramber. In due course the wealth and popularity of the Lord of Bramber excited the jealous hatred of King John, who only waited for an opportunity to effect the min of de Braose.

The Lord of Bramber was one of the confederate barons who had taken an active part in the endeavour to obtain a redress of public grievances and a better administration of the laws, and King John was determined to make an example of him. He could have seized de Braose in person but he knew that the man's great popularity would have resulted in all Sussex taking arms, so he devised another scheme. He sent his equerry, Sir Peter Maulue (who had assisted in the murder of Prince Arthur) to Bramber to demand de Braose's children as hostages for his good behaviour in the future. When de Braose sternly refused such a barbarous suggestion. King John swore he would be revenged and ordered an army to march against Bramber Castle.

The castle was not prepared for a siege and de Braose, powerful baron that he was, knew he had no hope of maintaining a war with the King of England, so he decided, for the safety of his lady and their children, to abandon Bramber and flee to his son in Ireland, which he did. The King, however, obtained word of what was happening, and no sooner had de Braose and his family landed in Ireland than they were seized and brought back to England and taken to Windsor Castle where King John then was.

Jubilant at the success of his plan, King John saw at last the opportunity of presenting an example to all rebellious barons and he commanded that the whole family should be imprisoned in one of the towers at Windsor and there starved to death. Another version of the story, King John's own in fact, tells of an agreement that was broken by de Braose, who escaped to France and that only Lady de Braose and her four children were starved to death.

The later history of Bramber Castle includes a story of a wronged husband, Sir Hubert De Hurst, and of his unfaithful wife, Lady Maud, and of her dying in strange circumstances after the murder of her lover, William De Lindfield. In 1954 some of the residents of Bramber reported hearing the sound of a woman wailing among the ruins of the castle. One resident described the cry as containing four notes. The belief at that time was that the noises were attributable to the ghost of the beautiful Lady Maud, sorrowing for her lover, who was said to have been trapped and walled-up alive by her madly jealous and older husband towards the end of the fifteenth century. The Lady Maud is said to have discovered her husband's grim revenge on the night that he surreptitiously laid the course of bricks that sealed the fate of the unfortunate De Lindfield. Next day Lady Maud herself was found dead.

Years later, when the castle was attacked by Parliamentarian troops, a skeleton was discovered crouched in a corner, the head resting on the hands, the elbows on the knees: the mortal remains of William De Lingfield. And there are other stories of intrigue and murder at Bramber, but the most persistent ghosts are said to be those of the three younger children of William de Braose, two daughters, Blanche and Jane, and the youngest of all, little Hugh.

It is now 800 years since a castle was built here on a natural mound above the River Adur; it is long centuries ago when William de Braose, that wealthy and powerful baron who owned forty manors, lived here in discord with his King but popular with his neighbours; but it is believed to be the ghosts of his children, a boy and two girls, who now appear as ragged ghosts holding out their emaciated hands as though begging for food — perhaps the most pathetic ghosts in all Britain.

Bramshill House, near Hartley Wintney, Hampshire

The present historic and majestic Jacobean mansion is built on the site of much earlier buildings: 'Bromeselle' is twice mentioned in Domesday Book and references to the house can be traced back to the days of Edward the Confessor. Today an ancient gateway and part of the cellars remain of a fourteenth-century building.

Several ghosts from different periods have been seen here in various parts of the house that is now used as a police training college, I learned when I visited Bramshill. First and foremost there is the famous legend of the Mistletoe Bough. This concerns a young bride, at her wedding celebrations or at a Christmas party, hiding inside a carved chest with a hidden spring that could only be operated from outside the chest, and the poor girl suffocating and the body only being discovered long after she had expired — a mouldering corpse dressed in white and clutching a sprig of mistletoe. The ghostly form of a girl in white, carrying a sprig of mistletoe, has reportedly been seen many times in different parts of Bramshill, but most frequently in what are now administrative rooms, especially the Fleur de Lys Room where other odd happenings have been experienced.

The Rumanian royal family, king, queen and two children, stayed at Bramshill after the Second World War, when the house was in private ownership, and they and their staff reported seeing the ghost of a beautiful girl in a white, old-fashioned dress. In fact the queen twice asked for her children to sleep in a different room because they were disturbed by a 'woman in a white' who ran through their room. Later an exorcism was performed here at the request of King Michael; he was worried by his children asking when the 'White Lady' was going to return to play with them. Other witnesses for the mysterious White Lady include police officers and their wives, a Red Cross worker, two builders, civilian staff and visitors.

Secondly there is the Grey Lady, probably a ghost of the Cope family who owned Bramshill for more than two centuries. This form, sometimes accompanied by the inexplicable aroma of lilies of the valley, has most often been seen in the early hours of the morning, disappearing through walls or passing through closed doors — a sad-looking ghost with golden hair and dressed in a straight, sleeveless grey robe. In 1962 the Grey Lady was seen by a Ministry of Works engineer who had been employed at Bramshill for many years and had previously been sceptical of the ghost stories. He described the figure as that of a beautiful young lady with auburn hair who walked sadly through the long gallery and disappeared.

The unexplained perfume of lilies of the valley, strong and unmistakable, convinced sceptical Colin Atkinson, the college engineer for the previous five years, when he encountered the scent in the summer of 1980. This report is based on that in an official police newspaper dated May 1981. He and his wife were in the company of the Assistant Staff

Officer's wife in the terrace drawing-room adjoining the college bar. It was one of the Bramshill Guest Nights. At this time the girls in the Accounts Office by the long gallery had been reporting the strong smell of lilies of the valley which they were totally unable to explain. The girls suspected a practical joker and searched each other's handbags but without solving the mystery.

Colin Atkinson takes up the story: 'It was about 9 p.m. The three of us had just had dinner and the women went up to the long gallery on a ghost hunt, if you like, while I got some drinks ready. When they came back into the room they stepped back quickly. As I went over to them I walked right into an area which held a strong smell of lilies of the valley. The area was about six by three feet and you could step in and out of the smell. There was nothing frightening about it but I thought afterwards that it was about the size of a grave — or a chest. It lasted three or four minutes. Being a sceptic I was so impressed that I spoke to the college parson. He pointed out that the floor had been taken up in the nursery and wondered what might have been disturbed.'

But it took more than that to turn Colin Atkinson into a believer. His twelve years in the Royal Navy and a similar period in the prison service had produced a hard-headed sceptic. 'After spending time with the Krays and the Richardsons you don't believe things that you don't see but I'm not the sceptic now that I used to be,' he says.

Sudden drops in temperature have sometimes accompanied appearances of the Grey Lady and this curious phenomenon has often been reported in the long gallery, now used as part of the library. One employee of Bramshill was making his rounds of the house one autumn evening, accompanied by his labrador dog, when he suddenly found himself face to face with the Grey Lady and at the same time the room felt icy cold. 'If I was mistaken,' he said afterwards, 'the dog wasn't. She gave a howl of terror and fell over backwards; then she ran home as fast as she could — and I wasn't far behind her!'

Then there is the ghostly Green Man, always seen in the vicinity of water, sometimes standing on the little bridge near the Tudor gatehouse and sometimes beside one of the lakes in the park. Oddly enough an eccentric Cope ancestor always dressed in green and drowned himself in 1806. Some witnesses have said the Green Man appears to be legless and it is a curious fact that the Cope ancestor obtained for himself a green suit, hat, gloves —just about everything, but he could not obtain green Wellington boots which were not manufactured at that time. One wonders whether at a distance black Wellington boots melt into the background and are not seen.

Other ghostly sightings outside the house have included at least one appearance of the White Lady. A man arriving at the house in a car to collect his wife after a dance saw a White Lady' seemingly step into one of the bridge recesses. It was past midnight and he stopped to give the girl a lift — but she had unaccountably disappeared. On another occasion (reported in an official police newspaper) in 1979 a woman in a long dress was seen walking on the grass. A motorist pulled up and called to her but she ignored him, turned towards the mansion and drifted through the wall surrounding the front of the house and disappeared.

In 1976 a security officer on night patrol encountered yet another Bramshill ghost, believed to be Ronald, the son of Bramshill's last private owner, Lord Brocket. Ronald died in tragic circumstances some thirty years previously.

The security man distinctly saw the figure of a young man in tennis gear and carrying a racket. Thinking it must be a student who had wandered out of bounds, the security man

Beautiful Bramshill - where there are a dozen haunted rooms; ghosts of a lady in white, a grey lady, a green man, phantom aromas and a carved chest that may be the actual one in the famous Mistletoe Bough legend.

[Image previously spread across two pages]

The Mistletoe Bough Chest,
Bramshill. Possibly the chest where
the bride hid - the bride who was to
became a famous ghost.

approached the figure; before he could reach it the form turned and seemed to look at him and then strode towards the fireplace and disappeared through the wall.

There is also a haunted path in the grounds of Bramshill. It is on the north-west side of the lake, a path which, where it is overgrown, forms a long tunnel of intertwining branches. Here the college engineer and others have discovered that their dogs sense something invisible to themselves. Colin Atkinson again: 'I've had two dogs while I've been at Bramshill and, along with other animals, they have both refused to go through that tunnel. The first was a little Manchester terrier and when I took her through she stopped, cowered and then suddenly shot through. She would never go near the place after that. At the moment,' he said in 1981, '1 have a border collie and he doesn't want to know either. He always goes round that spot, even though it means going down a banking and up the other side.'

The panelled hall with its stone screen and carved 'Bride's Chest' is haunted by the ghost of an old man with a long beard; the chapel drawing-room by a woman from the days of Queen Anne. An adjoining room has a ghost lady dressed in the tight bodice and full skirt of the days of Charles I and an upstairs bedroom is haunted by an invisible ghostly presence: a child's tiny hand is sometimes placed into the hand of a visitor. Another room on the first floor is occasionally peopled by ghostly forms that seem to float two feet or so above the existing floor and it is an interesting fact that this particular floor was lowered during structural alterations but the ghosts, it would seem, walk where they have always walked.

In 1972 a college security officer was in the hall when he saw a man on the path outside walking towards the house, a man dressed in a grey flannel suit. Later Mr William Chalk reported what he had seen: 'The man came in through the open door, crossed the hall and went straight through the wall opposite. The back of my neck went cold and I hurried round the corner to see where he had gone but he never re-appeared. Later I found out that where he had walked through the wall there used to be an archway, but the arch had been bricked-up years ago.'

As recently as 1980, according to Patrol, the official newspaper of the Sussex police, a figure was seen to appear and vanish in the college reception hall. The chapel and the drawing-room are situated directly above the reception hall and it is from here that security men on night patrol have heard footsteps, footsteps that have no rational explanation. So often have these sounds been heard and investigated with negative results that nowadays the strange sounds are accepted as part of the routine of night patrol at Bramshill and they are no longer even investigated.

The terrace, with its loggias, balustrading and elegant bay windows, is haunted by a mysterious woman in white. She appeared dramatically one evening in front of Sir William Cope and members of his family. Everyone present saw a white-robed figure leaning over the balustrade at the far end of the terrace. Thinking that one of the housemaids must be sleep-walking, Sir William sent for the butler and as he approached the figure it suddenly seemed to melt into the balustrade. After it had disappeared evidence came to light that a similar figure had been seen on the terrace previously and it invariably disappeared when someone approached it.

There are rooms at Bramshill where no dog will enter and parts of the grounds where animals show signs of fright; and there are other stories of strange happenings throughout the house and grounds; not without cause is Bramshill called 'the most haunted house in Hampshire'.

Brodick Castle, Isle of Arran, Strathclyde

'The delights of Brodick Castle on the Isle of Arran are many and varied,' says Peter Ryan in the first comprehensive guide to National Trust properties. 'It has a beautiful setting between the bay and the hills and an incomparable garden; its principal rooms contain a wealth of fine furniture, paintings, china and porcelain; and it has a long, eventful history.' He does not mention the perambulations of Brodick's mysterious Grey Lady.

The Vikings had a fortress where this red sandstone castle now stands; they yielded it to the MacDonalds, Lords of the Isles. Robert the Bruce was here in 1306 when he claimed the castle as a royal property, but frequent inter-dynastic quarrels in succeeding centuries caused Brodick to change hands many times. Eventually James III gave the property to his nephew James Hamilton in 1502, and it was held by that family until the Duchess of Montrose, daughter of the twelfth Duke of Hamilton, bequested it to the National Trust for Scotland on her death in 1958.

Today this Scottish baronial mansion seems to watch over Brodick Bay and there is a rarefied and distinct feeling, noticed by many visitors, of former generations of occupants being present.

The Property Controller, John M. Forgie, tells me that the Grey Lady is supposed to be one of the three victims of the plague of 1700 when three ladies, who were thought to have the plague, were immured within the massive walls of the oldest part of the castle. 'One is supposed to walk the corridors from time to time although neither myself, my wife nor our family, who have been in residence in the castle for some ten years, have yet seen the apparition. I did hear that the Lady Jean Fforde's son was said to have seen the ghost when he was a child.'

Brodick Castle on the Isle of Arran - where a Grey Lady has been seen in the servants' hall dressed as a dairy maid.

[Image previously spread across two pages]

When I spoke to Lady Jean she told me that following publication of her fascinating Castle in the Air in 1982 she planned a second volume which would deal in detail with the Brodick ghost. In the meantime she has been kind enough to give me some details and it seems that there has always been a story of a Grey Lady ghost at the castle.

When a 'somewhat psychic housekeeper', Mrs Munsey, was there, the form appeared several times. She was seen from different viewpoints and was usually described as looking like a dairy maid. She was most often seen going down a back stairway, dressed in grey with a white collar. Sometimes the form was followed into the servants' hall, where she always disappeared. One morning the butler noticed the figure walk down the stairway and pause beside an odd-job man who was scrubbing the flooring in the passage, and she seemed to speak to him before passing on. When the 'girl' had disappeared in puzzling circumstances the butler asked the odd-job man who the girl was who had spoken to him, whereupon the surprised man denied all knowledge of seeing or speaking to any girl while he had been scrubbing the floor that morning.

The housekeeper saw the same figure several times and, since she professed to have the gift of being able to produce 'automatic writing', she was badgered by other members of staff (and some of the family) to try and find out what she could about the Grey Lady. The story she unfolded by this somewhat dubious means revealed that the girl was a serving wench at the castle at the time that Cromwellian troops were billeted there; the general in command had had an affair with her and she was pregnant. In those days such girls were simply thrown out of the place where they were employed and this poor girl is supposed to have gone out of the castle and committed suicide by the old quay below the castle.

I also learned of a completely different ghost here; a man in a long green jacket and breeches and wearing a wig. He has been seen on occasions in the library, usually seated in a chair beside the fireplace; but who he is and why he appears is not known.

Lady Jean Fforde, daughter of Mary, Duchess of Montrose, tells me there is a long-standing tradition that a ghostly white deer always appears when the head of the ancient family of Hamilton dies. Such an 'animal', she tells me, was certainly seen at Brodick after the death of two successive heads of the family within living memory.

Brodie Castle, Forres, Morayshire, Grampian

This castle has been the seat of the ancient family of Brodie since the eleventh century, but little is known of the early history of the Brodies for practically all the family papers and documents were destroyed when Lord Lewis Gordon set fire to the property during the Montrose campaign of 1645. The castle was rebuilt and today contains many valuable paintings; some fine French furniture; English, Continental and Chinese porcelain; and a room where a former Brodie manifested after death.

Hugh, the twenty-third chief and grandfather of the present Brodie of Brodie, died in Switzerland in September 1889, having been treated for 'neuralgic pains at the heart' at Aix-les-Bains. When he had left Brodie Castle some two months earlier the whole castle had been let (the only time in its long history that this had happened) with the exception of the laird's ground floor study or business room, which was kept locked and shuttered.

During the evening of 20 September 1889 the butler startled the tenants by going up to the drawing-room and announcing: 'There is someone in the Master's study!' The family in residence hurried down and sure enough, although the door of the room was securely locked and no lights were visible, distinct noises emanated from the room, as of someone moving objects about inside the room accompanied by the sounds of papers being shuffled, and they heard too a strange and frightening moaning sound. Eventually all was silent.

Next day, the first news reached the castle of the death of Brodie of Brodie; an event which had taken place the previous afternoon. No explanation was ever found for the mysterious sounds heard by the butler and the occupants and other servants. In answer to my inquiries the present Brodie of Brodie tells me: This, I'm afraid, is the only ghost I can offer you and that was a one-night stand — it has never been heard again.'

Curiosities at Brodie Castle include the bones of a young child, preserved in a glass-fronted cabinet in the charter room, a small and windowless area where all the available family documents are kept. In the eighteenth century a spiral staircase was removed from a comer turret in one of the towers and the skeleton of a young child was unearthed; the origin of these bones has never been established and there is no legend or story to account for them.

A far more valuable find occurred in 1970 when Mrs Helena Brodie of Brodie discovered by accident some books in the old stables. One of them proved to be a previously unrecorded tenth-century English religious manuscript, a working Pontifical, a book which only a Bishop would have used. No one knows why such a valuable property came to be among the dust and rubbish of the stables or how it managed to remain there for so long before being discovered. It is now preserved in the British Museum.

Buckland Abbey, near Tavistock, Devonshire

Reputedly completed, from start to finish, in three days by preternatural means, this house that was once a monastery and became the home of Sir Francis Drake after his circumnavigation of the world, is said to harbour the sound of plainsong chanting; strange, dark, unidentified and muttering figures; and even the occasional appearance of Drake himself, taking his 'wild ride' back to earth driving a hearse, drawn by headless horses.

Drake's famous drum, the oldest English drum extant, was restored to the Abbey in 1968 after spending four years in the vault of a London bank. It is supposed to be the one Drake took round the world with him aboard the Pelican and it was probably beaten when he was buried at sea in 1596. As he lay dying in Nombre de Dios Bay he is said to have declared that if ever England was in danger, the drum would sound by itself and he would return.

Well-authenticated stories tell how the drum was heard, beating by itself, before the outbreak of the First World War in 1914, in 1939 before the Second World War and at various other times, not always when England was clearly in danger; but that it has been heard sounding by itself by many people seems indisputable.

Reports of unexplained chanting and the occasional appearance of inexplicable dark and muttering figures here are fragmentary and comparatively rare, but I have spoken to people who swear they have seen and heard the fearsome sight of Devon's famous ghost: Drake driving a black hearse pulled by headless horses and accompanied by headless hounds whose baying causes or foretells the death of any earthly dog that hears it.

Burnmoor Tarn, Eskdale, Cumbria

The wide expanses of Burnmoor Tarn, beside the path leading from Eskdale to Wasdale, have long been the haunt of a phantom animal, a coffin-bearing fell pony that used to carry the bodies of cragsmen, dalesmen and their families across the enormous moor.

One story tells of the body of a young dalesman being taken to its last resting place one autumn afternoon when the pony, for some unexplained reason, took fright and bolted. In no time it had disappeared into the wintry gloom, with the coffin securely strapped to its back, and the straggle of mourners were left to make their sad way to the young man's home and there to inform his old and infirm mother what had happened. The news, so goes the story, was too much of a shock for her and she had a heart attack and within a day or two she was dead.

So a few days later another funeral cortege was making its way across Burnmoor Tam and this time it was the old woman's coffin that was being borne by one of the fell ponies.

As they reached the spot where the other pony had bolted, this animal too suddenly reared and for no apparent reason bolted off over the moor, carrying the old woman's remains in the coffin on its back. Some of the mourners attempted to give chase but the terrified animal galloped off at full speed and was soon lost in the freezing fog.

A few of the more hardy followers pressed on, however, and soon they came across the coffin of the son, lost some days previously. With some difficulty they carried it to the churchyard and completed the funeral But of the second pony and the coffin of the old woman, it is said that never a trace was found, although many have been the stories of people glimpsing the form of a horse with a dark box-like shape on its back — a form that suddenly appears out of the mist or swirling fog and then as suddenly disappears, with never a sound accompanying the apparition.

Cartmel: Priory Gatehouse, Cumbria

The vicinity of this Priory Gatehouse has long been regarded as haunted by some of the monks from Cartmel Priory who once acted as guides across the treacherous sands.

Over the years the quicksands and the fast incoming sea have claimed many victims. Either could trap an unwary traveller in minutes and it is said the quicksands could engulf a horse and carriage in half-an-hour.

Sometimes the bodies of the drowned would be recovered and many graves in the little cemetery adjoining the priory church and in that of nearby Conishead bear witness to this fact. But many more victims were never recovered and it may be these restless souls, as well as the spectres of those who died trying to save them, that have haunted this place for centuries.

Local people say that the sands are peopled with ghosts and that when the wind is in a certain direction, coming off the sea, the whole place seems to be alive with the cries of dying men and women. Imagination? Perhaps, but what of the phantom form that has been seen in the lanes about Cartmel Priory — especially in the vicinity of the gatehouse which has stood here for more than five centuries so that the very stones must be saturated with memories?

There are many stories of ghosts here. There is one that has been seen many times: the ghost of a middle-aged man dressed in double-breasted waistcoat, breeches, ankle boots and a tall hat. He appears to be friendly enough and then suddenly he is no longer there. He is just one of the ghosts that haunt the area of the old gatehouse at Cartmel.

Charlecote Park, Stratford-upon-Avon, Warwickshire

The building of this fine house was begun in 1551 by Sir Thomas Lucy, whose family had lived at Charlecote since 1189; the same Sir Thomas Lucy before whom a certain Mister William Shakespeare is said to have been arraigned in the great hall when he was caught on a midnight poaching expedition in the Park. Charlecote still contains the famous 'Shakespeare' herd of fallow deer — and incidentally a flock of Spanish sheep of scarce breed whose ancestors were brought to Charlecote by a member of the Lucy family more than 200 years ago.

After his appearance before Sir Thomas Lucy the wayward Shakespeare was kept a prisoner for the rest of the night at Charlecote, 'held over' for interrogation or, more likely, punishment. There are various versions of what happened but it seems likely that Shakespeare retaliated by writing a rude poem about Sir Thomas and affixing it to the gates at Charlecote, an act that so infuriated the knight that Shakespeare, deciding that 'discretion is the better part of valour', deemed it prudent to hasten to London and 'disappear' for a time. Subsequently he took a more permanent revenge by lampooning Sir Thomas Lucy as Mr Justice Shallow in The Merry Wives of Windsor and in *Henry IV, Part Two*.

Sir Thomas Lucy entertained Queen Elizabeth I here to breakfast one day in 1576 when she was on her way to see her favourite Robert Dudley, Earl of Leicester. Much of the house has been altered since those days but the gatehouse is exactly as Shakespeare and Queen Elizabeth must have known it. The shadowy figure of a ghostly girl here may have its origin in those far-off days, or perhaps in later days when some of the Lucy family were no better than they should have been, as the following historical incident shows.

The bust of Shakespeare in the
hall of Charlecote Park.

The gatehouse at
Charlecote.

George, Duke of Northumberland, had become enamoured of pretty Catherine Lucy, widow of Captain Lucy of the Royal Horse Guards, but she insisted on matrimony. Within a year he had grown tired of her and he and his brother (who was a young man who welcomed all kinds of adventures) put their heads together and decided to kidnap Catherine and deposit her in a convent on the Continent.

These two, both illegitimate sons of Charles II by Barbara Castlemaine, managed successfully to inveigle Catherine aboard a ship, and in due course took her to a convent in Ghent where they also succeeded in persuading the Mother Superior to certify that Catherine had entered the convent voluntarily. In high glee at the outcome of their plan the brothers returned to England, but Catherine was a young woman with determination and spirit and she proved to be more than a match for the sly schemers. She escaped from the convent, made her way to London and sought out her husband. Threatened with scandal Northumberland came to terms, but one wonders what kind of life and how much happiness Catherine enjoyed thereafter.

Could she or some other unlucky Lucy be the ghost? The ethereal figure of a girl has repeatedly been seen running down to the willow-shaded water and there disappearing, making no disturbance to the surface as the form sinks and is submerged. Could Shakespeare have seen this ghost himself, for there is a persistent legend that this is the place where he was inspired to write his lines on Ophelia's death? Some people even say that the sad ghost of the drowned girl still floats in her watery grave.

Lady Fairfax-Lucy is in no doubt about Charlecote, having its haunted room, and she says: 'Our wing is very much impregnated with a sense of the past; that is with the three generations who lived in it since it was built in the 1830s. The Green Room is in the original part of the old house and had a door opening on to the Minstrels' Gallery (taken down in the 1870s) above the great hall, and still has a small room off it. I have myself been conscious of a pressure of people and an unidentifiable hubbub of voices when alone in the room. My daughter slept in the Green Room bed and confirmed this — she awakened in the night to find herself on the floor with a crowd milling round her. But at the same time I have to say that others have slept there and heard nothing.' But, as Lady Fairfax-Lucy so rightly says: 'Ghosts are not to be commanded and in my experience appear to the most unlikely people.'

In answer to my questions about Charlecote's ghosts, Lady Fairfax-Lucy explains that this Green Room, a bedroom in the south wing, long reputed to be haunted, is now used by the Lucy family. The confused noise of raised voices in the little room, once used by the musicians, has been heard by people, including herself, and it sounds as if an argument is taking place, accompanied by violent actions. Lady Fairfax-Lucy also tells me she heard from an old servant, who had been with the family for sixty years, that a footman who drowned himself 'is sometimes seen; a black figure standing by the waterfall'.

Chartwell, Westerham, Kent

In this delightful home for forty years of Sir Winston Churchill (1874-1965) which is furnished much as it was during his lifetime, it is not surprising that something of the great man still seems to linger, and that his form has been seen on at least one occasion, as recounted in Churchill and Chartwell by Robin Fedden. Understandably perhaps the studio in the garden, where there are some of his paintings and where he spent many happy hours, is regarded as especially haunted.

Against a large tapestry that once hung in the Belgian Parliament there stands a white marble bust of Lady Randolph Churchill, an old leather armchair and a damaged portrait.

Sir Winston's only son, Randolph, has described how once, when copying this portrait, he clearly saw his dead father sitting in the leather armchair nearby and furthermore they had a long discussion of men and events and of the changes which had overtaken the world in more than half a century.

Many visitors to Chartwell remark upon a somewhat disconcerting atmosphere, an intangible feeling that the dominant personality of the man who made Chartwell what it is today still lingers here.

Chingle Hall, Goosnargh, near Preston, Lancashire

'One of the best authenticated examples of a haunted house in England.' So James Wentworth Day described Chingle Hall, a fascinatingly hidden house built in the form of a cross, that lies at the end of a long drive. I have lost count of the number of times I have been there, for the place has an intriguing and puzzling atmosphere and it does seem indisputable that ghostly forms have been seen and heard here many many times.

I remember the late Mrs Margaret Howarth telling my wife and I, unequivocally, 'this house is undoubtedly haunted'. And she went on. 'We hear ghostly footsteps constantly in some rooms and passages and sometimes heavy footsteps walk over the bridge across the moat, through the old front door and across the hall .... Once eight people heard these footsteps ... door latches move, sometimes night after night and then not for a while ... doors open by themselves ... dogs' hackles rise at something they can see or sense ... objects are moved, water appears from nowhere, monk-like figures have been seen inside the house and in the garden .... Once my brother and I watched a cloaked form for fifteen minutes before it faded and finally disappeared; no, we were not afraid; now I can't think why we weren't, but we never slept in that room afterwards.'

This charming 700-year-old house, tucked away at the end of its lane, is believed to have been the birthplace of one John Wall, a Franciscan priest who was one of the last English Roman Catholic martyrs. Certainly Chingle belonged to the Wall family in 1585 and John was born in 1620. He was executed at Worcester in 1679 and his head is said to have been conducted on a grand tour of the Continent before being smuggled back to Chingle. Here it was either buried in the grounds or immured somewhere inside the house, where several secret hiding-places have been discovered and probably there are more yet to be found.

The ghostly form of John Wall is thought to have been seen here many times, 300 years after his death elsewhere. A local Chief Superintendent of Police and his wife; a former guide; Mrs Howarth's brother; Miss Ann Strickland (the present owner); Fred Knowles, the Manager of Chingle Hall; the Revd Peter Travis, and scores of visitors, believers and sceptics alike, have all experienced odd and apparently inexplicable happenings.

The cowled head of a monk once peered through a window — a pale face described to me as 'hardly human and surrounded by a dark cowl' which appeared for a moment and then vanished. A similar cowled form was seen in the garden. A visitor saw two figures, dressed like monks and in the act of praying, in a downstairs room; figures that seemed to melt into the wall when they were approached. A little later, in the haunted Priest Room upstairs, the figure of a man with shoulder-length hair has been seen to walk past outside a window, yet the window is all of twelve feet from the ground.

Another visitor met a greenish diffuse figure in the porch; as she stopped the figure turned and walked back into the dining-room — and disappeared! It was here, in the comfortable dining-room with its 1000-Year-old beams, in front of a roaring log fire, that my wife and I were entertained to tea one afternoon in March 1977 and heard, for the first time, something of the strange experiences reported from this interesting old house.

We heard about Mrs Walmeley who received a violent push in the back while she was standing alone in the centre of the lounge; about sceptical Mrs Moorby who was frightened when she found the air around her suddenly become icy cold and she had the distinct feeling that she was not alone and was in fact being watched: not a pleasant feeling; about Mrs Robinson who heard footsteps ascend the stairs followed by three raps from inside the priest's hole in the deserted room; about Mrs McKay who felt a wave of cold air sweep over her in the Priest Room and watched in astonishment as some flowers lifted themselves out of a vase and a table lamp and a picture shook without anyone being near them; about Mrs Rigby having a cup of tea with Mrs Howarth in the lounge when they both saw an old wooden plaque shoot off the wall over the fireplace and land in the centre of the room.

Once a visitor and her young son looked back at Chingle Hall as they left after a visit and saw a human form looking out of the window of the Priest Room, a form they described as 'a white or light-grey robed figure', but when they turned their car headlights on the window the form was still there but appeared to be black or dense.

Michael Bingham, a young New Zealander, once heard sounds like bricks being moved when he was in the Priest Room. The sounds seemed to originate in the area of the opened priest's hole, and when he peered inside he told me he saw what appeared to be part of a human hand moving one of the bricks! As he watched the hand froze and then disappeared. Michael spent hours attempting to record on tape the footsteps that he heard many times and to record on film the cowled figure he had glimpsed from time to time. He ran for us a recording of the heavy footsteps and a film showing a shadowy shape that he told us he had obtained after keeping out of sight in a room off the corridor and taking the film by remote control when he heard the footsteps.

Many people, including the present Manager, believe that the ghost at Chingle Hall is that of the Blessed John Wall and that there is nothing to be frightened of. He was in life a man of God, they will tell you; why should his spirit worry us when he is dead!

In May 1979 two Ghost Club members paid a preliminary visit with plans to spend some hours in the haunted Priest Room. They arrived about 7.30 p.m. and met Fred Knowles who proceeded to show them around and finally left them alone in the Priest Room.

After a couple of hours both investigators began to feel very bored and frustrated. By the time that light had faded it was very dark in the Priest Room where no light was used. Without any warning loud bangs and thuds sounded in the direction of the priest hole and then seemed to move across the floor towards one of the investigators and when the sounds were — or seemed to be — virtually under his feet and the floor actually vibrated, he moved across the room towards the other investigator. The violent bangs continued until they reached the window facing the chimney on the opposite side of the room and there they ceased. Both investigators were very surprised; after a long period of complete inactivity and the continuing noise of the owners' television downstairs, they had been lulled into thinking that nothing unusual would happen.

A window in one of the haunted rooms at Chingle Hall, Lancashire.

The haunted
Priest Room
at Chingle
Hall.

The noise really was very loud, so loud that it completely drowned the television noise. Shortly afterwards the noises began again, this time in a different part of the room. Scratching sounds and loud bangs seemed to come from the region of the priest hole beside the chimney and to proceed out into the room. They then moved towards and seemingly into a cabinet, then out again and across the floor with such power and force that a chair, on which one of the investigators sat, literally shook. The bangs travelled across the floor in front of the fireplace and then seemed to move outside the room, in the region of the doorway. After a short pause the bangs sounded yet again; this time they seemed to travel from the floor to the ceiling, by way of one wall, and then across the ceiling, where they ceased. The total duration of this exhibition was about two minutes.

Soon afterwards, at 10.30 p.m., Knowles came into the room and asked whether anything had happened. When he was told about the very loud raps, he said nothing but called on the name of Jesus Christ and banged loudly three times on the cabinet with his hand, asking the 'spirit' to answer him. Immediately three loud knocks came in reply, seemingly from within the room itself. A few more bangs were heard and then the investigators left the house at 11.30 p.m.

The second investigation by the same two Ghost Club members was on 28 July 1979. They arrived at the house at 7.00 p.m. to find that a party of nurses and ambulance men from Preston were in the house on a sponsored Ghost Hunt! They decided to join the party. This time they had brought full recording apparatus and extension leads and were able to obtain a record of the whole proceedings. At 10.00 p.m. the bangs started and again they seemed to move across the room. Various members of the assembled party were sitting on the floor and they said they could feel the floor vibrate with the banging noises. One member became very cold but the bangs were in no way as loud or as powerful as on the previous occasion. Later Knowles came into the room and a few more knocks were heard.

The third investigating party consisted of the two previous Ghost Club members and four additional members. This was in September 1979 and lasted from 7.00 p.m. until 11.30 p.m. One member felt something invisible brush against her leg as she sat with her back to the wall facing the centre of the room. A few knocks were heard but of no real strength or duration and only when Fred Knowles joined the party. This was easily the least eventful investigation.

The fourth investigation took place on 15 August 1980 and lasted all night from 7.00 p.m. until 5.30 a.m. the following morning. Again the entire session was recorded. There was no unusual variation in temperature recordings and the party consisted of ten Ghost Club members and two mediums from the Northern Society for Psychical Research. A few light taps were heard but nothing of great interest until Knowles joined the party just after midnight when, in direct answer to his request, loud and distinct knocks were heard on no less than six occasions. A recording machine just outside the room recorded no sounds whatever so it would seem that the loud knocks were confined to the Priest Room and were not heard outside the room. After Knowles left, one of the recordings — where he asked for his raps to be answered — was played back and a single rap responded to his recorded request!

In 1983 Manager Fred Knowles told me: 'There is still plenty of noise phenomena ... BBC Radio Lancashire recorded many bumps, bangs and footsteps; and an apparition has briefly been seen entering the haunted bedroom ... there have been numerous instances of cameras malfunctioning inside the house and ghostly monks have appeared on instant snapshots taken on the south lawn.'

Late in 1983 a photograph was published in Amateur Photographer showing the apparently haunted corridor leading to the Priest Room. The picture was taken by Andrew Usher as he heard footsteps going towards the haunted room, and the microphone he was using, which can be seen in the picture, picked up the sound of the footsteps but nothing unusual came out on film.

Subsequently Andrew told me that he became interested in such matters some ten years previously after he had visited Samlesbury Hall and while there, attending a wedding reception, he caught a glimpse of the famous White Lady ghost walking through the grounds! He decided that he would see whether he could discover more about spontaneous psychic phenomena.

Two years later he met the late Mrs Howarth who allowed him to visit Chingle Hall repeatedly and conduct experiments there; he tells me: 'The first night I went to Chingle I was wondering what was going to happen. Fred Knowles introduced me to Michael Bingham at 7.30 p.m. and we all went upstairs. We sat in the corridor so that we could see down towards the stairs and towards the John Wall Room; we had the light on in the Priest Room and the John Wall Room but no light in the corridor. We put orange bulbs in the sockets to counteract the harsh white light. About 8.00 p.m. I heard footsteps coming towards us from the stairs sounding like shoes on a wooden floor (although the flooring was in fact carpeted) and I put my hand down towards the floor, holding the microphone there. The footsteps stopped just in front of my hand and I felt icy fingers grasp my hand! I pulled myself free and the footsteps then continued towards the John Wall Room; then they turned left and into the airing cupboard which, it is believed, was once an old doorway into the Priest Room. The footsteps entered the room and then, for about half-an-hour, banging could be heard coming from a hide in the room, very loud banging, and then all was quiet and nothing more happened that night.

'Two days later I was in the porch when I heard footsteps coming across the stone bridge over the old moat and as they reached the door and stepped into the porch, I prepared myself to bid "Good Afternoon" to a visitor — but there was nobody there. This happened several times and once when I heard the footsteps I saw a faint dark figure pass through the porch into the house; I followed immediately but it quickly vanished.

'One night, about 6.45 p.m. I was looking through the window in the chapel and saw a monk dressed in brown walking towards the drive and I ran outside to meet it but it had disappeared; visitors to the house have also seen the ghost monk. The barn across from the house feels evil and depressing, a sensation that is shared by Fred Knowles, and I think something horrible must have happened there in the past which has left its mark .... When Michael Bingham saw bricks being moved in the hide I was a witness. I saw four black fingers pulling at a brick; I was filming with a sound cine camera at the time and on the film you can hear the sounds but the image is rather dark because I had to put the camera into the hide .... We ran downstairs into the chapel and found several bricks scattered over the floor .... I heard and saw things that I didn't believe were possible .... I have seen and felt some strange things in other places, but never as much as at Chingle Hall.... I hope the house will be investigated from top to bottom as there is so much to be found there.' Not without cause does Chingle have the reputation of being one of the most haunted places in Britain today!

Clandon Park, West Clandon, Surrey

In 1896, over the signature 'X', Miss Ada Goodrich Freer contributed an article to the now defunct Borderland magazine, quoting two continental publications and remarking that she had had the advantage of making inquiries on the spot on behalf of the Society for Psychical Research on the question of ghosts at Clandon Park.

The stories circulating on the Continent stated that a recent tenant of Clandon House had demanded the termination of his lease from the owner Lord Onslow because the place was rendered uninhabitable by the appearance of phantoms. 'Every night,' it was stated, 'about three hours before dawn, the servants of Clandon House saw, advancing across the lawn surrounding the house, a lady, dressed in a long robe of cream-coloured satin, and carrying a hunting knife in her hand. Several shots were fired by the keepers at this apparition, which disappeared into the castle, passing through the granite walls or through the massive oaken doors .... More than twenty witnesses, most of them well worthy of belief, affirm that they have seen this lady in cream colour, and had in vain opposed her progress in the house.' Furthermore, it was specified that Lord Onslow himself and his solicitor had both seen the ghostly lady in cream and Lord Onslow had also seen two other phantoms, 'a young girl in black and a man with a long beard'.

Miss Freer pointed out that, for the previous five-and-a-half years, a widow lady had been the tenant of Lord Onslow at Clandon Park. Earlier in the century the fine old mansion had been untenanted, with the result that it had acquired, 'on no evidence at present available', the reputation of being haunted. Yet, she goes on to say, 'the servants of the present tenant and a few other persons, have believed that they have seen figures about the house but how far there is any evidence for this...'. Miss Freer also mentioned that Lord

Onslow was at that time in Nice and, while she had made some inquiries, 'the evidence so far obtained has not yet justified a formal report to the Society and any expression of opinion on the matter might, in the meanwhile, be justly regarded as premature'.

In a later issue of Borderland (Volume 4, 1897) Miss Freer wrote again about the ghosts of Clandon House and of her claim to have seen the apparition herself. She prefaces her article by saying that at that time details of the true story were already known to herself and other members of the SPR 'but as a matter of courtesy to the owner of the house publication was deferred until permission had been received to make known the real circumstances'. She went on to describe the case as 'a really good, well-attested ghost story,' and says, 'the traditions of haunting have been well known in the neighbourhood for many years past', and at the suggestion of the Vice-president of the SPR, Lord Bute, she was invited to collect and examine all the evidence obtainable. She accordingly visited Clandon House in the company of Mr G.P. Bidder, Q.C., a fellow-member of the Society and they stayed overnight at the invitation of the occupants, Captain and Mrs Blaine. But let Miss Freer tell the story herself, as she did at a meeting of the SPR at Westminster Town Hall on 29 January 1897, with the President of the Society, Sir William Crookes, O.M., F.R.S., in the chair.

'The evidence was not far to seek .... It was abundant and varied in kind. We ascertained that the witnesses amounted to nearly a score. They were diverse as to age and class — adults and children, educated persons and servants .... The evidence extended over a lengthened period and was in many cases especially definite and clear .... At the time of my visit I knew that the house had the reputation of being haunted. I knew absolutely nothing of any details .... I arrived at the house in the dusk of an autumn day .... We had tea cheerfully in the hall. The subject of the hauntings was mentioned, but I begged, for evidential reasons, that it might be dropped at once. Should any phenomena present themselves, I did not wish to have to discount more than was necessary for expectation. I was permitted to sit alone, in the dark, in four rooms alleged to be haunted, but entirely without success. When I went up to dress for dinner, my hostess left me at the door of my room, with a promise to send the maid. I followed her out a moment later to ask her to send an additional message as to something I wanted. Nothing else was for the moment in my consciousness. I ran in the direction from which she had come, but my hostess had disappeared, and I turned back towards my room.

'As I turned I saw a lady coming towards me, perhaps twenty feet away. I stood for a moment, waiting for her to get nearer before deciding — I am slow-sighted — whether this really was my hostess. No, it was evidently someone who had come to dine: I had heard that guests were expected. She was cloaked and hooded, her dress of yellowish white satin gleamed where her cloak parted — she had jewels on the low bodice.

'The costume was quaint, the hood of the kind known to our great-grandmothers as a "riding-hood". I happen to possess one of the kind, about a-hundred-and-twenty years old, and the outline is quite familiar to me. She should be interesting and original, I reflected, and moved forward. Just as we met — when I could have touched her — she vanished. I discovered later that my description of her corresponds with that of other seers who have met the same figure before and since.'

It has to be stated that Miss Freer has recently been shown to be a most unsatisfactory psychic investigator but the manifestations at Clandon House cannot be wholly attributed to her lack of objectivity.

A tenant of Clandon Park once
refused to go on living there
because of the number of ghosts
in the house.

[Image previously spread across two pages]

Clandon House was built about 1735, on the site of an earlier house, by the Venetian architect Giacomo Leoni. A porch to the front door was built in 1876 but otherwise the exterior is virtually unchanged and the interior too — with its magnificent plaster decoration, especially of the two-storey entrance hall — is basically unaltered. The house occupies an area which a charter of Henry III confirmed as being in the possession of the Knights Templar and the home farm in the grounds is known as Temple Court and is likely to have once been a grange of the Knights Templar.

It was the second Baron Onslow who employed Leoni to build the present house. He had married one of the richest heiresses of the day, Elizabeth Knight, a member of a well known Jamaican family. Her portrait in the ground floor Palladio Room, shows her to have been a dark girl with small pretty features, wearing a silvery dress. Some people have suggested that she seems to be looking shy and almost apologetic. This is interesting, for although she brought great wealth to Lord Thomas Onslow she was considered to be socially a disadvantage; old letters suggest that Royal visitors were merely polite to the lady of Clandon, preferring the company of more obviously noble ladies. There seems little doubt that she was a sad and lonely person and legend has it that she drowned herself in the lake and that it is her ghost that haunts the house.

In the history of Clandon House (1964) Pamela, Countess of Onslow writes: 'Legend has it that the heiress was unhappy and it is said that her spirit still haunts the house that her riches built.' There are stories of those who have caught a glimpse of the dark lady dressed in cream-coloured satin' subsequently recognizing the figure they have seen from the portrait of the sad and lonely Lady Elizabeth Knight who died in 1730, before the house had been built over the foundations.

The thirty-nine acres of park, covenanted to the National Trust, were laid out by Capability' Brown, the fashionable landscape gardener who acquired that odd title from his habit of frequently remarking that such and such a piece of land was 'capable of improvement'.

Claydon House, Middle Claydon, Buckinghamshire

I first visited incomparable Claydon in 1962 at the invitation of the late Sir Harry Verney, whose family had owned land at Claydon since the fifteenth century. Claydon House was built by the second Lord Verney and the present delightful edifice is part of what was intended to be a much larger house.

With money made by his grandfather from trading with eastern countries after the Restoration, Lord Verney embarked on some ambitious building programmes. At Claydon he built first a brick stable block and then altered and extended the existing house, which was altered again in 1860. His further plan was for a 250-foot west wing that included a ballroom and a hall with an observatory over it; sadly he ran out of money before the house was fully furnished. Some of his handiwork was pulled down by his niece when she inherited, and of Lord Verney's west wing only one block remains.

Sir Harry Verney was full of stories of ghosts and ghostly happenings at Claydon and he invited me to bring down a party of Ghost Club members which I did as part of the Club's centenary year celebrations. I shall always remember the welcome he and Lady Rachel gave us as they met us, took us into their gracious and beautiful and historic home and Sir Harry began by recounting the ghost story of one of his ancestors, Sir Edmund Verney, Royalist standard bearer, who was killed in battle at Edgehill in 1642.

According to this story Sir Edmund had been captured by Cromwell's men who demanded that he give up the colours but Sir Edmund refused, saying, My life is my own but my Standard is the King's', and so he was killed. But when the Roundheads tried to take the Standard from his hand, they found they could not unlock his grip, so they cut off his hand. Later in the battle the King recaptured the Standard, Sir Edmund's hand still grasping it, recognized by the signet ring which bore the King's portrait. Sir Edmund's body was probably buried somewhere on the battlefield, no one knows where, but his hand was sent home to Claydon for burial.

When the family vault was opened some years previously. Sir Harry Verney told us, there was no coffin for Sir Edmund, only a casket large enough to take a hand. In honour of our visit Sir Harry brought out the treasured ring for us to see and handle: it is exquisitely beautiful. The present custodians at Claydon may tell you that this story is very sensational stuff, but Sir Harry Verney had no doubt about the matter and he said the ghost of Sir Edmund had long been reputed to haunt the vicinity, wandering pathetically about the little chapel and also within the present house, seemingly looking for his lost hand. Sir Harry told us that he had in his possession a number of signed and witnessed reports of sightings of the ghost of his ancestor. He was hoping to encounter the ghost himself one day.

Among other reported ghosts at Claydon Sir Harry Verney told us about the experience of Mrs Walker, a forester's wife who lived on the estate; a very reliable, truthful and responsible woman who was at the house in 1923 looking after the children while everyone else was away.

In the house, at night-time, she repeatedly heard the sound of very heavy footsteps, apparently emanating from the corridors near her. She knew there was no human being in the house, apart from herself and the children, who were certainly not responsible. Time and again she noticed that the footsteps seemed to take the same path and they always stopped at the trapdoor entrance to the priest's hole. Yet, each time she investigated, no one was up there and she discovered no explanation for the very distinct sounds.

Years later exactly the same sounds were heard by Mrs Walker's sister, who hurriedly returned to her home, almost shaking with fright, after a night looking after the children and hearing the same heavy and unaccountable footsteps. Yet she had spent many nights in the house alone and was completely familiar with the place. Her description of the sounds corresponded in every detail with the sounds heard by her sister and, very occasionally, by other people who had no knowledge of these unexplained footsteps.

There seem to have been two secret hiding-places at Claydon. One, mentioned by a writer in order to compare it with a similar unusual priest's hiding-place that once existed at Mancetter Manor House in Warwickshire, would seem to have been a staircase with a break half-way down where a man must let himself down several feet'. Such a hide would be almost unique, my friend Glanville Squiers told me. As an expert on secret hiding-places he informed me that a second hiding-place was found at Claydon House in 1860 and destroyed by workmen who were carrying out the renovations which inadvertently resulted in the discovery of the hiding-place. This hide was arranged next to a chimney and concealed a false wall. It was said to have been large enough to take ten men standing upright, but which hide was approached by the disembodied footsteps does not appear to have been established.

Inside the house we explored what the guide book described as 'the most astounding rococo suite of rooms in Britain' and the quite exceptionally fine staircase with its ironwork balustrade. This contains a continuous garland of ears of corn so delicately wrought that they rustle when anyone walks up the stairs — no ghost this, simply the remarkable work of a somewhat mysterious man named Lightfoot about whom practically nothing is known except that he was extremely eccentric. Sir Harry Verney told us that a ghostly figure, thought to be Lightfoot himself, had been glimpsed in various shadowy parts of Claydon House. As appropriate to someone so-named, his shade is seen but no sound is heard.

We were told that it could have been the ghost of Lightfoot that was seen during some demolition many years earlier. An estate carpenter had assisted in the destruction of the enormous ballroom and cupola, and while working among the rubble he had chanced to look up and he had seen a strangely dressed man standing nearby and looking at the devastation. When the carpenter called out to the figure, for he knew the stranger did not belong to the house, the figure suddenly and quite inexplicably disappeared.

Sir Harry had also taken the trouble to obtain a written account of an apparition seen by his sister on the red staircase and he remarked that this was probably the same apparition that other people had seen when staying at Claydon. Afterwards he very kindly gave me his sister's account and I cannot do better than quote verbatim: Written by Miss Ruth Verney, bom 1879. It must have been about 1892, when I was thirteen, that I ran up the Red Stairs at Claydon House, and turned left and left again on the first landing and then took a few steps towards the Cedar Room. I noticed without surprise that a man was halfway down the upper floor. After I got nearly to the door of the Rose Room, I quite suddenly thought, "But who was he?" and I ran back to look. He was gone and there hadn't been time for him to reach the top or the bottom of the flight. I saw him on the third step of the second flight and he was coming down. He was tall and slender, and wore a long black cloak, beneath the hem of which peeped the tip of his sword: he carried a black hat with a white feather gracefully curled round the crown. That was all I saw. Mother said he was just where the secret stair had been.

'There was a curious little sequel which may or may not have been merely a coincidence. Some time later a little school-friend was coming to spend a weekend. She was, of course, all agog to see the ghost, but in the interval we both forgot him completely. We were going up to the top of the Red Stairs and as she put her foot on the third step, she said: "By-the-bye, where did you see the ghost?" Alas! he has never come back. Other people have seen ghosts here and heard unaccountable noises. Andrew Lang, sleeping in what used to be called the Rose Room, was much honoured to be awakened one night and to see a lovely lady in grey, but she quickly vanished into the wall of what had been a secret room.'

A ghostly Lady in Grey has reportedly been seen quite recently in a room habitually used by Florence Nightingale who knew the house well, and one researcher has posed the question as to whether this could be the ghost of Miss Nightingale herself, but there seems no positive evidence for such an assumption.

Some of the custodians at Claydon pour scorn on Miss Ruth Verney's ghost story; they point out that the Red Stairs — and for that matter the house as we know it today — did not exist in cavalier days, so how can a ghostly cavalier haunt the Red Stair? But such logic cannot be applied to ghosts and ghostly phenomena. The ghost cavalier — if ghost it was — may have been appearing at the spot where it had appeared in life irrespective of what may be there now; or the ghost' might be a 'thought form' projected from the mind of a living or dead person that is perceivable to some people. It cannot but be interesting to observe that, according to Sir Harry Verney, the same figure was seen in the same place nearly a century earlier. Among the legion of theories for ghosts is one that proposes that ghosts are some form of telepathetic projection, possibly triggered by a traumatic event and perhaps unconsciously fed by the presence of a certain type of person. If this were so, the present surroundings that a ghost might appear to be part of may be nothing whatever to do with the ghost or its appearance. There does seem to be good evidence for thinking that some ghosts are the product of the minds of the people who see them — and yet the same ghosts are seen again in the same place by other people who have no knowledge that such a ghost has been seen there. An entirely different theory suggests that certain events, under certain conditions, may be stored or preserved in some way in stones and brickwork, to be released when the requisite conditions prevail.

My happy memories of Claydon House are clouded by a little disappointment. During the course of our fascinating visit I took many photographs and at the end persuaded Sir Harry and Lady Rachel Vemey, who was dressed in purple robes, to pose for a final photograph in front of the Ghost Club members. Back home I found my camera had jammed and, not wanting to spoil the film by opening the camera in daylight, I took it to a leading photographic establishment in Bedford Street, London, and explained the position, asking the assistant whether he could examine the camera in his dark room to avoid losing the photographs by exposing the film to daylight. The assistant took the camera from me and looked at it and then, before I could protest, he suddenly snapped it open — and I had lost my irreplaceable photographs of Claydon House!

Florence Nightingale frequently stayed at Claydon after her sister married Sir Henry Vemey in 1858 and against my disappointment of a few lost photographs I have the lasting memory of having talked with Sir Harry Verney about the happy times he spent with the girl who was to become the much-loved 'lady with the lamp' during the Crimean War.

Many objects associated with her are preserved at Claydon, but as far as I know her ghost has not been definitely recognized there although she certainly haunts at least one other house she knew — but that is another story!

Cley Hill, Warminster, Wiltshire

This 800-foot high chalk hill, with its univallate Iron Age hill-fort, is full of fascination and mystery.

At the time of the Spanish Armada, Cley Hill was one of the heights which blazed with a warning beacon; centuries earlier it probably blazed with the fires of pagan festivals; more recently there have been many reported sightings of unidentified flying objects from the top of this strangely shaped hill and there are those who feel that the place is a centre of psychic power.

Until the early years of the present century it was customary to fire the grass and gorse bushes on Cley Hill each Palm Sunday, ostensibly to drive out foxes and hares or, some claimed, to drive out the Devil. It seems likely that the custom was a survival of a magical, religious witchcraft or nature rite. Today the National Trust frowns on fires being lit on Cley Hill yet lights have sometimes been seen burning here at dead of night; fires that apparently have no objective reality since no trace is ever found of them next morning.

On certain nights, the ides of March and June, 31 October and 2 November are four, local people and visitors have reported strange sights and sounds on Cley Hill. Dim figures silhouetted against the sky for a brief second before disappearing; the sound of muffled voices, high and singing and deep and primitive has been heard, coming in waves and gone almost as soon as it is heard; but of course all this is pure imagination and has no reality outside the minds of those who hear it... has it?

Clouds Hill, near Bovington, Dorset

This prim and whitewashed cottage, nestling amid rhododendron bushes, was fast becoming a ruin when T.E. Lawrence, Lawrence of Arabia, first rented it in 1923. He repaired and altered the ramshackle cottage, put in some simple furnishings, and spent much time here; dreaming, writing, reading and listening to music on his ancient gramophone that is still in the pretentiously named Music Room.

Here Lawrence revised the text of his monumental Seven Pillars of Wisdom, talked the night away, ate and drank; but only water or China tea — no alcohol ever entered Clouds Hill. He bought the place in 1925 as a home for his retirement and had almost completed an extensive series of improvements when he left the Air Force in March 1935, and retired to Clouds Hill to live there for the rest of his life. In May he wrote to Lady Aston 'Nothing would take me away from Clouds Hill. It is an earthly paradise and I am staying here...'. Five days later, on his way back to Clouds Hill from Bovington Camp, Lawrence had his fatal accident. By this time there can be no shadow of doubt that Clouds Hill, as stated in the official guide, had 'become for him "an earthly paradise", which he did not want to leave'.

And it would seem that part of him never has left the vicinity of Clouds Hill. When I visited Clouds Hill in 1970 I did so because Lawrence of Arabia had fascinated me for as long as I could remember, and because I had known men who had served with him and I wanted to see the place where he had found some peace at the end of a troubled life. I was surprised to learn that stories of his ghostly form, in Arab dress, usually entering Clouds Hill at dusk, had begun to circulate soon after his death and that there had been irregular but persistent reports of the same figure being seen ever since.

Clouds Hill, near Bovington, Dorset - the home of Lawrence of Arabia. The phantom form of that tortured man is said to have been seen disappearing into the cottage he loved and said he would never.

Lawrence of Arabia on his Brough Superior motorcycle; the machine on which he had his fatal accident. It is said to be the ghostly roar of this machine that haunts the spot to this day.

I also learned that the roar of a powerful motorcycle had been heard in the area of the accident at dead of night.

A number of local people claim to have heard the throaty roar of a powerful Brough Superior coming towards them, often just before dawn. When the machine was still seemingly some distance from them the noise of the motorcycle would cease abruptly. Some of the witnesses were people who remembered hearing Lawrence roaring along the lanes during his lifetime; others were motorcycle fanatics who said there was no chance of their mistaking the unique sound of a Brough Superior, the machine that Lawrence possessed. A certain Mrs Little of Eastbourne heard the sound in 1973, according to Andrew Green.

I remember asking Lawrence's friend, Knowles, who had built himself a bungalow nearby, on that initial visit or possibly a subsequent one, about the ghostly associations and he said it was all nonsense; and yet I wonder. A friend of mine, who knew Lawrence well and today treasures several souvenirs of his travels in Arabia, tells me that she has no doubt that Clouds Hill is haunted. Some years ago she regularly visited the cottage, as she had done so often during Lawrence's lifetime, and she has repeatedly felt his presence there and sometimes caught a glimpse of his phantom form. Once, as she was leaving in the evening, she turned and saw him disappearing into the cottage, dressed in the Arab costume that he loved. Another time, when she was accompanied by a psychic friend, they both saw the ghost of Lawrence coming toward them; only to disappear when they could almost have touched him. They too have heard the roar in the roadway that has no objective reality.

Perhaps that last journey that Lawrence took has somehow become impressed forever upon the atmosphere and perhaps his love of the place has lived on and sometimes becomes crystallized into a visible form; at all events it seems indisputable that the moving spirit of the Arab revolt is seen from time to time, visiting again the little cottage that he loved, as he did so often during his lifetime — but in Arab costume? Perhaps that is how he most often thought of himself, who knows?

Corfe Castle, Purbeck, Dorset

Picturesque from any viewpoint, Corfe Castle, one of the more recent acquisitions of the National Trust, has long had the reputation of being haunted, as well it might for its history is long and gory.

King Edward (later known as The Martyr) succeeded his father in A.D. 975, when he was only fifteen years of age, in spite of the opposition of the dead King's second wife, Elfrida, who had borne the King another son, Ethelred, for whom she sought unsuccessfully to secure the crown of England.

The queen retired to Corfe with her son and a few years later she achieved her ambition. King Edward happened to be hunting in the area in A.D. 978 and becoming detached from the rest of the party, he decided to visit his ten-year-old half-brother of whom he had always been fond.

The former queen met him and he was offered a stirrup cup of wine which he had no sooner put to his lips than he was stabbed in the back on the instructions of the treacherous queen dowager who saw the opportunity to dispose of Edward and have her son Ethelred crowned.

The King, realizing that he had walked into a trap, turned his horse and raced away but the wound was a deep one and half-way down the hill he fell from his mount; one foot was caught in a stirrup and the King was dragged to the bottom of the hill.

Corfe Castle - where a
headless woman in a
nightgown has been seen
on several occasions.

The queen's retainers hastily hid the body in the nearby cottage of a blind woman where it was disguised with old and mean clothing. Before the night was out, so runs the story, the room in the cottage where the body lay hidden was filled with such a heavenly light that it even penetrated the old woman's blindness and she saw that the dead body was that of the King. Another version has it that the body was hidden in a well where a mysterious ray of light appeared to glow over the mouth near the castle, a well that became known as St Edward's Fountain. At all events the body was eventually recovered and buried at Shaftesbury but meanwhile Ethelred did succeed to the throne to become known as Ethelred the Unready.

It is said the boy Ethelred was deeply shocked at the assassination of his beloved step-brother and he became hysterical and screamed that he did not want to become king at such a price but his mother seized a candle and beat him into silence. The effect of the murder and the punishment he received always stayed with Ethelred and for the rest of his life he banned candles from any ceremonial or religious procession in which he took part. It matters little that there was no castle here in those days and the incident must have occurred at a hunting lodge on the site; the beautiful but wicked Elfrida did remove Edward in the manner described.

King John made the castle a royal residence and used it as his treasure house; he also starved to death there twenty-two French nobles in the dark dungeons.

During the Civil War the treachery of an officer of the garrison allowed the parliamentary troops to gain possession and the castle was undermined, blown up and brought to total ruin. So much wickedness, painful deaths and human treachery has perhaps provided the atmosphere for ghosts and strange happenings. For many years the castle ruins were said to be haunted by flickering light and dark figures but reports were less frequent after a gang of smugglers were caught!

Yet phantom figures have sometimes been seen in the vicinity of the castle, as evening darkens the sky, and there are reports of an odd, vague figure seen here over the years; a figure that resembles a headless woman. A local resident who saw the mysterious form in 1967 wondered whether it might be connected with the nearby manor house which is reputed to have a ghost and a secret underground passage that is said to lead to the castle.

At first John Seager, approaching Corfe Castle at night, thought the figure ahead of him was a woman in a nightgown, but as he drove nearer he found himself braking hard and he said afterwards: 'It was a white figure, headless, that drifted across the road in front of me. It moved on down the path at the foot of the castle hill, near the bakery. I suddenly found myself trembling with coldness ... it was an experience I would never want again.'

In 1971 the same figure was seen in approximately the same place by a visitor to the area and again in 1976 by three visitors. Historians have suggested that the ghost is that of someone concerned in one of the many tragic events that have contributed to the history of Corfe Castle.

Cotehele, Calstock, Cornwall

Lovely and romantic Cotehele is a fine example of the late medieval home of a squire; it is one of the least-altered houses in the county, being built between 1485 and 1520 on the foundations of an earlier house.

To wander through Cotehele is to step back in time. There is the splendid hall, the evocative kitchen with its mysterious square hole to the left of the hearth: the kitchen court with its cressets (early medieval lamps); the old dining-room with its rich tapestries; the chapel with its fascinating clock, the earliest clock in England still unaltered and in its original position; the Punch Room with its gay bacchic tapestries and stone steps within the wall that lead up to the north tower; the White Room with its walnut four-poster bed with Jacobean hangings; the Red Room, so-named from the huge, crimson-draped four-poster bed that dominates 'this mysterious room' as it is described in the official guide; the staircase lobby with its pair of mid-seventeenth century chairs, carved and ornamented with grotesque contrivances and an infinity of knobs and rings, of which the origin and purpose is wrapped in mystery; the old-drawing-room visited by George III and Queen Charlotte in 1789; Queen Anne's Room — no one knows why it is so-called; King Charles's Room, where Charles I is said to have rested in 1644, a dark room full of atmosphere that is only lit by two small windows ... and there have been ghostly happenings at Cotehele in the past and it may be that something remains of long-forgotten past events here where time has virtually stood still.

With its long history of feuds and outlaws, and of hiding and ambush and plans of murder, it is not surprising to learn that there was a tragedy of some kind in the archway leading to the entrance and that a man was killed there or died in some unremembered episode. The spot where he fell and died was marked forever afterwards by an irremovable bloodstain; and hereabouts the mysterious, unidentified and ghostly form of a man in something like seventeenth-century costume has been seen many times over the years. Later the bloodstained' stone was removed to the little bridge by Cotehele Quay. When I was at Cotehele in 1981 I was told that the bridge had recently been painted and the 200-year old curiosity had been obscured. In actual fact the mysterious stain was probably red ironstone which contains veins that can look like blood when the stone is wet.

Cotehele, Calstock, Cornwall - where the unexplained scent of herbs and ghostly music has been reported; and where a White Lady walks.

[Image previously spread across two pages]

Another gruesome story told about Cotehele, and repeated by S.P.B. Mais, concerns Caroline Augusta, Countess of Mount Edgcumbe, who died in 1881. It is said that a thieving sexton was surreptitiously removing the jewellery from her body after death, when she suddenly sat bolt upright on her bier — and the sexton fled empty-handed!

More recently and more plausibly a strong herbal fragrance has been noticed by many people all over the house, including visitors who have no knowledge that such an inexplicable scent has long been noticed at Cotehele; and, more rarely, the sound of ghostly music has been heard here. The weekend before my last visit in September 1981, a friend of the Administrator had asked whether the house was haunted, having walked round the house when it was empty and devoid of visitors. He had experienced puffs of herbal fragrance, heard strains of phantom music and encountered other experiences which he was loath to relate, in various parts of the house. Another visitor had remarked on the fragrance in King Charles's Room and indeed several of the guides will tell you that they have themselves experienced this very pleasant odour in this lovely house. Other ghostly incidents and experiences are less talked about.

Cotehele belonged to the Edgcumbe family from 1353 until it passed to the National Trust in 1947. It is said that during the last illness of the fifth Earl a nurse from Tavistock was sitting by his bedside when a woman dressed in white passed through the room. At this period one could walk right round the house through the various rooms surrounding the courtyard and the nurse took little notice of the person she had seen, thinking that it must be the housekeeper. A little later she saw the housekeeper and, noticing that she was dressed in black, commented: 'Have you changed your dress because when you passed through the Earl's room you were in a white dress?' The housekeeper replied: 'You must have seen the ghost, for I have worn this dress all day and have not been near the Earl's room today.' Apparently the ghostly figure of a girl in a white dress was repeatedly seen in certain rooms, including what was then the Earl's room, some years ago. Mrs Phyllis Julyan, who has lived at Cotehele for many years, tells me that what may have been the same figure was seen at Christmastide 1980.

A friend had called with her husband to wish Mrs Julyan the compliments of the season. Afterwards she called on the telephone and asked whether Mrs Julyan had a young girl staying with her, a girl with long hair and wearing a white, flimsy dress. They had seen such a girl going down the main staircase on their way out. Mrs Julyan assured her friend that there was no one in the house but herself. It seems that this lady is interested in the subject of ghosts and has seen ghostly forms on other occasions: she spoke to Mrs Julyan because she felt there was something strange about the figure. Such experiences (someone seeing a figure that has been seen by others but having no previous knowledge of this) lead one to wonder whether ghosts are frequently present but are only visible to certain people. Mrs Julyan tells me that she is not able to see or feel these things and for her the house has a lovely atmosphere and she is sure that people living there before her have been very happy. Many of the thousands of annual visitors to this lovely house will, I am sure, echo these feelings; but still some of them may see ghosts.

Coughton Court, Alcester, Warwickshire

The central gatehouse here was built in 1509 but in 1780 the Gothic-style stone wings were added; by contrast the rest of the house consists of Elizabethan half-timbered upper storeys of brick. Inside the house there is exceptionally fine panelling of different periods, porcelain, furniture and portraits pertaining to the Throckmorton family who built Coughton.

Historically Coughton is connected with Sir Walter Raleigh, who married Bessie Throckmorton, a lady-in-waiting to Queen Elizabeth; possibly with the Gunpowder Plot — according to tradition the wives of some of the plotters assembled in the drawing-room to await news of the outcome of that affair; and the house was the scene of bombardment during the Civil War. It is not known to which period the ghost belongs.

The phantom was known as the Pink Lady and is said to have walked from the Tapestry Bedroom, across the dining-room, and on to the front stairs — odd how so many ghosts are associated with bedrooms and stairways. One cannot help wondering what tragic episode gave rise to the appearance of the ghost... and although the present Custodian, who has been there many years, tells me she has never seen or heard any ghost, it must have been very troublesome at one period, for about the turn of the century the wife of Sir William Throckmorton's agent had a Catholic priest in to lay the ghost. Perhaps, unlike most exorcisms, this one was successful.

According to Meg Elizabeth Atkins the ghostly footsteps always follow the same route — 'down the main staircase, across the drawing-room and towards the south-west turret, where the footsteps die away into silence'. A 'marked change' in the atmosphere has been reported when the ghost footsteps of Coughton Court walk.

Craigievar Castle, Lumphanan, Aberdeenshire, Grampian

Here Scottish baronial architecture is generally regarded as having reached its greatest pinnacle of achievement and Cecilia, Lady Sempill told me in April 1982: 'Yes, I am sure Craigievar is haunted.'

Lady Sempill once
saw a crowd of
people in olden dress
in the hall at
Craigievar.

Legend has it that the Blue Room is haunted by the ghost of a member of the Gordon family (traditional feudal enemies of the Forbes, the family who built the property in the seventeenth century). This Gordon is said to have been forced through the window of the Blue Room by the third laird, the Red Sir John, to fall four storeys to his death and he retaliates by returning in ghostly form. For many years the Forbes-Sempill family would not sleep guests in the Blue Room for fear of their being disturbed by the ghost although his presence was usually felt rather than seen.

Cecilia, Lady Sempill, widow of the late Lord Sempill and last of the family to live at Craigievar, has been good enough to tell me about the ghosts and I cannot do better than quote from her fascinating letter to me of 21 April 1982:

'I am sure Craigievar is haunted, but by very benign ghosts on the whole. I have often slept in the castle, and had no qualms. I did once feel a "presence" in the Blue Room, and was very momentarily afraid, but I didn't see anyone. Oddly enough the next night my husband told me he had felt someone in the room. (He was away the night I felt someone was there.) We used to sleep in that room because it was supposed to be haunted and we didn't want to alarm our guests.

'The story was that a Gordon was pursued and forced out of the south window, which was then bricked up. The window was re-opened by the National Trust seven or eight years ago. Many people have heard footsteps going up and down stairs at Craigievar, but no one was ever seen.

'The most notable ghost story of the castle (so far as I know) was when I saw a number of people in olden dress in the hall late one night when the family was in some trouble and our solicitor came up to talk matters over. He and I were talking in the withdrawing room by the light of one lamp until after midnight. There were only four candles in the hall, on the table. We were

waiting for my husband to come and join the talk, but after midnight he still didn't appear. I got up to go to the hall and saw a man in a philabeg or kilt picking up something from the chest opposite the hall door. I assumed (light was bad of course) this was my husband and went towards him asking him why he hadn't joined us in the withdrawing room. He retreated into the hall and I followed him, asking him why he hadn't joined in the talk with our solicitor. He didn't speak and seemed to hurry ahead of me. Now comes the odd part of this story. When I entered the hall it seemed full of people which, at the time, didn't seem odd to me — I was so anxious to speak to my husband that I just brushed aside the crowd, saying: "Wallie — where are you? It's too late to be funny." (He loved playing practical jokes.) I looked in the secret stair and the pantry and behind the lugget chairs, pushing through the throng. But I was so intent in my search that I didn't take in the crowd or notice what they were wearing — except that their clothes were unfamiliar. I saw our solicitor looking at me in a puzzled way and I suddenly felt exhausted. I offered him a drink and then went up to bed. My husband I found fast asleep in the Blue Room.

'*Only the next morning did I think how strange it was to have seen all those people ... I told my story to two elderly Scots women, who both (at different times) said the same thing: "My dear, didn't you know that they would come back when you were in trouble."*

'*I am told the most interesting and convincing part of my tale is that at no time did I think I was seeing ghosts ... I have an open mind about them really. Certainly I was not alarmed.*'

Crathes Castle, Crathes, Kincardine, Grampian

A dramatic survival of sixteenth-century baronial architecture, Crathes Castle has been lived in continuously ever since it was built and it retains its interior decoration, including the remarkable painted ceilings, and some of the original furniture.

Historical associations go back to 1323 when the Lands of Leys were granted to the Burnett family by King Robert the Bruce and indeed the jewelled Horn of Leys, said to have been given by Bruce as a symbol of the gift, is still preserved in the four-storey building with its immensely thick walls. The Burnett family built Crathes Castle and a Burnett gave the castle to the National Trust for Scotland in 1951.

Crathes has long been famous for its Green Lady, a ghost that is said to have appeared on many occasions and usually before a death or some other grave trouble in the Burnett family. Queen Victoria often visited Crathes and there are reports that on one occasion she saw the Green Lady gliding across a certain room towards a carved fireplace.

There the form stooped and lifted up a ghost child before fading away, as she has done so many times before.

No one knows the story behind the appearance of this ghost or ghosts or why she should most often appear before misfortune in the Burnett family, but it was beneath the hearth of the fireplace where the ghosts disappear that the skeletons of a woman and child were found some years ago; perhaps the mortal remains of the Green Lady of Crathes and her child.

Croft Castle, near Leominster, Hereford and Worcester

Croft Castle looks every inch a castle from the outside with its fourteenth- and fifteenth-century walls and towers but inside the hall and the gallery belong to the eighteenth century. There is a wealth of delightful plasterwork and some fine panelling, some imported from other houses — which perhaps accounts for the variety of ghosts.

Over the years there have been a number of strange and ghostly incidents reported here, including the sightings of at least two unidentified ghosts, one being seen in what is now the Oak Room, another in the hall, and others elsewhere.

In the 1920s a friend of the late Sir James Croft (eleventh baronet) was playing billiards in the room now known as the Oak Room. He turned round and saw the ghostly figure of a huge man dressed in leather. There have been other sightings of a similar figure here, as we shall see, and some people think the ghost is none other than the redoubtable Owen Glendower: it certainly seems only fitting that the ghost should appear somewhere of the man who claimed to be able to 'call spirits from the vasty deep'.

There was the time, also in the 1920s, possibly 1926, the present Lord Croft tells me, when some of the Oxford boat race crew were staying at Croft for the weekend. Among the guests was the Oxford stroke of the day, a very tall and powerful man. Sir James Croft was an Oxford cox in his time and coxed the Oxford crew in the Boat Race of 1926.

On one occasion this prosaic oarsman came downstairs rather late just before dinner and in the dim light of the portrait gallery he saw the figure of a man with bobbed hair and a leather jerkin, a figure that he estimated was at least seven feet tall. The apparition faded away within a few seconds. Later Sir James and other members of the family and some of the guests set out to attend a hunt ball.

The cars were at the door and everyone was outside when one of the guests realized that he had left his cigarettes in the Oak Room. He ran back and on reaching the Oak Room he almost collided with 'an enormous man' who, a moment later, was no longer there. Another member of the party said afterwards that the unimaginative and burly fellow-guest, an Oxford oarsman, was 'green and shaky all evening'.

While I feel that these two incidents, recounted to me by two different people, may have their origin in a single episode, there is no doubt that something of the kind did happen. Lord Croft tells me that he heard the story from Sir James himself and three other people who were present. Lord Croft went back to Croft Castle as a tenant of the National Trust in 1956.

I have been told that often, of an evening, in the 1920s, the girls and young men at Croft would play card-guessing games with friends in what used to be called the Billiards Room, now known as the Saloon. Sometimes they would indulge in table-turning and planchette (a board with a pencil through it) that seemed to answer questions.

One evening they became very worried when they all heard tapping from outside, at each window: the Oak Room, Blue Room, Saloon, library ... and then it seemed to turn and come back. Even the dogs showed every sign of distress, their hair literally standing on end. This 'staggering exhibition of psychic force' took place at a time when Sir James was thinking of pulling down the Elizabethan wing and one planchette message read: 'Croft must not destroy Croft'.

There were other occasions when the unrecognized figure of a man was encountered in the Oak Room; once by a cousin of the family in the day-time. At first she thought it must be a carpenter or workman until 'he' disappeared as she watched.

An Elizabethan ghost has been seen in one of the tower bedrooms. The present Lord Croft tells me: 'The late first Viscount Bledisloe, who I knew quite well as he had been a friend of my late father, told me once that when he was Governor General of New Zealand he had occasion to visit Australia on official business and was present at a dinner party in Canberra, the capital. During the course of conversation after dinner the subject of ghosts cropped up and the whole party became respectfully silent when the then

Archbishop of Brisbane told how he had had a ghostly experience in the *[...text continues on page 129]*

The redoubtable figure of Owen Glendower has been seen a number of times at Croft Castle.

[Image previously spread across two pages]

mid-twenties when as a Canon of the Church of England he was staying at an old castle on the Welsh border. It was at Croft Castle and the experience occurred while he was drinking his early morning tea in bed in his bedroom. Suddenly he saw very clearly an Elizabethan gentleman in ruff, puffed sleeves, breeches and hose with buckled shoes, walking across the room. The apparition paused and looked in his direction but made no sign and walked on, disappearing into the wall. Later he was shown the portrait of Sir James Croft, the Comptroller of Queen Elizabeth Is Household, which then hung in the Blue Room and recognized him as the ghost he had seen before breakfast.'

Lord Croft adds that when he was at Croft Castle in 1949 (before it passed to the Trust), 'my wife read out an account in the Leominster News about a gentleman in full Elizabethan costume being seen walking on Bircher Common, which is only about two miles distant from Croft Castle. The person who saw him recognized him instantly from having seen a reproduction of his portrait in a book called The House of Crofi by the late Major Owen Croft. It was Sir James Croft (the Comptroller) who died in 1591.'

Oddly enough another Elizabethan ghost — or possibly the same one — has been seen on the ground floor at Croft. During a fancy dress dance in the early 1920s one of the guests spotted someone whom she thought must be a gatecrasher: a most elaborately dressed Elizabethan gentleman. She informed several companions who all saw this person', apparently mingling among the guests. When a check was made the figure had disappeared but several people who had seen the figure said it resembled the Croft portrait of the sixteenth-century Sir James Croft.

During and after the Second World War Croft Castle was used by a Catholic school. Altars were placed in the rooms used as classrooms; nuns, quiet and contemplative, were everywhere; a priest lived for a time in one of the towers. There seem to have been few sightings of ghosts at Croft since that time; perhaps it was all too much for preternatural appearances, and yet, in 1980, a twelve-year old grandson of the family told his grandmother that he had seen the form of 'a little bent old lady in black' entering one of the bedrooms. He wasn't at all frightened and described the experience simply and in a very straightforward manner as a matter of fact. The grandmother, who knew that no such person was in the castle, investigated the idea that it may have been a shadow or trick of the light but came to the conclusion that the distinct form that had been seen was not to be explained in this way.

Once, too, a woman writer was staying at Croft as a guest and, when her host had to go to London and stay there for the night, the lady absolutely refused to stay alone in the flat, although this was situated above the Custodian's premises and sounds of movement and the television could be faintly heard so one did not really feel alone there.

And then there was the curious incident that happened at the time the family were trying to collect the endowment for the National Trust. A lady who lived in Wales was interested in the family who lived at Croft in the eighteenth century. She contributed handsomely to the fund and was about to return to Wales after being in England for her sister's funeral. She looked in at Croft Castle, which chanced to be empty at the time. It was a beautiful, still summer evening. She stopped her car and walked round the outside of the house. As she did so she became aware of some very pleasant eighteenth-century music apparently emanating from the Saloon (which is now used for concerts). She may well have been in an emotional state after the funeral and not in her normal frame of mind, perhaps not on her usual wavelength'; but that she did have some kind of paranormal experience seems indisputable.

One day in October 1978, the Assistant Custodian of Croft Castle was talking to a schoolmaster in the hall. Suddenly the teacher spun round and said he had seen a reflection in the glass covering a map, the reflection of someone walking across the hall behind him. The Custodian, facing the teacher, had seen nothing. The Birmingham schoolmaster took his class to Croft several times, he spent a good deal of time there one way and another, but that occurrence in the hall was a never-to-be-forgotten experience; strange, inexplicable, pointless it may have been but it certainly happened.

In the old days, I have been told by someone who knows, at Croft Castle, when it came to ghosts, it was always a case of 'don't talk about it or the servants won't stay'; perhaps now, with no servants, the ghosts will come into their own again, or have they gone forever?

Culloden, east of Inverness, Highland

The National Trust for Scotland has in its care the Graves of the Clans, the Well of the Dead, the Memorial Cairn, the Cumberland Stone and Old Leanach farmhouse, now restored as a battle museum; here where Prince Charles Edward's army was defeated and the '45 Rising ended. And hereabouts linger without doubt some of the ghosts of those doomed Scotsmen. Here, where the fate of the house of Stewart was sealed, the setting has changed little since the last pitched battle in Britain was fought on 16 April 1746.

Bonnie Prince Charlie's 9000 tired and hungry Highlanders met 9000 government troops under the Duke of Cumberland, third son of King George II, and it was all over in sixty-eight minutes. The Highlanders' losses were enormous, the victors cruelly massacring their wounded enemies; the English dead only numbered fifty. A cairn and green mounds

The Cumberland Stone on Culloden Moor, where, on the anniversary of the battle, the atmosphere can be strange and sombre.

mark the soldiers' burial-place and from time to time visitors to this sorrowful place report strange happenings.

On occasions, the dim form of a battle-worn Highlander has been seen at dusk in the vicinity of the impressive cairn and one visitor, while looking closely at the Highlanders' graves here, lifted a square of Stewart tartan which had blown down from the stone on the grave-mound and distinctly saw the body of a handsome, dark-haired Highlander lying, at ease it seemed, full length on top of the mound. The visitor sensed that the figure she was looking at was dead. His clothes were dirty, muddy and of old-fashioned cut and material. His tartan was the red Stewart. As she fully realized that she was seeing something of supernormal character, she turned and fled from the field of memories.

Miss Wendy Wood has related some of her unusual experiences in her autobiography. At Culloden the redolent atmosphere may not be as apparent during the summer months when the area is full of visitors, but in the winter months it is very strong and in spring too, around the anniversary of the battle, the whole region takes on a sombre and reflective character. Each time it has been outside the summer season when Miss Wendy Wood has encountered something very strange at Culloden.

As she and a party of Scottish patriots visited the museum, the Cairn, the Graves and the Well, she recalled a previous visit, many years before, when she had leaned over the Well of the Dead and saw in the water, not her own reflection, but that of a man with a drawn face, wild eyes and long black hair....

This time, she again looked over the Well — and was confronted with the reflection she had seen before: it was the same man, she had never forgotten that face, the eyes filled with agony, an open cut across the forehead ... blood-clotted hair ... and suddenly Miss Wood experienced a searing pain in her own brow. With the greatest difficulty she somehow wrenched herself away from the Well and returned to her friends, trying to hide her distress; but her appearance left no doubt that she had had a very curious and disturbing experience and she records that it took her three days to recover fully and a further four days before she lost the pain over her left eye.

Culzean Castle, Maybole, Ayrshire, Strathclyde

Picturesque Culzean Castle was built by Robert Adam between 1777 and 1792 around an ancient tower of the Kennedys — and a Kennedy piper haunts the place to this day, especially on Piper's Brae, between Happy Valley and the sea and particularly on winter nights when the cold wind howls across the Firth of Clyde; then the sound of the ghostly piper is said to be most likely to be heard.

Another ghostly sound associated with Culzean goes back 400 years. It is said that here (or possibly at nearby Dunure Castle, now all but disappeared) Gilbert Kennedy, fourth Earl of Cassillis, arranged for Allan Stewart, Commendator of Crossraguel Abbey, to be seized when he visited Culzean, which had become Crown property after the Reformation. The story goes that the unfortunate Stewart was dragged to the ominously named Black Vault in the depths of the castle and there stripped naked, bound to a spit and roasted before a fire, care being taken to liberally baste him with oil every few minutes to ensure that he did not burn!

After repeatedly pleading for mercy or for death, he signed a document surrendering the lands of the Abbey to the Earl, and he was taken away to recover. Six days later, however, he refused to sign a confirmatory document and the Earl ordered him to be roasted again. When he was near to death, he signed the land away, and was again carried away and *[...text continues on page 136]*

The Oval Staircase at Culzean - where a misty shape has been seen, which is supposed to be the ghost of one of the Kennedy's.

allowed to recover. When the matter came to fight Kennedy was fined £2000 by the Privy Council and bound to keep the peace with Stewart to whom he had to pay a fife pension, but he kept the lands.

Occasionally, and especially it seems on quiet autumn mornings, the crackling and roaring sounds of a great fire are heard from within these old walls, accompanied by faint, smoke-smothered screams and agonized sighs that soon fade away into silence.

A furnished apartment in the castle was presented to General Dwight D. Eisenhower in 1946 as a token of Scotland's appreciation for his services as Supreme Commander of the Allied Forces in the Second World War — an area of the castle that is haunted by the ghost of a beautiful girl.

One afternoon at five o'clock a visitor, Mrs Margaret Penney, met a lovely, dark-haired young woman coming towards her along a corridor. The figure was dressed in an evening gown which Mrs Penney immediately thought strange at that hour, but by the time the thought crossed her mind the figure was almost upon her. The corridor was a narrow one and Mrs Penney quickly squeezed herself to one wall to allow the girl to pass, saying as she did so: 'Not too much room for passing when you're as plump as I am!'

The young woman passed quickly by, but as she did so Mrs Penney felt her entire right side, the side nearest to the beautiful form, suddenly become icy cold, and as she realized that the form had actually walked through her and she must be seeing a ghost, she seemed to hear the words, 'I do not require any room nowadays ...'. And as the words faded away the figure suddenly and completely disappeared leaving the corridor deserted.

In 1972 three servants at the castle reported that they had independently seen an indistinct and inexplicable shape, on different occasions, in one of the passages leading to the dungeons; while in 1976 two visitors saw a 'peculiar misty shape' near the oval staircase. They watched the shape travel up the stairway and out of sight and afterwards a member of the castle staff told them: 'What you have seen is not uncommon. Several people have said they see things on that staircase. It is supposed to be the ghost of one of the Kennedys although the castle they knew is the old tower in a different part of the building. Whatever or whoever it is goes back many years.'

At the foot of the rock on which the castle stands are the Coves of Culzean, rock caves used as smugglers' hiding-places and, it is said, the rendezvous of fairies on Halloween.

D

Dunstanburgh Castle, near Alnwick, Northumberland

Today there are only ruins where once proud Dunstanburgh Castle stood, begun in 1316 by Thomas, Earl of Lancaster and enlarged by John of Gaunt; the only castle of importance mentioned in the list of sixty licences granted by Edward II. Cadwallader J. Bates, writing in Border Holds of Northumberland describes the savage grandeur of the place: A crescent of black cliffs rises a hundred feet straight out of the waves to form the northern rampart of the castle.

You almost expect to be challenged by the basalt giants that are drawn up like so many warders round the base of the stately Lilburn Tower, and might reasonably conclude that the shattered turrets of the great gatehouse were sustained by power of enchantment, so much do their fantastic outlines, peering mysteriously over the green slope of the western escarpment, seem to set all known principles of gravitation at defiance. High as these turrets are, in a strong north east gale the sea dashes up through the Rumble Churn into a fountain above them.'

The one-time owners of this melancholy pile, the earlier lords of Dunstanburgh, might almost have been the prey of some mysterious hereditary malady for they became extinct in 1244. In Henry VIII's time the stronghold is described as 'a very ruinous house and of small strength'; but as a superb ruin the castle remains to this day.

Dunstanburgh Castle was already a ruin when the events occurred that gave rise to the ghost story associated with this picturesque and vast edifice; once it was the largest castle in Northumberland.

It is said that a knight by the name of Sir Guy was making his way down the Northumbrian coast when a violent storm caused him to look for shelter. The only place in sight was mined Dunstanburgh Castle and Sir Guy spurred his horse forward, amid the pouring rain and flashes of lightning, looking forward to some shelter among the mins.

As he reached the castle he dismounted and led his horse to the archway in the keep gatehouse and there, with the wind and rain for company, he waited beside his steaming horse for the storm to pass.

Suddenly a figure appeared before Sir Guy, a shining form that commanded him in a voice that brooked no argument to follow if he wished to find a 'beauty bright'. Puzzled and bewildered, Sir Guy followed his ghostly guide who led him beneath the castle and through a labyrinth of passages until they reached a brass-bound door.

The dramatic ruins of
Dunstaburgh Castle.

[Image previously spread across two pages]

Beyond the door, which was opened for him, the knight discovered himself to be in a huge, cavern-like chamber, lit by hundreds of flickering lights that shone on dozens of knights in armour who lay, deathly white and with closed eyes beside their sleeping horses. Sir Guy was led through these columns of sleeping or entranced warriors to the far end of the hall where he beheld, to add to his amazement, a beautiful lady lying on a bier. The 'sleeping beauty' was guarded on either side by two corpse-like figures, one of whom held a horn and the other a sword. Sir Guy's guide intimated that he must choose either the horn or the sword and that upon his choice depended the fate of the sleeping lady.

For a moment Sir Guy thought about the choice before him and then he decided that if he blew on the horn it seemed logical that it would wake the sleepers so he seized the horn, put it to his lips and sent a high-pitched blast echoing through the vast chamber.

Immediately the horses and the warriors awakened from their sleep and rose to their feet, the knights' hands already reaching for their swords; but the beautiful lady slept on and then, as Sir Guy felt everything begin to spin faster and faster about him, the whole vision faded and he awoke outside the walls of Dunstanburgh Castle with a couplet running through his head:

Woe to the coward, that ever was born,

Who did not draw the sword, before he blew the horn.

Sir Guy sought diligently for the entrance to the passages that led to the great door that imprisoned the sleeping beauty; indeed it is said he searched for years afterwards but he never found it.

Practically identical legends are told about the Eildon Hills in Scotland and Sewingshields Castle, Northumberland;

but amid the mins of Dunstanburgh to this day there are stories of the sounds of a high-pitched horn blasting the silence at dead of night and of visitors suddenly encountering a dark figure resembling a knight in armour of long ago, among the crumbling mins and in the vicinity of the gatehouse towers.

Dunvegan Castle, Sligachan, Isle of Skye, Highland

Formerly accessible only from the sea by means of a gateway with a portcullis opening on the rocks and now having an entrance over a bridge across a ravine which once served as a moat, this historic castle with walls in places ten feet thick, stands amid delightful gardens, in sharp contrast to the rugged wildness of its surroundings.

From time immemorial the castle has been the seat of the MacLeod of MacLeod and the early thirteenth-century clan stronghold is visited by MacLeods from all over the world. Dunvegan is claimed to be the oldest castle in Scotland still inhabited by the original family.

At first sight this venerable edifice does indeed look, as Dr Samuel Johnson put it, 'as if it had been let down from heaven by the four corners, to be the residence of a Chief. It dominates the village at the head of Loch Dunvegan, and the famous Fairy Bridge has long had an evil reputation — for years it was said that no horse could cross the bridge without shying. Horses and dogs are, of course, notoriously super-sensitive.

The castle contains a host of interesting and historical objects including relics of Prince Charles Edward, letters from Dr Johnson and Sir Walter Scott referring to their respective visits in 1773 and 1815, and Jacobite and St Kilda mementos. There is also the Dunvegan Cup, made of Irish bog-oak; the

Haunted Dunvegan
Castle, Isle of Skye,
has a bridge that no
horse could cross.

drinking horn of Rory More, Sir Roderick MacLeod, the twelfth-century chief, knighted by King James VI; and, in the Fairy Room in the south tower, the fascinating Fairy Flag of mysterious origin.

This banner was credited with the power to bring victory to the clan that waved it; to make fruitful the marriage bed of a MacLeod chief who spread it on the nuptial couch; and to charm herrings and other edible fish into the loch when it was unfurled. One condition of its effectiveness in victory is that the flag can only be waved on three occasions and so far it has been used twice. In 1490 at the Battle of Glendale and in 1580 at Trumpan; on both occasions the MacLeods were the victors.

Legend has it that the flag was given to the MacLeods by a member of the fairy fraternity who, in the guise of a mortal woman, married a member of the clan; the gift being made at the Fairy Bridge which stands nearby.

Dunwich Heath, Dunwich, Suffolk

South of Dunwich, along these acres of sandy cliffs, there have been heard, it is said, the ghost-bells of churches long since submerged; and there is also, it seems, a ghostly Victorian squire riding a ghostly Arab thoroughbred.

The squire is a member of the wealthy Barne family who, in Victorian days, owned nearby Sotterley Hall and some 3000 acres in the region of Dunwich. Miles Barne was a splendid horseman and bred Arab horses, exercising them on Dunwich Heath and elsewhere in all weathers, attired in a tall white hat. During the First World War soldiers billeted hereabouts reported seeing the ghost of the old squire riding on a ghostly horse, a beautiful beast with proudly arched neck and magnificent tail, totally different from their troop horses. Over the succeeding years there have been sporadic reports of such a mounted figure being seen in the area, most often when the moon is full or on the wane — a silent figure that passes proudly along the heathland and disappears among the sandy cliffs.

Here too, in this eerie place, the ghost of an unidentified Elizabethan lady has been seen walking down towards the sea ... and disappearing.

Old Dunwich now lies buried beneath the waves; once a prosperous city possessing no less than nine churches, a bishop's palace, a mint and immense bronze gates of great antiquity, it was a sea port of power and significance. Now all has gone, borne away by the ceaseless erosion of the sea. The phantom bells, for some reason, are most often reported just before Christmas and frequently late at night.

Nearby Grey Friars has a legend of lost love. Here a maid and a local son of the lord of the manor fell in love and used to meet secretly and walk together among the sandy dunes. The noble family found out what was happening. Forbidden to meet his love, the young man died of a broken heart and his ghost still wanders along the beach, amid the heathland, leaving no footprint in the sands.

Dunwich is one of the areas in East Anglia known as the haunt of Black Shuck, the phantom black hound that goes padding across the desolate countryside, his coat black as ebony, his eyes burning like live coals .... All imagination you say, more likely a disordered digestion, a hallucination or trick of the light and shade. Tell that to the local people. Many claim to have seen the fearsome hound and have no wish to bring back the memory by talking about it; if you don't choose to believe them, well, that's your affair.

E

East Riddlesden Hall, Keighley, West Yorkshire

This manor house, typical of the district, has been discoloured by centuries of industrial grime but otherwise looks much as it must have done when it was completed in 1692; the great bam in the grounds is much older than the hall and is in fact one of the finest medieval barns in the north of England. There are several ghosts here from different periods of history.

First, there is the Grey Lady, a female form attired in grey, that has been seen flitting aimlessly along corridors and in and out of bedrooms, seemingly without object or destination; but very much a part of the atmosphere of the house. The Administrator, Major W.D. Morris-Barker, tells me this is the ghost of one of the ladies of the Manor and the story goes that her husband returned home one day to discover his wife with her lover. Not wishing actually to shed blood, he 'kindly' decided to lock his wife in her room and then promptly bricked-up the boyfriend. Consequently, of course, they both starved to death and her ghost is said to mount the stairs, walk along the landing and enter the master bedroom. An old lady who was caretaker at the Hall many years ago used to see the Grey Lady quite regularly; she became quite used to seeing her and could minutely describe the dress she wore. She was rather annoyed with the Grey Lady because it seems that although she always greeted the figure and said 'Hallo' to her, the Grey Lady never replied! Major Morris-Barker adds; 'We have never seen the Grey Lady, but both my wife and I and our family have heard footsteps on the stairs and landing on a number of occasions; and three times a disembodied voice has bade me "Goodnight" from the top of the stairs.'

The haunted stairway at East Riddlesden Hall and a photographer's idea of the ghostly 'Grey Lady'.

Another ghost, Major Morris-Barker tells me, is known as The Head at the Window. This is reputed to be the ghost of the lover of the Grey Lady and his head is supposed to appear at the Rose Window in the room where he was bricked-up. The son, now elderly, of a former caretaker here tells me that many years ago this room was in fact bricked-up and when it was broken into, a male skeleton was found.

'A third ghost is known as the White Lady and this is supposed to be the ghost of another of the Ladies of the Manor. This time our White Lady had been out riding or hunting on the estate and was seen to enter the gates on her return. However, only the horse arrived at the house and although a search was made she was never seen again and it is thought that the horse perhaps shied, threw her into the lake, and she drowned. Her ghost is said to be seen walking round the lake.

'Then there is the Ghost Coachman. The horse of the coach he was driving is said to have shied for some unknown reason and bolted, pulling the coach into the lake. The coachman was drowned and his ghost is said to be seen walking across the lake, presumably looking for his coach.'

Yet another ghost at East Riddlesden Hall is known as The Highlander. His ghost, according to some reports, is seen peering through the circular window over the front porch; according to other accounts he walks up the drive leading to the Hall or, more rarely, walks leisurely round the old fishpond at dusk. It could be that some of the ghosts have been incorrectly identified but that ghosts do walk here seems indisputable.

The story of the Highlander ghost tells of a Scottish wool buyer, or some say a 'Packer', who had attended a market at Bingley in the eighteenth century, when the owner of the Hall was one of the richest men in the area, riches made in the rag trade. But the nefarious deeds of this master of the Hall were, apparently, legion throughout the district — it was even believed by the local peasants that the lordly River Aire, disgusted at the practices and carryings-on at the Hall, changed its course as a protest! But still the wily and wealthy owner of East Riddlesden looked out over the river, enjoying the spectacular views from some of the 280 windows in the house.

The Scotsman, carrying a great deal of money on his person, either for the purpose of purchasing wool or the result of a good day's trading, whichever story you may prefer, was caught in a blizzard and sought shelter at the Hall. He was taken upstairs by the steward and shown into the small room over the front door and soon afterwards coldly murdered and his body buried secretly at dead of night. There are various stories of the murder and some say that the Scotsman was in debt to the master of Riddlesden Hall and that the steward acted on the orders of his master; others have it that the steward had caught sight of the large amount of money he carried and acted on his own initiative. At all events an account of the subsequent trial and hanging of the steward is on record at York for the year 1790. Whatever the truth of the matter, the ghost of the unfortunate Scotsman seems to have lingered here, making irregular appearances at the most unexpected times.

On the other hand, another apparently paranormal manifestation at East Riddlesden Hall consists of the rocking of a carved wooden cradle in one of the bedrooms and this is said to take place each New Year's Eve. The seventeenth-century cradle is that used by generations of previous owners and occupants of the Hall and it stands in the master bedroom. Each New Year's Eve, I am told, the cradle has been seen to rock and to contain a ghost baby, and it has been suggested that Riddlesden's ghostly Grey Lady is responsible for the rocking. Perhaps she is looking for the cradle when she is seen wandering about the house throughout the year and for some unknown reason only finds it on New Year's Eve. Major Morris-Barker tells me: 'I have popped up to this room at various times of the night on two New Year's eves but have not seen anything to date ... it could be, of course, that my timing was wrong!'

One recent ghost book mentions a ghostly figure of 'a middle-aged lady in a greyish-blue dress' that frequents parts of the garden, her gown long enough to trail on the ground although it is noticed that when she passes over lawn or flowers there is no movement of either; and it has been observed that she casts no shadow, which is surely hardly surprising.

A final word from Major Morris-Barker: 'Although we seem to have a lot of ghosts for a smallish property, I personally do not see anything odd about this in view of the fact that there has been a dwelling here for well over a thousand years. Quite apart from this the site has certain "mystical" features about it: it lies on a ley line and the dividing line of two Saxon Wapentakes (the Staincliffe and Skyrack) passes directly through it and the site had certain sacred connotations in as much as it is reputed to stand on a hill with a river flowing beneath it .... Saxon and probably pre-Saxon chiefs would meet here to pass laws and punish wrong-doers...'

The past seems to overlap the present at Riddlesden Hall.

F

Felbrigg Hall, Felbrigg, Norwich, Norfolk

This is a fine seventeenth-century house with a wealth of eighteenth-century furniture and pictures, a walled garden, woodland and lakeside walks and a haunted library.

The first Earl of Norfolk took the name de Felbrigg, adopted it as the name of his manor and built the first house on the site. Some medieval arches and doorways still remain in the cellars of the present noble Hall. The estate passed into the hands of wealthy merchant, John Wyndham, and his son, Sir John, who married Margaret Howard, whose father became Duke of Norfolk in 1483 and was knighted by Henry VIII. Sir John was eventually beheaded on Tower Hill in 1502. A later member of the family, 'Mad Windham' (1840-66), became notorious for his passion for trains, persuading railway officials, strictly against regulations, to allow him to drive engines, collect tickets and wear a guard's uniform. Towards the end of his life he may have achieved some kind of happiness when, totally bankrupt, he became the driver of the express' train that ran between Norwich and Cromer at wages of a guinea a week.

After his death the house, contents, park, woodland and farmland were acquired by John Ketton, a successful Norwich merchant who had made a fortune out of cattle feed in the 1830s and 1840s. He and his Quaker wife loved the house and made very few alterations. Thirteen years after Ketton's death, in 1872, author, traveller and collector of ghostly legends, Augustus Hare, visited Felbrigg and saw the two Miss Kettons. They seemed to have adopted the Windhams and all their heirlooms and traditions as though they were their own ancestors and in particular they were convinced that William Windham (1750-1810), a man who had made many alterations in the library and added to it many valuable volumes, still visited the house and especially the library in ghostly form.

The fine library at Felbrigg was described by a visitor as long ago as 1795 as 'well furnished with the most valuable authors'. The large Gothic library table, a pair of green leather armchairs, the three splat-backed chairs and the celestial and terrestrial globes — all must have been familiar to William Windham II; as familiar perhaps as the books he loved and collected for his family library. These included large folios on architecture and classical antiquities which he brought back with him after his prolonged Grand Tour of 1737-42, his copy of Gauffecourt's Traite de la reliure (which stimulated a practical interest in bookbinding) and the manuscript Ragandjaw, a short satirical play written by David Garrick and dedicated to William Windham in 1746. Windham also owned a large collection of bookbinding tools and materials and in the library there are some 300 quarter-bound calf volumes thought to be his work. Small wonder that he is popularly believed to have so loved his books and his library that even death could not separate him from them.

During the course of his visit to Felbrigg in 1885 Augustus Hare was told by one of the Miss Kettons: 'Mr Windham comes every night to look after his favourite books in the library. He goes straight to the shelves where they are. We hear him moving the tables and chairs about. We never disturb him, though, for we intend to be ghosts ourselves one day, and to come about the place just as he does.'

It is hoped that it is not the Misses Ketton who are responsible for the ghostly smells of rotting flesh that have been reported in recent years from Felbrigg Hall! I hesitate to dwell on anything so repulsive as this strange smell but the fact, as reported to me by more than one National Trust official, is that in the past, undoubtedly, there has been an unexplained smell, limited in scope to an area of no more than a few feet, within a passageway; a smell which has sometimes been noticeable on the ground floor and on other occasions in a certain upstairs corridor — but most often not at all. It was emphasized to me that many investigations were carried out and as far as could be established the occasional smell was not due to drains or had any logical explanation. The smell was sickly sweet and very strong and most people who encountered it said it was a smell they would have associated with rotting flesh.

David F. Musson, B.Sc., is presently Regional Director of the National Trust, Southern Region. For some years he was at Felbrigg Hall and he has been kind enough to send me an account of his experience; he prefaces this by saying, 'I should state that I am not really a believer in ghosts, but that might just make what I have to say more interesting:

'During December, 1969, the last squire of Felbrigg Hall, Windham Ketton-Cremer, died leaving the house and all its contents, together with the park and estate, to the National Trust. The house was absolutely full of a magnificent collection of ephemera of many kind. I had just moved to the East Anglian Region and was given the responsibility of sorting out the financial situation, taking over the property and opening the house to the public. This involved examining the contents of every drawer and trunk, as well as all the nooks and crannies on the estate.

'One winter's afternoon at about five o'clock I was working in the library on the first floor of the house sorting through the contents of the library desk. Light was fading fast and it was a very cold afternoon. I had an electric fire close beside me. The only lighting was a standard lamp and a table lamp. I was engrossed in my sorting work when I suddenly became aware of the feeling that someone else was in the room, and I looked up to see a gentleman sitting in an armchair in front of the fireplace, apparently reading a fat leather-bound book. I did not react immediately and carried on with my work, before it dawned on me that there was no-one else in the room. I looked up again; the gentleman was still sitting there but gradually faded from view. The experience was in no way worrying.

Later I asked the butler to the late squire whether there had ever been a ghost in the library. He said: "Oh yes, — the ghost of William Windham has regularly been seen sitting in the armchair on the far side of the fireplace reading a book. He always likes to read one of the collection of Samuel Johnson's personal library which he bought for the Felbrigg Hall library, and we keep two or three volumes from this collection on the table by the chair."

As far as I know the ghost has not been seen subsequently, perhaps because on security grounds, with the room being open to the public, we have had to lock up the valuable books which William Windham found so interesting.

'I myself had some doubts as to the identity of the gentleman in question, in that he was dressed in a very ordinary-looking suit which was not what I would have expected from someone occupying the house in the 1750s and 1760s. However, my doubts on this score were completely overruled when after many months of attempts we managed to get into one of the trunks in the attic at Felbrigg, in which we found wrapped in newspapers of the 1830s three-piece suits of the 1750s and 1760s, remarkable in being ordinary day-to-day wear, rather than special-event clothing. These clothes were very ordinary and would hardly have drawn attention to the wearer had they been put on at the present time.

'There is a further mysterious twist to the story, which I do not fully understand, nor am I sure of the details. After I left Felbrigg in 1975 to become Regional Director of the Southern Region, I heard that one of the portraits of William

Windham which had been painted in his youth on a Grand Tour of Italy, had an inscription on the back of the frame which apparently said something in Italian to the effect that his spirit would return to his home. He was not to die, however, for a considerable number of years.

'There is a further ghost story relating to Felbrigg, quite different in character. It was told to me by a previous Agent for the Estate, John Mottram, if I remember correctly. Apparently the late squire was dining with his younger brother, Dick, and a friend of their own age, Dick Bagnall-Oakley, probably in the early thirties when all three were young men. As I remember it, they had left the dining-table and were sitting in front of the fireplace with a glass of port in their hands and with three gun dogs at their feet; when suddenly all three dogs pointed at the door at one end of the dining-room and, with the hair of their backs on end, they followed the movement of something along the length of the room and out of the other door, after which they very slowly settled down. All three of the men also felt that a presence had gone through the room, although this was invisible to them, and at the time of the event there seemed to be a very chilly atmosphere in the dining-room.'

It has long been accepted that certain animals and in particular most dogs are acutely sensitive to psychic activity, and it would appear that the elegant dining-room at Felbrigg may well be haunted in addition to the comparatively austere but very atmospheric library which has seemingly been haunted for more than a hundred years.

Formby coast, Merseyside

The sand dunes and foreshore west of Formby, the nearest unspoiled coastline to Liverpool, have been reputed to be haunted since time immemorial by the fearsome 'Old

Trash', a hound whose appearance is reiterated by legendary giant dogs all over the country.

The ghastly resident of Formby beach is an immense black hound with luminous eyes, the sight of which is said to bring death or misfortune to the beholder. Belief in such Hell Hounds' abound throughout Europe and appear to be folk memories that date back to the days of pagan Nature gods and to the old Norse mythology of the 'Wild Hunt' and 'Wolf of Hell'. Demon dogs, harbingers of doom, huge supernatural creatures with howls that make the blood run cold — surely such legendary beasts have no place in the world of today? But 'Old Trash' (a local name derived from the noise the creature makes as it paces through the wet sand) was reportedly seen as recently as 1962 when two staff reporters and a photographer from a local newspaper paid a Halloween night visit to Formby Beach in search of the ghost animal.

Two of them heard and saw a 'huge, dark shape moving about in clear silhouette atop a nearby sand dune'. As they moved forward, the 'strangely compelling' shape began to move about in circles, much as a dog would. The watchers hurriedly climbed the high sand dune but when they reached the top there was nothing to be seen, nor were there any footprints or any disturbance of the sand. A typical newspaper invention? Perhaps. The three men added at the end of their report: 'It is impossible to describe exactly how we felt in print. Though it may easily have been a trick of the imagination, or perhaps even a stray dog, we are sincerely convinced that what we saw and heard was not of this world.'

G

Gawsworth Hall, Gawsworth, Macclesfield, Cheshire

Gawsworth Hall has several ghosts and a few years ago the then occupants, Mr and Mrs Raymond Richards, told rne all about the beautiful sixteenth-century half-timbered manor house with its tilting ground formed by the Fitton family and about the ghosts and strange happenings that have been reported there over the years, but, as Raymond Richards said, 'all ancient houses must have unaccountable occurrences which are difficult to explain; a dwelling cannot have occupied the same site for 900 years without acquiring some influences.'

Gawsworth Hall is the capital house of the ancient Manor of Gawsworth and we are fortunate in knowing a good deal of the history of the people who lived there since medieval times. Here, through the ages, lived the Norman earls, the Stanhope family, the Earls of Macclesfield, the Earls of Harrington and the Roper-Richards family; each in turn being Lord of the Manor and Patron of the Living.

And for more than 300 years, from 1316 to 1662, Gawsworth was the home of the Fitton family, one of whom, the wayward Mary Fitton, may well have been the Dark Lady of Shakespeare's Sonnets, although Dr A.L. Rowse believes that the Dark Lady was Emilio Bassano, the wife of an Italian count. At all events a ghostly lady is reputed to walk in the beautiful courtyard and elsewhere at Gawsworth; a ghostly form described as a 'lady in ancient costume'.

In February 1971 Monica Richards, who occupied a bedroom immediately below the Priest's Room, complained of the smell of incense that sometimes pervaded her room. Next to the Priest's Room there is an oratory with an escape hatch leading to the cellars. In 1921 a macabre discovery was made following the removal of an old cupboard: a human skeleton. The bones were later interred in the churchyard. No one has ever been able to discover whose body was hidden there but surely no one could have wished for a more beautiful place to die.

The 500-year-old mansion now known as the Old Rectory at Gawsworth is also said to have once been the home of Mary Fitton, the charming and promiscuous seventeen-year-old who so enjoyed herself when she was a member of the court of Queen Elizabeth I. The fifty-year-old Comptroller of the Queen's Household, Sir William Knollys, thought himself to be in love with her; so did William Herbert who found himself in Fleet Prison after giving her a baby and getting her sacked from the Court. Her passions led her and Sir Richard Leveson, an old friend of the family, to have an affair and some say he gave her two children (letters exist in which he addresses her as, 'My deare sweet wyff').

Certainly she had a child by Captain William Polewhale before she eventually married him — and what of William Shakespeare, a close friend, it is said, of William Herbert; could he too have fallen for the gay and bright-eyed Mary — and made her immortal?

Be that as it may, her ghost has long been said to walk on autumn evenings through the avenue of lime trees from the old hall to the Harrington Arms, a countryman's inn that stands on the site of a farmhouse or lodge that Mary must have known and perhaps even used as a trysting-place. It Seems that when she returned from Court after the birth of her son by the Earl, her mother would not allow her inside the Hall, and she was forced to live at the Rectory; 'Poor Mary' had her unhappiness as well as her happiness.

Gawsworth Old Rectory
is haunted by the ghost
of promiscuous Mary
Fitton and an
unidentified man.

[Image previously spread across two pages]

In 1964 the Old Rectory was purchased by a former Stockport alderman, Mr Idris W. Owen. He became interested in the possibility of encountering the ghost of the amorous Mary and he waited up no less than eight times in the room where she is reputed to appear, but with no success. 'Still,' he said in November that year, 'I've not given up hope of seeing her one day.' He was addressing a luncheon to celebrate the opening of the Abbey National Building Society's first Stockport office, attended by Sir Geoffrey Shakespeare, deputy chairman of the Society and a direct descendant of the Bard. He suggested that he might visit Mr Owen's home one day, adding dryly; 'The Dark Lady might put in an appearance for a Shakespeare.'

In March 1977, my wife and I met Raymond Richards and his wife Monica and, over sherry in the beautiful ground-floor library, she told us of the ghosts and ghostly happenings at Gawsworth Hall and Gawsworth Old Rectory. We talked first of Mary Fitton and learned that the ghostly figure of a girl has been seen in the vicinity of the church as well as the Old Rectory, the Hall and the roads between. Once, a man who does odd jobs at the Hall was returning very late one night when he saw a cloaked female figure which at first he thought was Mrs Monica Richards. He saluted her but she gave no indication that she had seen him and carded on across the road and he had to brake very hard to avoid hitting her. When he had stopped he got out of his Land Rover to find no sign of her anywhere; this was about 2 a.m. in the morning.

At one time there were serious attempts to establish whether or not Mary Fitton was buried in Gawsworth Church and, before the ecclesiastical authorities stopped the investigations, a coffin was located bound with narrow leather straps decorated with a floral design: an identical design to that pictured in some portraits of this remarkable individual who deserves a ghost.

Monica Richards told us that the incense had been noticed in particular on three occasions and each time it seemed to precede the visit to the Hall of an archbishop. Once the archbishop commented as he entered the Hall on the thoughtfulness of the family to welcome him with incense; the family had been thinking that he must have brought it! Each time the overpowering but localized odour has been experienced by upwards of four people; on the last occasion, at the beginning of March 1977, it lasted only about three minutes but on the previous two occasions it had lasted considerably longer.

When the Richards had lived at the Old Rectory all sorts of odd things had happened: the sound of smashing glass, a woman's voice, various raps and bangs for which there seemed to be no logical explanation and once Mrs Monica Richards saw the form of a man with dark eyes and a little pointed beard. At that time her husband was busy with his book, The Manor of Gawsworth, and any visitors were directed to her, upstairs. The house is a fascinating place, full of history and interesting features and lots of people used to call and they were never turned away. It was after eight o'clock one evening when Mrs Richards came out of the upper room and saw a man standing at the bottom of the stairs, almost hidden in an alcove. At the time her immediate thought was that he had left it rather late to call and she was a little surprised that her husband had sent anyone up at that time. However, she felt that she obviously had to show the visitor her customary courtesy and she went down the stairs towards him. Looking back on the experience afterwards she realized that she didn't notice anything about the figure below the neck but .the face always remained very clear in her memory and she always wanted to see him again. When she was almost up to the figure it seemed to retreat and at the same time she felt a sudden pain in her chest, almost like a dagger being plunged into her. By then the figure had disappeared and she never saw it again.

At one time, when they were at the Old Rectory, a student priest was staying with them and after he had been there some time Mrs Richards chanced to comment that she hoped he liked his room and always slept well. Oddly enough, she was told, he had found that he could never sleep until two o'clock in the morning so he had got into the habit of studying until the clock struck two and then he went to bed and always slept without difficulty. It will be remembered that the odd job man who saw the ghost of a female (Mary Fitton perhaps?) found that the time was two o'clock in the morning.

Somewhere within nearby Maggoty's Wood lie the mortal remains of Samuel 'Maggoty' Johnson, perhaps the last professional jester in England, an eccentric eighteenth-century dancing-master and dramatist, and his ghost haunts the spinney that bears his name.

Perhaps his final jest was to be buried in unconsecrated ground to test the theory that people so buried cannot find rest and are likely to return to haunt the land of the living. If so he seems to have been successful for his prancing form, a dim silhouette, is seen in the vicinity of the tombstone where verses seek to justify his unusual choice of 'resting' place. Maggoty's lion-headed fiddle, dated 1771, resides in the dining-room at Gawsworth, where he lived.

A visitor once found himself in Maggoty's Wood one bitterly cold winter day and was astonished to encounter a prancing form with tight breeches, a motley coat and a head-covering resembling a monk's cowl ornamented with long ears and a cockscomb, with bells hanging from various parts of the form; yet no sound reached the ears of the visitor who, a moment later, found that the figure had disappeared as suddenly and as inexplicably as it had appeared. Puzzled, the visitor hesitatingly approached the spot where the form had pranced and sprung so lightly only seconds before but there was no disturbance in the even snow that covered the ground.

Another time, one of Raymond Richard's servants, a trusted and respected and responsible man, told his master that he thought he had seen someone in Maggoty's Wood. He had entered the wood while he could still see someone or something springing and bounding about in the area of Johnson's grave, but when he reached the spot where the prancing form had attracted his attention the place was totally deserted. This happened on a bright summer afternoon but the man said the spot near Johnson's grave seemed icy cold and he had been glad to hurry away. To the end of his life he always remembered that odd experience and he was never able to explain it satisfactorily.

Glamis Castle, Glamis, Angus, Tayside

With a background of the Grampian Mountains, in the wooded and fertile Valley of Strathmore, stands historic Glamis Castle with its soaring towers, battlements and chimneys, grey-pink and majestic, full of mystery and probably the most haunted building in Britain.

It is an unforgettable experience to approach Glamis Castle along the impressive, tree-lined drive, even on a shimmering summer day, and well it might be so for this is the oldest inhabited and most striking of all the castles in Scotland. Parts of the present structure date from about 1430 — the crypt and the lower part of the main central tower; a castle that was well-known to King James V of Scotland, to his daughter the enchanting Mary Queen of Scots; perhaps to Duncan who, according to tradition, was murdered here, and certainly to most of the succeeding monarchs including the present Queen and of course to Princess Margaret who was born at haunted Glamis.

Inside Glamis Castle, Scotland's house of mysteries.

Glamis, the grim castle with stories of a family monster and half-a-dozen ghosts; its famous secret room; the mysterious ringed stones in the floors of several bedrooms; the everlasting bloodstain that marked the spot where the murder of Duncan is said to have taken place; the doors that open by themselves no matter that they are locked, bolted or wedged with heavy furniture.

Among the ghosts there is the fearful apparition of the huge and bearded Lord Crawford; he appears high up in an uninhabited tower where 'Earl Beardie' (as he was called) is supposed to have gambled with the Devil himself. and to have died soon afterwards. Ever since the ghost of Earl Beardie has gambled, stamped and swore with 'something' in the empty room with its two doors and ominous trap-doors. A daughter of Lord Castletown is said to have seen the ghost of the huge old man; Lady Granville, elder sister of the Queen Mother, told James Wentworth Day that when she lived at Glamis, children often woke up at night in the upper rooms in that part of the castle, screaming that a huge and bearded man had leaned over their beds; Sir Shane Leslie told me that his Aunt Mary saw the ghost of Earl Beardie when she was a visitor at the castle; and according to Gordon Gregory, 'only a few years ago a week-end guest at Glamis claimed to have seen the spectre. He stared at it horror-struck for a few minutes, then, with an agonizing scream, the apparition vanished.' He adds; Other people claiming to have seen it allege that the furnishings and decorations are transformed to those of another age at the moment the ghost appears.' All the furniture has long been taken out of these rooms and they are never used these days but still stories continue of sounds of movement and muffled oaths emanating from one atmosphere-laden room.

Where but at Glamis could there be a room called the Hangman's Chamber? A room haunted by the ghost of a butler who hanged himself there; and of course there is too the

Haunted Chamber, sealed for many years now but which still contains some lingering essence of the ghastly fate of men and women of the unfortunate Ogilvy clan who, fleeing from the Lindsays, sought shelter from the treacherous owner of the day who had no sympathy for their cause and promptly locked them in the remote chamber and left them to starve. Years later, disturbed by the nocturnal sounds of frantic cries and bangings, a Lord Streathmore and some companions ventured to explore the Haunted Chamber but he is said to have collapsed when he encountered the contents of the unventilated chamber .... Today the bare, white-walled rooms retain a brooding sense of unease.

Then there are the occasional reports of a tall, dark figure in a long coat, fastened at the neck, that is seen entering a locked door halfway up a certain winding stairway; a figure in armour that passes silently through a certain bedroom and into an adjoining dressing-room; a ghostly little black boy who sits on a stone seat beside the door into the Queen Mother's sitting-room: he is supposed to be a servant who was cruelly treated two centuries ago.

When my wife and I were at Glamis we were told that the ghost most frequently seen these days is the so-called Grey Lady who haunts the quiet little chapel. One sunny day Lady Granville saw a grey figure kneeling in one of the pews and although the details of the dress seemed dear and opaque, she noticed that the sun shone right through the figure and made a pattern on the floor. The last Lord Strathmore also saw the Grey Lady in the chapel several times. Once he was checking the details of some of the interesting de Wint pictures one afternoon when he saw the kneeling figure and, not wishing to disturb her, he tiptoed quickly away. When he looked again there was no one there. My wife and I spent some time in the chapel, examining the pictures and keeping half an eye on the empty pews but we saw no ghost.

There is also a ghost known as the White Lady, and on one memorable occasion this particular phantom was observed by three people independently at the same time, from different vantage points. Then there is a strange, illusive unidentified figure, known as Jack the Runner, who speeds across the park on moonlit nights; and a terrifying apparition of a tongueless woman looking out of a window, a woman who is supposed to have been mutilated so that she could never reveal one of the many secrets of Glamis — the monster story or perhaps the vampire legend. It is said that a servant was once caught in the act of sucking the blood from one of her victims and was hurriedly bricked-up in a secret room. There undoubtedly are secret rooms at Glamis yet to be discovered; the last Lord Strathmore told me he had no doubt that there were many secrets yet to be uncovered in mysterious and haunted Glamis Castle.

The lure of Glamis has endured for several hundred years and it is as strong today as ever it was, a fact that can be verified any summer day when hoards of visitors from all over the world descend on the impressive castle, wander about the gardens and explore those rooms that are open to the public. Sir Walter Scott visited Glamis for he wanted to experience the atmosphere for himself and although during the night he spent there he saw no ghost he wrote afterwards: 'I must own that when the door was shut I began to consider myself as too far from the living and somewhat too near the dead.'

Gunby Hall, Burgh-le-Marsh, Lincolnshire

Built in 1700 by Sir William Massingberd this unpretentious' country house illustrates the sustained use of bricks of a beautiful deep plum colour to produce a simple but satisfying design; and also the fact that the least ghostly-looking house can be haunted.

It is difficult to realize that this fine Hall was built in the reign of William and Mary, standing as it does serene and elegant among the great trees of the 1500-acre park, and seeming to look away to the sea and the Norfolk coast beyond the Wash. Preserved in the Hall is a copy of Tennyson's verse, written in his own hand, which is an apt description of the house, verse that ends with the line, 'A haunt of ancient peace'.

But peace has not always reigned within these solid walls. Soon after the house was built trouble seems to have plagued the family. The story varies in detail but either the mistress of the house or, more likely, the daughter, fell in love with one of the servants, possibly a postillion, and their plans to elope were discovered by Sir William Massingberd.

Some versions of the story say that both were shot before they could carry out their plan; others have it that the young man only was murdered and his body dumped in the pond near the house; a crime that resulted in a curse being laid on the family which foretold that no male member of the family would inherit the house. The ghost of the murdered man is said to haunt the path beside the pond, known to this day as the 'Ghost Walk'.

Those who lean towards the story of both lovers being murdered point to the evidence of those who have seen the 'vague outlines of a young couple' moving slowly along the same path, accompanied by a sensation of extreme coldness. After a few seconds the figures fade and disappear and the atmosphere returns to normal and the temperature is again found to be that of the surrounding area.

Hame House near Petersham, Surrey - haunted by the old and powerful Duchess of Lauderdale, who murdered her first husband; and by a yapping King Charles Spaniel.

[Image previously spread across two pages]

H

Ham House, Petersham, Greater London

Almost hidden by trees amid the Thames-side meadows between Twickenham and Richmond, one is almost surprised to come upon the stately and magnificent Ham House, a silent reminder of a more leisurely past, its ancient iron gates, at what is now the back but was once the front of the house, unopened since the flight of James II.

Ham House was built by Sir Thomas Vavasour, Knight Marshall to James I, in 1610 and intended, according to tradition, as a residence for the eldest son of the King. But the young prince's sudden death in 1612 brought whispers of murder — although it is not Prince Henry who haunts Ham House, but the old Duchess of Lauderdale who is said to revisit the scenes of her triumphs and infamies during the days of Cromwell and of King Charles II.

The scheming and powerful Duchess, formerly Countess of Dysart, reputed to have been Cromwell's mistress, was daughter of William Murray, First Earl of Dysart, who had served in his youth as 'whipping boy' for the misdemeanours of the Prince of Wales, later Charles I. Elizabeth, his only child, while still married to Sir Lionel Tollemache, chose for her lover John Maitland and in 1672, with Sir Lionel dead, she married this later member of Charles IPs Cabal Ministry, 'within six weeks of his Lady's decease'. She also built the magnificent great staircase at Ham. Maitland lived to become the unpopular Duke of Lauderdale, favourite of King Charles II. Ham House was enlarged, sumptuously decorated and furnished anew with lavish splendour: these were the compensating deeds of the villainous Lauderdale and his wicked wife who were known to send innocent people to the rack.

For years after her death the Duchess's boudoir remained as she had known it: her silver-headed ebony walking-stick where she had left it. It is this stick which is thought to be the original source of the mysterious tapping noises heard about the history-laden rooms of Ham House. At dead of night that noise would be heard — tap, tap, tap —just as the old Duchess used to hobble about in her later years.

The story that is supposed to account for the haunting concerns a butler at Ham whose little girl of sue stayed at the house on a visit at the invitation of the Ladies Tollemache. Very early in the morning the child awoke suddenly to see an old woman scratching and clawing at the wall close to the fireplace. At first more curious than frightened, the little girl sat up in bed to see better what was happening but the sound of her movement apparently made the old woman turn round. She came to the foot of the child's bed, grasping the bed-rail with her bony hands and stared long and fixedly at the now terrified child who screamed and buried herself beneath the bedclothes. Hearing the screams, servants and occupants of the house rushed to the child's room and although they saw no old woman, they comforted the child, listened to her story and then turned their attention to the wall by the fireplace. There they found papers which, it is said, proved that Elizabeth, Countess of Dysart, had murdered her husband to many the Duke of Lauderdale.

When I was at Ham House some years ago with Dr Peter Hilton-Rowe, Life-member of The Ghost Club, we were told by one of the guides that the more active ghost these days was a phantom King Charles Spaniel that was often seen and heard running, yapping, along the terrace in daylight. Other reports state that the cheerful little animal has been seen roaming through various rooms of this handsomely furnished house and once, again in daylight, it was seen to run from a room along the west passage and disappear into the skirting-board. Once, on the terrace, a woman visitor went to approach the animal, but it bared its teeth at her and then promptly vanished!

It is also from the terrace and again in broad daylight that the ghost of a woman in white has been seen, looking out of one of the windows. On one particular occasion when this happened the house was closed to the public and a check by the resident officer's staff seemed to prove that nobody could have been in the room where the ghost was seen.

There are also occasional reports of phantom figures in period costume being seen in various rooms of the house and of inexplicable noises, banging and whispering and footsteps, that emanate from empty rooms behind locked doors.

Near the house, on the towpath of the quiet Thames, a figure wearing high boots, a large cloak and a hat with a drooping brim has been seen many times; he is thought to be a courtier who visited Ham House with Charles II, a cavalier who became drunk and ended up drowned in the river. He was seen by a lady acquaintance of F.W.H. Myers, one of the pioneers of psychical research, at 5.30 p.m. on a sunny July afternoon. Elliott O'Donnell told me he saw a similar figure in the same place one evening. In 1978 a visitor to Ham House, who had heard nothing about a ghostly cavalier on the towpath, told me she had seen such a figure; she assumed that some sort of pageant was in progress but then realized that the 'cavalier' was alone; when 'he' suddenly and inexplicably disappeared from view, she began to accept that she had encountered something very strange; she had never previously had any kind of psychic experience. One summer evening in 1980 two residents of nearby Kingston-upon-Thames saw a man dressed like a cavalier coming towards them along the towpath near Ham House; they were quite amused at his appearance (although he seemed quite oblivious to everyone) and they were preparing to make some comment as he passed when suddenly, when he was perhaps ten feet away from them, he was no longer there.

Hampton Court Palace, Hampton Court, Greater London

At least a dozen different ghosts have been reported from this magnificent country house on the banks of the Thames that Cardinal Thomas Wolsey built in the reign of Henry VIII. When the King stripped the most powerful man in England of all his possessions. Lord Chancellor Wolsey, in a desperate bid to regain favour, presented his manor, its buildings, furnishings and plate to the King; but Wolsey's days of glory were over and the house was enlarged to become one of the most luxurious palaces in the kingdom and the home, successively, of five of the King's wives: Anne Boleyn, Jane Seymour, Anne of Cleves, Catherine Howard and Catherine Parr. And the spirit of King Henry VIII seems to brood heavily over the mellow Tudor palace to this day.

The best know ghost here is probably that of Catherine Howard, the shrieking phantom of the Haunted Gallery. Christina Hole, of the Folklore Society, told me that many residents' of the palace had heard the terrified screams of Queen Catherine in the Haunted Gallery and occasionally some of them had glimpsed a figure in white, with loose-flowing hair, gliding swiftly along the panelled passageway.

The story goes that on 4 November 1541 the Queen escaped from her guards as she was being held a prisoner and rushed along the gallery towards the chapel to make a last appeal for her life to the King, only to be taken back, sobbing for mercy and shrieking with terror, to her room which she was only to leave when she was sent to the Tower and there beheaded on 13 February 1542. It cannot but be interesting that the Queen had lived and loved and had happy and unhappy times at Hampton Court, but it is only that poignant and traumatic moment of her life that remains, perhaps forever, imprinted on the atmosphere that is perceivable to some people, under certain conditions, at certain times.

A century ago the gallery was locked and used as a storage room for pictures. At that time nearby rooms were occupied by residents; more than one of whom maintained that they were sometimes awakened in the middle of the night by horrifying shrieks for which no explanation was ever found, but they seemed to come from the direction of the Haunted Gallery and they were noticed especially in the late autumn.

When the gallery was first opened to the public an artist was busy sketching some of the beautiful tapestry that used to hang there when he was astonished to see a human hand with a ring on one finger appear on the tapestry he was sketching. He hurriedly sketched the hand and the ring which had an unusual jewel; later the ring was found to be very similar to one known to have belonged to Queen Catherine.

Those who have heard and seen this famous ghost include Mrs Cavendish Boyle and the Lady Eastlake, in addition to many servants and employees at the palace. All agree that the figure has long and flowing hair and that it invariably disappears so quickly that there is no time to observe it closely. In recent years one of the occupants of an apartment at the palace, situated near the Haunted Gallery, related that she had witnessed the shrieking figure so often that she took it as a matter of course!

Another well-known ghost here is that of Jane Seymour, Henry's third wife. Her phantom form, 'dressed' in white, perambulates Clock Court, having emerged from the entrance to Catherine of Aragon's Rooms in the Queen's Old

The rooms at Hampton Court Palace -
once occupied by Mistress Sybil Penn,
beloved foster-mother of Edward VI.
The ghost of Mistress Penn is said to
have been seen and heard many times
hereabouts.

Fountain Court, Hampton Court - once haunted by the ghosts of two cavaliers; when their remains were discovered and buried elsewhere, the disturbance ceased.

Apartments. The ghost of Queen Jane also wanders noiselessly about the stairway and immediate vicinity of the Silver Stick Gallery, carrying a lighted candle; she seems to have been seen most frequently on the night of 12 October, the anniversary of the birth of her son Edward VI. She died a week after bearing the King's only legitimate son. It has been reported quite recently that servants have given notice because they have been frightened by the repeated appearance of a 'tall lady, clad in white, with a long train and a shining face', a form that glides noiselessly down stairways and along passages and passes through closed doors, carrying a lighted candle with a flame that never flickers.

Yet another famous ghost at Hampton Court is that of Anne Boleyn, a phantom that has been recognized from a portrait that hangs in the palace. The form that has been seen wears the same blue dress, which shimmers in the light of late afternoon sunshine as it glides, noiselessly along corridors that once the second wife of Henry VIII must have known and loved during her few short years of happiness. Palace servants at the end of the nineteenth century reported seeing the figure of Anne wandering, disconsolate and downcast, among the rooms and passages where once she walked as Queen.

Here too there is good evidence for the ghostly activities of Mistress Sybil Penn, foster-mother to Edward VI. The sounds of her voice and the whirr of her spinning-wheel must have been some of the first sounds heard by the baby prince. Mistress Penn seems to have been much loved, and certainly the sickly Edward never forgot his old nurse. Elizabeth I granted her a pension and residence in Hampton Court where, incidentally, both she and the Queen suffered an attack of smallpox. The Queen recovered, although marked for the rest of her life, but the old servant died and was buried in nearby St Mary's Church, Hampton. There it seems she rested in peace until the church was wrecked in a thunderstorm and pulled down in 1829. During the demolition the grave of Sybil Penn was desecrated and her remains scattered; an outrage that coincided with reported disturbances at Hampton Court Palace, the place she had known so well during her lifetime. A family named Ponsonby then occupied Sybil Penn's old rooms and they began to complain of continually hearing the sound of a spinning-wheel and a woman's voice, which they were totally unable to account for; the sounds seemed to originate from a wall in the south-west wing. When other occupants of nearby grace and favour apartments made similar complaints the Board of Works was called in and they discovered a sealed room which was found to contain a much-used spinning-wheel.

The discovery did not however bring the disturbances to an end: a ghostly figure in a long, grey, straight dress with a hood or close-fitting cap was repeatedly reported inside and outside the old apartment of Mistress Penn. This figure was, among others, reported by two sentries independently, and they both asserted that the figure they saw resembled closely the stone effigy that had decorated the grave of Sybil Penn. Later the haunting degenerated into the sound of footsteps, and Christina Hole, writing in 1940, said that the footsteps were still heard and that the ghost was still seen occasionally by residents and servants at the palace. One sentry is reported to have deserted his post after seeing the grey form disappear into a wall and there were other reports of muttering sounds, loud crashing noises, stealthy footsteps and rooms bathed in 'a ghastly, lurid light'.

Princess Frederica of Hanover, who knew nothing about the reported appearances of the ghost of Mistress Penn, once found herself face to face at Hampton Court with a tall and gaunt figure, seemingly clothed in a long grey robe with a hood; a figure that held out its hands as though to take charge of a baby. Before it had disappeared Princess Frederica was struck by a likeness between the mysterious silent figure and the effigy of Mistress Penn that she had seen. This Hampton Court ghost is sometimes known as the Grey Lady.

Other witnesses for the ghost of Mistress Penn (or the Grey Lady) include a palace resident, Lady Maude. She was preparing to greet a guest when a tall lady in a long grey dress entered the room. At first Lady Maude thought she must be a housekeeper or servant of some kind and she asked for the light to be switched on. When there was no reply Lady Maude turned to see the gaunt figure glide silently through a closed door.

Hampton Court also boasts a White Lady, seen most frequently in the area of the landing stage; a vague and indistinct figure that has never been identified, but such a figure has been reported by dozens of visitors and by a party of anglers who saw the figure collectively one midsummer night.

Fountain Court used to be haunted by the ghosts of two cavaliers who were reportedly seen occasionally in daylight by those residents whose apartments overlooked the court, which is in the heart of the palace. One resident, Lady Hildyard, collected evidence for the phantom forms from other residents and servants, together with reports of strange tapping noises and other unexplained sounds and sent the result to the Lord Chamberlain. Soon afterwards workmen unearthed the remains of two young cavaliers. Lady Hildyard researched the matter and came to the conclusion that what had been discovered were the mortal remains of Lord Francis Villiers and another Royalist officer who were killed in a skirmish between the forces of the King and those of Parliament; at all events after these remains were removed and buried elsewhere there were no more reports of strange sounds or unexplained figures in Fountain Court.

Even the grounds of Hampton Court seem to be haunted and there are many stories of different ghosts being encountered in various parts of the palace precincts. One sighting figures in an official report. In February 1907 PC 265 T saw what he took to be a group of people walking towards him along Ditton Walk. As they came nearer, apparently chatting and laughing among themselves — although, looking back, he could not remember actually hearing any sound except the slight rustle of the ladies' dresses — he noticed that there were eight or nine ladies in long evening dress and one or two men, also dressed for dinner. The constable, an experienced officer with some twenty years' service to his credit, turned and opened the gate for them but when he turned back they had changed direction and were heading towards the Flower Pot Gate. As he watched, the group formed itself into two lines and then, to the utter astonishment of the watching policeman, the whole group suddenly vanished completely. As he said at the time: 'One moment they were there, lifelike and completely natural, the next they had completely disappeared.' — a curious incident in the history of haunted Hampton Court Palace that is still preserved in the station occurrence book.

Producer-actor Leslie Finch told me that after a costume performance of Twelfth Night, performed at Hampton Court Palace, he was walking towards one of the palace doorways, at the back of the old part of the building, accompanied by Lady Grant who lived in a grace and favour apartment, when he saw a misty, grey figure in Tudor costume approaching them. He thought at first that the figure must be one of the actresses and, since she seemed determined to walk straight into them, he moved to one side to allow her to pass. As she did so he experienced a sensation of sudden coldness and told me: My skin went stiff like parchment and I felt a shiver but apart from that it was not at all an unpleasant experience.' He resumed his place at the side of Lady Grant, who looked at him a little oddly and asked what had caused him to suddenly move in that way. He then discovered that Lady Grant had not seen the figure that had appeared to be completely lifelike and natural to him although, at the moment it had passed, she too had noticed a sudden coldness in the air.

During the 1966 season of Son et Lumiere at Hampton Court, a member of the audience wrote in to accuse the organizers of breaking the rules by introducing an actor into the production. The writer had seen the figure of Cardinal Wolsey walking through one of the gateways of his beloved palace. Christopher Ede, the producer, referred to the incident in his contribution to the 1970 programme, saying: 'For one member of the audience at least the magic had worked.'

There are other ghosts at Hampton Court in addition to those I have detailed: a 'figure dressed in period clerical robes and hat' in the cloisters beside the ancient tiltyard; a figure resembling Anne Boleyn in the Witch Hazel Avenue, leading from the King's Staircase to the banqueting hall and also in the audience chambers; the ghosts of the romantic youths, Dereham and Culpepper, who dallied with Anne Boleyn and so suffered agonizing deaths, haunt the little-known byways and narrow passages of the palace; a ghostly little old lady in grey haunts the Birdwood Apartments on the south side of the great gatehouse; a strange, rather frightening figure of a distraught woman in a long dress and with hair blowing in the wind runs out of the main entrance beneath the great gateway, across the bridge and turns towards the river where she disappears; a phantom monk has been seen at the rear of the palace on three separate occasions by different people; and a ghost dog on the King's Staircase. In addition, there are numerous stories of unexplained footsteps, ghostly music, the sound of furniture being dragged about, objects being moved paranormally, the sound of piano playing from empty rooms and so much more. Hampton Court Palace must be a strong candidate for the most haunted historic house in Britain.

Beautiful Hardwick Hall,
with its mass of windows, six
towers and magnificent
plasterwork.

[Image previously spread across two pages]

Hardwick Hall, near Mansfield, Derbyshire

Hardwick Hall

More glass than wall

runs an old jingle, and indeed this sixteenth-century house, the only one of all Bess of Hardwick's manors standing as she built it, is remarkable for the astonishing number of windows. Yet this masterpiece of Renaissance building with its six towers, wealth of magnificent plasterwork and Great High Chamber that Sacheverell Sitwell called the most beautiful room in the whole of Europe' does not appear to have a ghost within its walls, though phantoms and apparitions do seem to manifest from time to time in the gardens, laid out in a series of walled courtyards containing herb, shrub and flower borders.

When Bess of Hardwick, the scheming Elizabethan Countess of Shrewsbury, was not engaged in getting married herself (she married four times), marrying off her children, bullying her husbands, tormenting her captives or quarrelling with all and sundry, she was obsessed with building mansions. She completed Chatsworth after Sir William Cavendish's death and built Worksop, Bolsover and Oldcotes in addition to Hardwick. Indeed there is a story that tells of a prophecy saying she would not die as long as work was going ahead on one of her mansions — a prophecy she could well have believed. Oddly enough she died during a hard frost when her builders were unable to work on her new manor of Oldcotes.

Today the house that knew Mary Queen of Scots (some of her exquisite needlework is preserved here), the 'supreme triumph of Elizabethan architecture', houses a wealth of interesting portraits: Queen Elizabeth, Lord Burghley, James 1, Mary Queen of Scots and three of Bess herself; after the death of her fourth husband she was the richest woman in England after the Queen; even in the portrait of her when she was growing old, her beauty gone, her face still shows great authority. Hardwick Hall is thought to contain secret rooms and priests' hiding-places and perhaps there is a connection between a forgotten escapade involving a monk or priest and the phantom form seen in the gardens.

In 1976 Mark Gresswell and his fiancee Carol Rawlings were travelling through Hardwick Park when they both saw the figure of a monk 'in a black habit'. 'He was a big, tall chap,' Mark said afterwards. The figure seemed to walk towards them, clearly visible in the headlights of their car, then it turned off and disappeared. Mark swung the car round in the hope of seeing the figure again but it had completely vanished. Both Mark and Carol said they didn't see either the hands or the feet of the figure but the face seemed almost luminous', a brilliant white.

Furthermore the two occupants of a car which they had passed travelling in the opposite direction had also seen the figure; and according to the landlady of the Hardwick Inn, the ghost monk had been seen twice before within that past week. Other witnesses for this ghost form include two young ladies, visitors to the area, and two policemen. When I was at Hardwick Hall in 1980 I learned that visitors to the Hall have sometimes asked about the monk dressed in black' that they have noticed in the gardens; a figure that seemed to disappear in mysterious circumstances. As far as can be established no real person, answering such a description, has been at the Hall at the time. On the other hand, the Administrator in 1982 told me that a ghost monk at Hardwick was news to him.

Fraser Martin, co-founder of Chesterfield Psychic Study Group, revealed at the end of 1983 that during the time he worked at Hardwick Hall, he saw a shadowy figure cross the

Blue Room on several occasions, always in the same place, and invariably the figure disappeared straight through a window.

Harvington Hall, near Kidderminster, Hereford and Worcester

'Harvington Hall', says Allan Fea in his fascinating book Rooms of Mystery and Romance, 'is almost as elusive as its many hiding-places' and he goes on to speak of the 'ghostly atmosphere' of this moated sixteenth-century house.

Some twenty years ago Frank Burns, writing in Catholic Fireside, 'the Catholic Magazine for the Home', stated: Harvington Hall has more Priest's Holes than any other house in England,' and he continues: In the old days when people read ghost stories, real ghost stories, with white-clad ladies wandering along corridors, mail-clad knights, and pictures of cavaliers coming to life, Harvington Hall would have been the novelist's dream come true. If it is not haunted, it deserves to be.' And, oddly enough, perhaps, I have no knowledge of any well-authenticated ghost at Harvington but, as Allan Fea also says: 'In so mysterious a building who can tell but that there may be more wonders yet to be found?'

Harvington Hall dates from the time of Henry VIII and has additions of every period since then. The tall mass of sandstone and red brick, standing in dark and reedy waters overhung with gloomy trees, only came into Catholic hands about 1630, some fifteen years after Nicholas Owen's death, so that the many remarkable and ingenious hiding-places in the house cannot be put to his credit. From 1667 to 1678 there sheltered here a Franciscan priest named John Wall, the last priest to be captured and hanged in England — and his ghost has been seen and heard at Chingle Hall in Lancashire. Beyond these few historical facts we know little of the happenings at Harvington; and one is left wondering not only about the hiding-places with their pivoted beams and miniature lifts and the use of the preserved relics of past persecutors, but also the significance and use in days gone by of the subterranean tunnel, the secret doors, the false floor which could send unwanted persons hurtling to their death, the strange echoing rooms and the many thrilling hunts and escapes that this great house must have seen.

One wonders too about the ominously named Gallows Pool (did it really receive its name from the hanging of a dog?), while the ghost of a local witch haunts the neighbouring grounds and fields and highways. Mistress Hicks was hanged in 1710 after being found guilty of causing women and children of the locality to vomit pins and needles and for possessing the power to raise storms. She probably met her death at the crossroads of the present A448 and A450 and it is there that her ghost is most frequently reported, although, according to some people, the ghost occasionally flits through the grounds of Harvington Hall; with or without a ghost, one of the most interesting manors in the Midlands.

Hoghton Tower, Hoghton, Preston, Lancashire

The hill on which proud Hoghton Tower stands, visible for miles, is the last tip of the Pendle range; and the Forest of Pendle around Pendle Hill has long been known as witch country.

Even today there are witch covens, magic potions, and spell-casting in this vast, strange place. There are corners of fields that are never cultivated because the land has been poisoned'; there are haunted barns where the fear of being bewitched has resulted in suicide; there are stories of cattle that have been 'overlooked' trying to climb out of their pens on certain moonlit nights; and there are churchyards where a gravestone has iron spikes driven through it to stop the witch that is buried there from rising up and haunting .... There are marks in some churches where locks were once fitted to fonts to prevent witches from stealing Holy Water to use in their evil ceremonies; and if such tales of witchcraft seem far-fetched and out-of-date to most of us, in Lancashire the memory of the power of witchcraft lives everywhere and especially around Pendle.

But we have come to visit hauntingly beautiful Hoghton Tower and it was a strange experience for me to enter Hoghton on a winter's afternoon when it was deserted except for those who lived there. No one was in evidence as I quietly walked through the ancient archway and into the outer courtyard and up the lovely curved stone steps, through another archway and into the inner courtyard and so to the huge door of the King's Hall — and still no sign of anyone and no single sound disturbed the quiet of that overcast day. My echoing footsteps retreated as I made my way out of the inner courtyard and, across the outer courtyard, I mounted the steps towards the private apartments and then, in answer to my ringing, Philomena, Lady de Hoghton, welcomed me to her home.

We had first met when Lady de Hoghton had visited my wife's antique shop and soon we were being entertained to tea, my wife, our friends Freda and Steuart Kiemander and I. The talk quickly turned to ghosts for here, it seems, there is not only a ghostly lady in green velvet but other phantom forms that have made their presence felt and heard: the sound of loud laughter suddenly booming forth, or the rustle of a heavy silken skirt passing close by; several dogs and at least one cat have acted strangely in various parts of the house and we were to witness an example of this curious phenomenon during our visit.

Soon we were joined by Mrs Margaret Bagueley who helps with guiding in the banqueting hall when Hoghton Tower is open to the public, something she has been doing for over five years; and, quite often, she is completely aware and utterly convinced of ghostly feelings and ghostly presences in the house. Mrs Bagueley does wonderful black needlework and individual and artistic embroidery and sewing, some of which has been included in exhibitions; but when she is on duty Mrs Bagueley dresses in remarkably accurate costume as a Tudor Lady Margaret' and she talks to the ghosts that she knows are there and bows and curtsies to them.

During one turbulent period of history when the occupants of Hoghton were Protestant, the lovely daughter of the house, Ann, fell in love with a Catholic young man from nearby (and also haunted) Samlesbury Hall. They planned to elope and one night he rode quietly up the long, straight drive to the house, leading another horse for Ann, the horses' hooves covered to preserve silence. At the house Ann saw him arrive and quietly ran out of the house, down the graceful curved steps in the outer courtyard and leaped onto the horse he had brought for her. But the attempted elopement had been expected and was detected; even as Ann's heart leaped at the thought of being with her lover for always, a shot rang out and her lover slid off his horse, dead at her feet. Ann never recovered from the shock and she never forgave those who had killed her one and only love; she went into a nunnery and stayed there for the rest of her life. But how many times, in her thoughts and dreams, must she have travelled back to Hoghton Tower, to the ancient and solid home of her forebears and perhaps to happy days long past and merry meals in the banqueting hall.

Even earlier memories Ann must have had, perhaps of great colourful gatherings in the bedecked hall when she was too young to take part and then maybe she would steal a look at the boisterous scene from a vantage point of the Minstrels' Gallery or some dark comer, and it seems that sometimes Ann or some remnant of her being does indeed return to the banqueting hall at Hoghton Tower. Time and time again Margaret Bagueley told us she is aware of the presence of Ann.

When the house is open Margaret, dressed in immaculate Tudor costume, is usually to be found seated in the banqueting hall with her back to the Minstrels' Gallery, in that room so full of memories.

In this splendid hall with its beautiful woodworked ceiling and bow window, King James the First of England, the Sixth of Scotland, was entertained together with his favourite George Villiers, Duke of Buckingham and the Earls of Pembroke, Richmond, Nottingham and Bridgewater; Lords Zouch, Knollys, Mordaunt, Grey, Stanhope and Compton; the Bishop of Chester, and many baronets and knights and a crowd of local notables. They feasted here in the presence of their host Sir Richard de Hoghton — honest Dick, a mellow, good-hearted fellow with the reputation of being able to put six bottles of Rhenish wine under his silken doublet at one sitting; and he had risen to the occasion of entertaining his monarch.

Indeed it is said that the entire length of the sharp and steep ascent to Hoghton Tower had that day been carpeted with red velvet, especially woven in the Low Countries .... They had entered to a flourish of trumpets and an avenue of javelin bearers to be met by the owner's heir, another Sir Richard, already knighted by the King in 1606, sumptuously dressed in embroidered cloak and hose, his vest of cloth of gold enriched with precious stones, silver-worked ruffles and shirt band, and Spanish perfumed gloves. It was a day to be remembered, not least by those who, suffering from Scrofula, i.e., King's Evil, that day received the Royal touch in the King's Hall.

When the youth who had greeted King James the First was fifty-one the Civil War broke out and, while he supported the King, his son and heir Richard Hoghton fought in the ranks of the Parliamentary forces. In those days between the outer and inner courtyards there stood a great central tower (it can be seen in George Cattermole's picture) and from this vanished tower the house took its name and is always correctly referred to in the singular as Hoghton Tower. In those far-off Jacobean days Sir Gilbert lit a beacon on the top of the central tower as a signal to the country 'for the Papists and Malignants to arise'. Throughout the war Blackburn supported the Protestants while Preston was the Royalist headquarters and, although Sir Gilbert escaped the storming of Preston, Hoghton Tower itself fell and the central tower disappeared. Whether it was by accident or design has never been established, but the powder and arms in the tower caught fire and the tower blew up with great loss of life.

With the restoration of King Charles II the de Hoghtons gradually won the favour of the King. Catholics and Protestants, royalists and parliamentarians, courtiers and country gentlemen, the de Hoghtons have played many parts in the changing scene of English life; for many years nonconformist congregations met in the banqueting hall, and John Wesley himself was here. But soon, dissatisfied perhaps with the absence of a good water supply and other shortcomings, the family moved to Walton Hall (which has its own ghost) and Hoghton Tower fell into romantic decay. In 1848 Harrison Ainsworth described the property as '... consigned to the occupation of a few gamekeepers ... rotten ... broken and ruinous ... cracked and mouldering, Hoghton Tower presents only the wreck of its former grandeur...'.

A few years later Charles Dickens visited Hoghton and described the ancient rooms ... many of them with the floors and ceilings falling, the beams and rafters hanging dangerously down, the plaster dropping, the oak panels stripped away, the windows half walled up, half broken'.

Then in 1862 Sir Henry Bold Hoghton began the work of restoration; work that has been continued by the family ever since. In 1913 the house was sufficiently splendid to welcome a visit by King George the Fifth and Queen Mary and the King was able to record in his diary that he had dined at the same table as his Stuart ancestor nearly 300 years before.

Today the house gives an excellent idea of the structure its founder had in mind: a baronial hall with two courtyards, the buildings around the first courtyard housing the servants, the second consisting of the banqueting hall and state apartments for the family. Sadly many of the family portraits and heirlooms — including the pearls of Mary Queen of Scots — were destroyed by fire, either when Walton Hall was burned down in 1830 or in the terrible fire that gutted The Pantechicon, a warehouse in London where so many of the priceless possessions of the de Hoghtons were destroyed.

But what of the ghosts? Well, Frances de Hoghton lived at Hoghton Tower from the age of sixteen until she was thirty-two in late Victorian times and she had many 'inexplicable' experiences. In particular, Lady de Hoghton told us, was the 'lady in green velvet' that Aunt Frances often saw walking about the house late at night and especially in the vicinity of the Minstrels' Gallery. Then there was Lady de Hoghtons late husband, Sir Cuthbert, who sometimes complained of odd happenings in the Ladies Withdrawing Room which is off the Minstrels' Gallery. Once he was writing letters quite late in the evening when he suddenly became aware of a presence and strange sounds: loud laughter filled the air and he heard the rustle of silk, rather like a heavy-skirted figure close beside him. He sensed the presence was looking over his shoulder, reading what he had written, and he read again what in fact he had written and found it very amusing although he had not been aware of having written anything so amusing. It was a distinctly odd experience; not frightening, but so strange that he never forgot it.

After tea we toured this lovely house with Lady de Hoghton: the King's Anti-chamber, the ballroom, the King's

Bedchamber, the Buckingham Room, the haunted banqueting hall, the State Bedroom, the Guinea Room, the King's Hall and the private apartments — each fascinating and full of atmosphere; and then, accompanied all the time by Ginty the dog, we went down to the ancient but still-workable and unusual Tudor well (Hoghton Tower is 700 feet above sea level) and here the dog showed extreme and concentrated interest, looking up at the age-old beams and running round and round as though he could see something invisible to his human companions and it seems that he always acts like that in the area of that ancient well.

Nor is that the only area where dogs sense something at Hoghton Tower. Sir James de Hoghton was walking through the ballroom late one night accompanied by his Pekingese dog and Siamese cat when suddenly the dog started barking and running around in a circle, facing and barking towards the middle of the circle; while the cat, with its tail bolt upright, walked in a tight circle as if around a person's legs....

To leave Hoghton Tower, even after only a few hours, is like parting from an old friend. The ghosts here are friendly memories of past days, remnants of happenings and experiences in this beautiful, atmospheric and enchanting place. Yes, there are ghostly voices here and ghostly forms and ghostly sounds impressed upon the very air of Hoghton Tower — how could it be otherwise?

Horsey Mere, Norfolk

My old friend, Ghost-Clubber Charles Sampson, the well-known yachtsman, was quite certain that this 120-acre stretch of water, two-and-a-half miles from Potter Heigham, was haunted once a year by the voices of dead children who used to be buried in the Mere, and for those perceptive individuals to whom ghosts are no stranger, more spectacular events were glimpsed from time to time.

Years ago Charles Sampson talked with a local man who knew all about the hauntings. He said the ghosts went back to Roman times; in those far-off days when a child died they took the body out on the Mere, weighted it and lowered it to the bottom of the pool. He believed that the spirits of these children haunt the place, especially on 'Childers Night', 13 June, when 'all their little bodies come to life again for an hour and sing and play just as they did in the flesh'. The old man assured Charles Sampson that he had seen and heard the children himself, twice; once when he was a young man and again five years before Charles talked to him.

Sampson was no fool. He was fond of reminding sceptics that apparitions and ghostly phenomena are not perceptible to everyone: even psychically sensitive people cannot always see and hear the same things owing to the fact that certain perceptions can only tune in to certain wavelengths or vibrations, as can a radio set; equally, certain ears are capable of hearing certain sounds while others are note-deaf and cannot receive vibrations of particular notes. He often pointed to such accepted facts as X-Rays, gamma rays, infra-red and ultra-violet rays, none of which are normally visible; and he believed that some kind of light-ray or radio-active emanation exuded from the human body that might remain in a place after physical death.

At Horsey Mere, on 13 June 1930, Charles Sampson and an antiquarian friend spent the night on the Mere, fishing. At about 11.30 p.m. the sky began to grow dim and a quarter of an hour later it was dark. The watchers extinguished their light and before long they noticed a change in the atmosphere.

They noticed a gentle breeze stirring the reeds and the presence of fireflies, seeming very bright in the darkness. Soon they noticed the faint sounds of music that seemed to come and go with breaths of wind. Gradually the Sweet music became more definite, minute but clear, and then the reeds seemed to grow taller — until they realized that the water was sinking. Soon, in places, there was no water, only a beautiful green sward with flowers here and there, lit by a thousand fireflies. The music grew louder and then they seemed to see scores of little children, naked, dancing and clapping their hands. The night air rang with merry laughter and the children romped and played. After a while the light grew dim, the display of happiness gradually faded and the music became further and further distant until it died away altogether; the waters gradually rose to their normal height and all the little lights went out.

Charles Sampson always swore he and his friend heard and saw this phenomenon; he maintained that it was known and written about as long ago as 1692 and he also referred to some Archaeological Transactions of 1709 where it was stated that 'these mysterious manifestations are common knowledge to the folke of the countryside in these parts, but they do not speak openly of them, for fear of frightening their children, and also to preserve muchly the sanctity of the "Children's Mere"'.

Horton Court, Chipping Sodbury, Avon

This Cotswold manor house, with its wide courtyard and handsome doorway of sculptured stone (including a curious and quaintly carved little man) is one of the very few examples in England of an unfortified Norman house, with Tudor work by a bishop who was with Henry VIII on the Field of the Cloth of Gold.

The ghost, if ghost there is, in this lovely, lonely spot, seems to be a friendly spirit. Although the present tenants have never seen anything of a ghostly nature, they were told, when they went to Horton in 1954, that the cook's little boy, who was sleeping in the bedroom next to the Norman hall, asked on one occasion: 'Who is the little old lady, with a frilly cap, who tucks me up at night?' The date of this occurrence would seem to be about 1937 and as far as I know this ghostly little lady has not manifested again at this house by the ancient church where one of Shakespeare's contemporaries sleeps.

House of the Binns, Linlithgow, West Lothian

This historic home of the Dalyells — one of whom, the long-bearded General Thomas (Tam) Dalyell (c. 1605-85), defeated the Covenanters at Rullion Green — must look much as it did when he proudly surveyed it after its restoration.

When he was commander-in-chief of the forces of Scotland, in 1681, General Tam Dalyell formed the regiment that became known as the Royal Scots Greys and the first musters were held here. The mansion was presented to the National Trust for Scotland in 1944, after being in the Dalyell family for over 300 years.

According to those who live on the banks of this picturesque river, the countryside is peopled with native spirits. A little old man in a brown habit is to be seen gathering sticks on the hillside above Binns: a water-sprite lures the unwary to death in the dark waters of the ancient pond below the hill. Other primitive forms are glimpsed here from time to time, perhaps survivors of the Picts who made their last stand here against the Romans.

The ghost of General Dalyell himself has also been seen mounted on a white charger, galloping across the ruined bridge over the Errack Burn; in the vicinity of the Binns tower; and up the old road to his house, where the General's riding-boots, spurs and sword are preserved to this day.

House of the Binns, where the ghost of General Tam Dalyell has been seen, galloping across the ruined bridge mounted on a white charger.

In his lifetime, it is said, Tam Dalyell used to play cards with the Devil. Once, when Tam won, the enraged Devil threw the table they had been playing on at his head but it flew past him and dropped into Sergeant's Pond, outside the house. This is one of many strange stories told about General Dalyell, tales of which few people took much notice until, one day, during the dry summer of 1878, the water of the pond was reduced to a new low, and there, stuck fast in the mud at the bottom of the pond, was a heavy carved table that must have been there for all of 200 years.

It seems that the General had another argument with the Devil over cards, resulting in Satan threatening to blow Tam's house down upon him. General Dalyell retorted that he would build extra thick walls to protect the house. The Devil replied that he would blow down the house and the walls — to which the General answered that he would build a turret at every corner of the house to pin down the walls. Today you can see turrets at each corner of the historic old house, which certainly serve no purpose — unless they have prevented the Devil from blowing the property down!

Hughenden Manor, High Wycombe, Buckinghamshire

The ghost of Benjamin Disraeli, Earl of Beaconsfield, has, according to Antony Hippisley Coxe's guide to more than a thousand haunted sites, Haunted Britain, 'been seen on a number of occasions at the foot of the cellar stairs and on the upper floors'. My own researches and investigations suggest that this is indeed so, especially, it seems, the upper portions of this very individual house.

Disraeli (1804-81), British statesman and novelist, of adventurous and romantic temperament, much addicted to dandified apparel, was shrewd and gifted with a quick wit and a neat turn of phrase, and his patriotism, courtly deference and loyal affection (especially after Prince Albert's death) gained him the friendship and support of Queen Victoria. It is difficult to clear him of the charge of gaining his ends by flattering the Queen's self-esteem, tempered by romantic phraseology, exemplified by his calling her (following Spenser) the 'faery'. His inscribed copy of the Queen's Leaves from the Journal of Our Life in the Highlands can be seen at Hughenden, a publication that enabled him to say to her, on more than one occasion, 'We authors, ma'am'.

He purchased, with some difficulty, Hughenden in 1848, during his political wilderness years and he was able to write to his older wife (formerly Mrs Wyndham Lewis, whom he had married soon after the death of her first husband, the Member of Parliament for Maidstone and who brought him a house in Park Lane and a considerable fortune): 'It is all done, you are Lady of Hughenden.'

It is not difficult to see what had so attracted this 'undoubtedly mysterious personality' (Encyclopaedia Britannica) for Hughenden is a delightful property, the lawns and park sweeping away through magnificent trees and presenting fine views of the hills beyond. The Disraelis soon changed the plain, late-Georgian house, where they lived for the rest of their lives, both inside and outside, leaving their mark on every aspect of the place. They added the ornamental parapet, they decorated and furnished the rooms in their own individual style, and today the house is decorated and furnished in the style they adopted and much of the furniture now at Hughenden actually belonged to them.

Disraeli has been accused of 'shrouding his own character' and perhaps he was wise to do so. One recalls his romantic friendship with Mrs Brydes Willyams, an aged Jewess of Torquay, who left him her considerable fortune on her death in 1863, and she is buried in his family grave at Hughenden.

So: adventurous, romantic, shrewd, quick-witted, patriotic, affectionate, frustrated, lonely, secretive, happy and deeply attached to the house he lived in for more than thirty years; are these the ingredients — or some of the necessary composition — for the appearance of a ghost? Be that as it may, and notwithstanding the scepticism of some of the present staff at Hughenden, there is no doubt that the shade of the 'old Jew' has been seen at this distinctive and much-loved home. This is so especially in the vicinity of the staircase, with its 'portrait-gallery of friendship', and upstairs in Disraeli's study, which is little changed since he died, and still retains the armchair specially made for him, his ormalu inkstand, the black-edged notepaper that he always used after his wife's death, and a number of his books.

It is known that Queen Victoria visited this room, which 'Dizzy' called his workshop', after his death and spent some time in the room. It is also known that the Queen showed great interest in the mediumship of Robert James Lees, a prominent Leicester spiritualist. Lees was only twelve when Prince Albert allegedly communicated at a 'home circle' using a nickname, an endearing term used by the Prince for the Queen; a term known only to the Royal couple. The Queen seems to have accepted this evidence as proof of her husband's continuing personality after his physical death and Lees was summoned to the palace; indeed he paid nine visits in all and was asked to join the palace household as resident medium. Lees told the Queen that John Brown, son of one of the Prince's Scottish gillies, would be able to act as medium between Her Majesty and the Prince; and for many, many years the 'insolent Scottish gillie' had a strange influence over the Queen and regularly the Queen believed she communicated through him with her beloved Prince Albert.

Hughenden Manor, where the ghost of Benjamin Disraeli has frequently been seen.

[Image previously spread across two pages]

A portrait of Disraeli by
John Everett Millais.

Could the extended presence of the bereaved Queen alone in the favourite room of her favourite minister have contributed in some way that we do not yet understand to the subsequent alleged appearances of the ghost at the house where the spirit of Disraeli unmistakably broods?

During the course of a Ghost Club visit to Hughenden one of the members, an intelligent and critical observer, happened to be ahead of the main party and, wandering into the otherwise deserted study, she was occupied in examining a water-colour of Windsor Castle when she thought she caught a movement out of the comer of her eye, and turning she saw, as clear as day, the distinct form of the dandified Jew, his distinctive kiss-curl over his right eye and the fobbish and elaborately tied stock or cravat beneath the lightly bearded chin. Mrs M.M. Wynn-Williams stood looking at the figure which seemed to be completely natural and real but totally unaware of her presence. The form did not move and seemed preoccupied, in a day-dream perhaps; and then Mrs Wynn-Williams heard some of her fellow-members approaching the room, she turned to warn them of the presence, and when she looked back the form she had so clearly seen had completely disappeared.

As the Ghost Club party left Hughenden Manor that day one of the members hurriedly returned to the staircase to check on one of the portraits and saw a figure resembling that of Disraeli disappearing down the stairway. The hall was completely deserted at the time and astute John Watson watched the retreating figure for a second and noticed that it moved without making a sound but it quickly disappeared from view. Perhaps it was the elusive ghost of Benjamin Disraeli checking that all was well at his beloved Hughenden or putting in an appearance in honour of a visit by the Ghost Club, or maybe that particular figure had a rational explanation; John Watson was never quite sure and the puzzling incident was never satisfactorily explained.

Jack Hallam, in one of his ghost books, says that the ghost of Disraeli was once seen with papers in its hand in the vicinity of a staircase at Hughenden. One witness for the appearance of the ghost near the main staircase, within a few feet of a portrait of the Earl of Beaconsfield, is Mrs Ellen Cartwright of Cobham who told Andrew Green, author of Ghosts of Today, that she distinctly saw the form standing near the portrait. 'He appeared quite normal and, at first, I thought it was someone dressed up as Disraeli. I smiled and he vanished.'

One author has made the interesting observation that notwithstanding the present study being much as he left it at the time of his death in 1881, there have been no reports of his ghost being seen, seated characteristically at his desk, quill in hand; instead it would seem that Queen Victoria's favourite Prime Minister walks the upper floors, haunts the staircase, and generally pervades this perfect example of a Victorian gentleman's country seat.

I

Ightham Mote, Ightham, Sevenoaks, Kent

Macabre stories are told of Ightham Mote, a moated manor house of great beauty, character and charm, built in 1340 and outwardly little changed since those far-off days. For some 300 years, from the time of Elizabeth I to the middle of Victoria's long reign, the house was the home of the Catholic Selby family, and consequently there have long been tales of private escape routes and secret hiding-places; but my friend Granville Squiers, who was a mine of information on the subject, assured me that even the so-called dungeon is actually a space created when a modern fireplace was built and there is no space extending beyond the floor-level.

Over the years there have been many dominant and forceful personalities at Ightham Mote; people of dedicated purpose who may have unconsciously contributed to the reported ghostly experiences.

The earliest owner of Ightham Mote of which anything is known is Sir Thomas Cawne who may well have served with the Black Prince in France; he settled here some time during the first half of the fourteenth century and built the kernel of the present house. His great hall is still one of the features of this delightful place in its secluded and peaceful setting. After Cawne, the Haut family held Ightham for nearly a century and a half, Sir Richard Haut enlarging the house by adding two wings, after inheriting the estate about 1450. Sir Richard, a cousin of Elizabeth Woodville, the haughty, ambitious and unpopular Queen of Edward IV, took part in the attempt to seize the reins of power when he and the Woodvilles accompanied the twelve-year-old Edward V on his journey from Ludlow to London. Three of the conspirators were executed but Sir Richard seems to have lain low during the troubled years when the boy-king and his brother were held in the Tower of London and Richard of Gloucester became King.

The property changed hands several times before it became the home of the Selbys, who were to remain here from 1591 until 1889. This Northumberland family may have been involved in border raids, cattle thieving and fierce family feuds; certainly one Selby was suspected of being the chief culprit in an affray during which a man was killed in a church and several other people wounded.

Another member of this family, Dorothy Selby, is believed to have sent a cryptic letter to her cousin Lord Moneagle that resulted in the failure of the Gunpowder Plot of

5 November 1605. According to local tradition she was walled-up in a little room in the tower by those who were sympathetic to the conspirators, possibly by friends of Guy Fawkes himself. And so came into being the story of Dorothy Selby's once-restless ghost walking at Ightham Mote.

There is also a curious story concerning an event that is supposed to have happened in 1552. It concerns a young monk who acted as Priest in secret to the family of Sir Thomas (or Anthony) Browne, First Lord Montagu, at Cowdray, Midhurst, West Sussex and his wife Ethelred of Ightham Mote. It is said that after a scandal involving a young servant girl he died by his own hand and she was bricked-up alive in a section of Ightham Mote.

Certainly, in 1872, workmen came across a sealed doorway that led to the discovery of an ancient female skeleton. It is said that there had always been an unexplained coldness in the area of the immured skeleton and that for years afterwards there were those who were sensitive enough to be aware of a variation in the temperature in that part of Ightham Mote, even without knowing anything of the story, while others insist that the sensation of a sudden chill in the air of the tower bedroom to this day denotes the passing of the invisible and ghostly Dame Dorothy Selby. Some years ago a bishop sought to exorcise the ghost but, according to repeated reports, the peculiar chill remains.

Inveraray Castle, Inveraray, Argyllshire, Strathclyde

Passing through Inveraray a few years ago my wife and I visited Inveraray Castle, the home of the Dukes of Argyll, and the haunt of the strange little Harper of Inveraray'. Rob Roy MacGregor's dirk handle and sporran are among the relics displayed at Inveraray Castle; the ruins of Rob Roy's house being five miles away at the Falls of Aray.

Immediately prior to the death of the Chief of the Clan, or a near relative, a ghostly galley containing three ghostly standing figures is reputed to sail up Loch Fyne and then proceed overland in the direction of the castle. Those who have seen this arresting spectacle assert that the vessel resembles the ship on the coat of arms of the Campbells, Dukes of Argyll. And yet another death omen here is reputed to be the appearance of ravens wheeling in unusual numbers about the castle, before the death of a Chief.

The famous physician Sir William Hart was one of three men, walking in the castle grounds on 10 July 1758, who looked up and saw a battle taking place above them, visionary soldiers wearing Highland uniform desperately attacking a fort defended by French soldiers. After a few seconds the scene dissolved and disappeared. Soon afterwards two ladies, the Miss Campbells of Ederin, arrived at Inveraray to say they had been on the road near Kilmalieu when they saw a vision of a battle in the sky. They went on to describe exactly the same spectacle that the three men at Inveraray Castle had witnessed. There was some later speculation as to what it could have meant, and it was not until some weeks later that news came that Highlanders had been in action against the French at Ticonderoga and that the name of Duncan Campbell, master of Inverawe House (some miles north of Inveraray) was among those killed. The date of the battle was 10 July.

The part of turreted Inveraray Castle in the area of the Green Library has long been said to be haunted by a loud crashing sound. Many years ago, according to a former Duke of Argyll, a tremendous commotion took place one Sunday evening like books being thrown violently to the floor, and it continued for over an hour. Nothing was found to account for the sounds.

Unusually only the family hear the ghostly sounds when other people are present, although friends and visitors have shared the experience on one or two occasions. Nothing is ever moved and nothing has ever been discovered that might account for the loud sounds that have been reported from time to time for nearly a hundred years. The sound of harp music used to be heard in the area of the Blue Room, although no harp was in the castle at the time.

The Harper, described by the family as 'a harmless little old thing', is said to be the ghost of a man who was hanged at Inveraray when Montrose's men were hunting the first Marquess of Argyll. In fact, Argyll lived to see Montrose hanged in the Grassmarket at Edinburgh, but the castle was not built until the middle of the eighteenth century although doubtless there were many men and women hanged at the place once known as Gallows Foreland Point.

Occasionally the Harper is also seen. It has been noticed that he always wears the Campbell tartan and never harms or frightens anyone; he has most frequently been seen by the successive duchesses of Argyll and only rarely by the dukes. A number of women visitors have seen and heard the Harper', noticeably at the time of a duke's death and during a ducal funeral.

Inverary Castle, Argyllshire - haunt of the ghostly 'Harper of Inveraray'; his harp is heard most often in the Blue Room.

K

King John's Hunting Lodge, Axbridge, Somerset

This early Tudor merchant's house (much restored in 1971) stands prominently in the corner of the square and is used as a museum of local history and archaeology.

Here there is a somewhat doubtful Elizabethan ghost lady and a well-authenticated phantom tabby cat; both have allegedly been seen in the panelled room on the first floor.

The ghost of an Elizabethan lady dates from a reported sighting, recorded in the museum diary, for 22 August 1978, and subsequently written up in the Christmas Newsheet of the Axbridge Archaeological and Local History Society. The relevant item reads: Two people have reported seeing a lady in a beautiful white Elizabethan dress sitting in the Mayoral chair. The lady is not violent, we are told, but there is violence about her, so perhaps a duel was fought for her hand. The Custodian's diary entry reads: "Mediumistic lady says beautiful Elizabethan lady dressed in white haunts the panelled room. Hunting Lodge has seen very violent days. Violence centred in panelled room ..." The Mayoral chair, as far as is known, started life in the Guild Hall, which is now the Lambs Hotel and Alliance Food Store, moved to the Town Hall after it was built and then was placed in King John's Hunting Lodge when that building became a museum. Did the White Lady come with it, or has she recently found it a comfortable addition to her surroundings?'

Mrs Frances Neale, Vice-Chairman of the Museum Management Committee, tells me: We are somewhat sceptical about the Elizabethan lady. I have spoken to the Custodians who made the original entry shortly after the event and they told me that the visitor whom they described wryly as "mediumistic" was very much the sort of person who would enjoy receiving feelings about a place. The topic was taken up mildly by the local press and the more elaborate comments of the other two people are almost certainly derived from this; the versions that came back to us at the museum in 1979 became increasingly elaborate, unlikely — and tiresome. The Mayoral Chair, incidentally, is Stuart and not Elizabethan.'

Mrs Neale is however less sceptical about the ghost tabby cat. In the same issue of the Newsletter previously referred to this feline phantom is mentioned in these terms: Members of the Society would be sceptics except for the fact that the first night the tabby cat was seen entering the panelled room by two members on the first floor, the rest of the Society spent some time making sure that there was no animal in the building before locking up. The cat has now been seen on several occasions, including one when, in the middle of a lecture, it was seen to enter through the closed door, sit down, curl its tail comfortably round itself, then slowly disappear.'

Mrs Neale tells me: 'The tabby cat, on the other hand, carries more conviction by its sheer inconsequential nature: coupled with the fact that it has been witnessed on several occasions by a number of hard-headed, disbelieving archaeologists! It has not, as a far as I know, been seen during the day; only during the evening.'

Brian Rowland, of Axbridge Archaeological and Local History Society, wrote the piece in the Society's Newsheet and he tells me that as far as he knows the White Lady has not been seen again. On the question of the ghostly tabby cat, he writes: 'This is often seen around the doorway to the panelled room on the first floor, just near the top of the stairs. Most sightings seem to be of the "movement out of the corner of the eye" type when the door is ajar; these total four or five, myself included. Our Secretary claims to have seen its tail projecting above and from between cardboard storage boxes standing on the floor just inside the panelled room. About six months after the article was written I was standing about three feet inside the panelled room and another member, Mrs Frances Day, was out on the landing, about ten feet from me; the door was open so we were within sight of each other but I was not looking at her, rather at something in the room. Mrs Day attracted my attention by making a hissing noise, then, pointing downwards said in a loud whisper:

"It's at your feet!"

'I looked down but could see nothing. Looking up again I said, "Where?"

"Just there," she said, pointing again, "beside you."

'I could still see nothing. Mrs Day then walked towards me saying in a normal voice: "Too late, it's gone." That was the last definite sighting I can recall but we still occasionally have a member say: "Oh, I thought I saw a cat coming in!"'

It is interesting to note that the first alleged sighting of the 'White Lady' was August 1978, and that the first time that the ghost cat was seen was also about 1978.

L

Lacock Abbey, near Chippenham, Wiltshire

As a little girl Ela, Countess of Salisbury in her own right, had been carried off to Normandy and only after a search lasting two years was she found by a courtier, disguised as a troubadour. After the death of her husband, William Longespee, she founded Lacock Abbey, consecrated as an

Augustinian Convent in 1232. William may have been an illegitimate son of red-headed, hot-tempered Henry II and his young mistress, Fair Rosamund, whose ghost may walk to this day at Lacock Abbey.

The story of Rosamond is as fascinating as it is impenetrable. Most of the stones have it that her death was caused by Queen Eleanor, Henry's jealous and older wife. Some say that the Queen had the unfortunate girl bled to death in a bath at Woodstock; others that she trapped her in a maze and there 'delte with her in such manner that she lyved not long after'; others again say that the Queen stabbed Rosamond to death or forced her to drink poison; yet none of these stories are very probable.

It seems more likely that Rosamund died peacefully at Godstow Nunnery where her ghost used to haunt Fair Rosamond's Well, near the lake in the park — but why does her ghost apparently haunt Lacock Abbey? It can hardly be something conjured up by the mind and memory of her son William Longespee, a remarkable man by all accounts, for he was dead before Lacock was founded — or is this a possibility? An article in the Hatcher Review by Miss Burnett-Brown seems to disassociate Fair Rosamond from the abbey completely. Whose then is the ghost?

They were strange and visionary people, the Longespees, and Ela too had her moments. When William Longespee was returning to Ela from an expedition to Gascony in 1225, his ship ran into a tempest and when all hope of surviving seemed lost, William, to rid himself of earthly vanities, cast overboard his precious rings and golden ornaments. Suddenly, when it seemed that nothing could save them, he and all the men aboard 'beheld a great light shining at the masthead, encircling a maiden adorned with exquisite beauty'.

Lacock Abbey

The men were in great awe but devout William had no doubt that it was the Virgin Mary, sent to save him, forever since he had been knighted he had kept a light burning before her altar. The story of the divine intervention and deliverance was accepted without question and no one was really surprised when, at his funeral procession from Salisbury Castle to Salisbury Cathedral the following year, neither wind nor rain could extinguish the lights borne by the mourners.

Their eldest son, another William, joined a Crusade against the Saracens in 1250 and was killed in a courageous skirmish in which the Saracens cut off his left foot with their long swords. William, supporting himself on the shoulder of a friend, promptly proceeded to cut off the head of every Saracen whom his right arm could reach. When they managed to cut off his right hand, he transferred the sword to his left, and continued to fight until he had lost both hands and both feet. Over his tomb, declared those who buried him, a miraculous light hung for hours.

The night before the death of her son, Ela had a vision. She saw a knight in full armour enter the gates of Heaven. The vision was so clear that she recognized, with trembling apprehension, the device upon the knight's shield and she cried out, 'Who is it? Who is it?'; and a gentle voice replied, 'It is William, your son!' When friends went to break the news to Ela of her son's death, they found not a sorrowing mother but a woman full of exultation.

When she founded Lacock Abbey Ela took the veil herself; the following year she was elected Abbess and there she remained until she died, a much respected old lady.

Years later, at the Dissolution of the Monasteries, Henry VIII sold Lacock to Sir William Sharington who was succeeded by his brother Henry whose daughter Olive in turn inherited. She wanted to marry a certain John Talbot but her father disapproved; eventually Olive decided to risk all for love and she leaped into her lover's arms from the tower. Her voluminous skirts acted as a parachute and the only injury she suffered was a broken little finger. John Talbot was knocked unconscious but her determined act softened her father's heart and he declared that, 'since she had made such a leap, she should een marry him'. Thereafter Talbot succeeded Talbot at Lacock until the property passed into the possession of the National Trust in 1944. So the candidates for the female phantom at Lacock include the villainous Ela, Countess of Salisbury; just possibly the murdered Fair Rosamond; and the spirited Olive Sharington. Incidentally, the best-known member of the Talbot family was William Fox Talbot, who was born at Lacock in 1800 and died there seventy-seven years later; a pioneer of photography, he invented the photographic process named after him and there is a Photographic Museum in Lacock village.

I have before me as I write a report from a leading photographic expert who visited Lacock and saw, on the drive in front of the double steps at the west front, the figure of a 'most beautiful girl'. She was standing, looking at the abbey, and my friend who always has a camera at the ready, made sure the figure was in the centre of his viewfinder and took a photograph. Afterwards he approached the stationary figure, and when he was no more than a few yards distant and was already beginning to address the girl — suddenly there was nobody there. On making inquiries at the abbey and in the village he discovered that such a figure had been seen from time to time, usually on bright, still, summer days, both inside and outside the abbey.

When my friend's photograph was developed he found an excellent pictorial representation of the west front of Lacock Abbey but of the beautiful lady there was no trace.

Lanhydrock House, Bodmin, Cornwall

Lovely Lanhydrock was originally one of the many possessions of the great Augustinian Priory of St Petroc. It was surrendered to Henry VIII in 1539, passed quickly through three families (Glynn, Lyttelton and Trenance) and was then bought by Sir Richard Robartes in 1620. The estate remained in the possession of the Robartes family until it was given to the National Trust in 1953. The house itself was built between 1630 and 1642, a quadrangle surrounding a courtyard. In 1780 the east wing was removed and then in 1881 the house suffered a disastrous fire which destroyed most of the building. The house was at once rebuilt and so the present house is almost entirely of the late Victorian era.

Although it is not generally accepted as being a haunted house, I rather think that a ghost does occasionally walk here. Tim Belton, the Administrator when I was there in 1981, told me that on occasions the odour of fresh cigar smoke has been reliably reported, appropriately enough, in the vicinity of the Smoking Room. While it may be possible that the smell of a stale cigar might linger in the air (although no smoking is permitted inside the house), the aroma of fresh cigars is, it was suggested to me, something quite different.

At Lanhydrock, too, there are occasional reports of the appearance of a little grey lady or a lady in black, glimpsed briefly in the vicinity of the gallery, the great room of the house, and the oldest part of the present building; and also in the area leading from the gallery to the drawing-room with its ginger-coloured oak panelling and granite chimneypieces. These portions are remnants of the original house as are the walls which escaped the unfortunate fire of 1881.

After the fire, when the house was virtually demolished, only the gallery and parts of the drawing-room remained standing, so the ghost walks, if it walks at all, in the original part of the house that has seen so much happiness and as much anguish and unhappiness as any ancient inhabited building.

It is in the gallery too that one of the most fascinating curiosities of this fine house is to be seen, although it is something not usually shown to visitors. At the far end of the gallery, on the right-hand side, there is a little hinged window of stained glass, dated 1675. John, Earl of Radnor, married first Lady Lucy Rich, daughter of the second Earl Warwick and secondly Isabella (Letitia), daughter of Sir John Smith. There is a story that one of these beautiful wives was frequently visited by the current Duke of York and, as the Earl was often away from home, there are suggestions that he had his wife fitted with a chastity belt. At all events the beautifully decorated little glass appears to depict the Devil attempting to remove the belt while the Duke (or is it the husband?) looks on. This curiosity is said to have been found in the grounds of Lanhydrock, near the church, and to have been preserved by the Lord Clifden of the time who may have hoped that the glass was one of a pair and that the other would come to light one day and be preserved on the left-hand side of the gallery window. Certainly the little glass door has been there for many years, for no known purpose.

The ghostly Grey Lady also seems to have been seen walking down the gallery towards this curious little stained glass about which so little is known; but when the same figure is seen in the drawing-room or thereabouts she is usually seated and is at first taken for a real person. When I was there in September 1981, I was told that a presence' had also been felt by a number of visitors in Her Ladyship's Room, with its immense four-poster bed, the Dresden china and the glowing little Madonna' to the right of the bed and, to the right of the door. Her Ladyship s jewel safe. What stories this room could tell!

The gallery at Lanhydrock House, the oldest part of the house, where a ghostly lady has been seen.

A ghost dog has
been seen on several
occasions at Leeds
Castle in Kent.

[Image previously spread across two pages]

Leeds Castle, near Maidstone, Kent

A fairy-tale castle built in the middle of a lake, known to the medieval Queens of England, has in its history a sort of family ghost. Here you can see a pair of Anne Boleyn's shoes and England's oldest pendulum clock and, just possibly, a phantom black hound. Whether or not the ghostly dog dates from the fifteenth century — when Henry VI s aunt, Eleanor of Gloucester, was imprisoned here for the rest of her life after being found guilty of practising Necromancy, witchcraft, heresy and treason' — the appearance of the ancient animal was usually regarded as an ill omen for those living at the castle and there are a number of stories that bear out this idea.

But the old owners, the Wykeham-Martins, departed after the First World War and today Leeds is virtually a new castle. Gone are the old and atmospheric rooms and tapestries and instead we have the mock-medieval; but still the walls rise sheer out of the lake, and there is a stone bridge across the moat and chilly dungeons and narrow passages within these massive walls where a skeleton was found curled within a cell only four feet square.

The Wykeham-Martins used to relate stories of a medium-sized, black, curly-haired, retriever-type ghost dog suddenly appearing in a room and then as suddenly disappearing. A seemingly harmless phantom — sometimes that dog would dissolve into a wall or fade into a closed door. There were those who associated the appearance of the dog with disaster, but these reports tend to be selective and sound almost coincidental. There was the appearance of the dog a few days before a young member of the household died; or an old and trusted servant passed to her last resting place; or some other death or calamity happened as must happen in any family. On one occasion an under-housemaid came across the ghost dog trotting towards her in a passage and shortly afterwards she was jilted by her young man. But some of the stories suggest that the appearance of the ghostly animal was benevolent or a warning of some sort.

Jimmy Wentworth Day told me that he had heard first-hand from an old Wykeham-Martin lady one of the most famous of the stories told me about the ghost dog of Leeds Castle.

It seems that she was sitting sewing one autumn afternoon at one of the great mullioned bay-windows, which overhung the moat and looked out across the park beyond. As the sunlight faded the ghost dog appeared for the first and only time to that lady of the house. Without feeling any apprehension or coldness or awareness that anything was different, she saw a large black dog walking across the room. She looked at him with mild wonder, thinking the door must have been ajar, but she could not recall such a large, likeable-looking dog belonging to the household and idly thought that he must be a new addition. As she prepared to make friends with him she watched him approach a wall on the opposite side of the room and simply vanish into the wall! Very surprised at this turn of events, the lady rose and crossed the room to examine the wall where she had seen the dog disappear and, even as she left the window-seat and before she reached the wall she was heading for, the whole of the bay-window, including the window-seat she had so recently been occupying, fell with a crash into the moat below! Had she not seen the ghost dog, she would certainly have plunged to her death that day with a ton of centuries-old bricks on top of her.

So, it would seem, an appearance of the Black Dog of Leeds did not always portend doom and disaster for those who saw it; but reports of appearances of the ghost dog grow fewer with the passing years and, with the disappearance of the old castle, perhaps this canine phantom, the only paranormal heritage at historic Leeds Castle, has vanished forever.

Leigh Woods, Bristol, Avon

Opposite Clifton Down (the site of an early British camp), on the banks of the River Avon by the famous suspension bridge, Leigh Woods covers more than 150 acres and includes Nightingale Valley and an Iron Age promontory fort at Stokeleigh; and it is a haunted place.

Both sides of the river here are delightful places on summer days, and many a skipper has gladdened a pilot's heart by telling him that the seaway to Bristol is the most beautiful approach to any city he has ever seen. As Brian Waters puts it in his book on The Bristol Channel: 'For the landsman there are finer approaches to other ports in other lands, but not for the sailor, who on his way to dock passes through meadows grazed by sheep and cattle, before entering the shadow of Leigh Woods ... the suspension bridge spans the river, like an archway to the city.' The suspension bridge was designed to enable the tallest sailing-ship to reach Bristol Docks; a quarter-of-a-century earlier that most versatile engineer, Brunei, had designed the Great Eastern, launched from Bristol Docks in the year that Queen Victoria came to the throne.

Did the thought ever cross the mind of Isambard Kingdom Brunei (1806-59), who died five years before the bridge he designed was opened, that his unquiet spirit would one day walk in the shadow of his greatest achievement?

Be that as it may there are many reports of the ghost of the great man having been seen hereabouts: a slightly stooping, hurrying figure in double waistcoat, high-collared cut-away overcoat, breeches, a high and straight top hat and the inevitable cigar. Brunei died relatively young, largely through overwork and the excessive smoking of cigars.

Incidentally, Brunei's other outstanding achievement, the giant Great Eastern, was a haunted ship. Scores of workmen were killed and injured during the building and launching of the 'Wonder of the Seas', the mother of ocean liners, a ship that, fully laden, outweighed the combined tonnage of Britain's 197 ships which fought the Spanish Armada. During the first launching, throughout the life of the ship, and in particular on the day before Brunei's death, the unexplained sound of 'constant hammering from below' was heard. Captain Harrison complained to his chief engineer, who investigated the matter; but no one could account for the deafening noise that always seemed to be heard before a misfortune. During the breaking-up of the ship that became 'the white elephant of the seas' the wall of a compartment in the inner shell on the port side was broken down and inside workmen found a carpet bag of rusted tools and a human skeleton. They were thought to be the remains of a workman accidentally entombed between the hulls during some stage of the construction and whose ghost, for thirty years, haunted a hull to warn of approaching misfortune.

Leigh Woods have an eerie reputation, especially on dark winter nights, when frightful screams and other weird noises have been heard; noises for which no natural explanation has ever been discovered. Of course there could be a normal explanation, but some of the circumstances in which these disembodied sounds have been heard are very difficult to explain in rational terms. And then there is the behaviour of the dogs. Most dogs will behave quite normally in Leigh Woods, but occasionally well-behaved dogs will suddenly show all the signs of extreme terror. Perhaps, from time to time, the ghost of Brunei or some other ghostly manifestation revisits this strangely unquiet place, an invisible presence that can be sensed by super-sensitive dogs and some people.

Leith Hall, by Kennethmont, Aberdeenshire, Grampian

When the American author of historical novels, Elizabeth Byrd, lived at this unusual house for five years, she and her husband both saw and heard ghosts and experienced a wealth of ghostly manifestations. It was a 'strange and seeing time' that resulted in a full-length book devoted to that dramatic period of her life.

Leith Hall, built around a courtyard and looking more like a French chateau than a Scottish mansion, has parts that date back to 1650 but most of it was built during the eighteenth century. For 300 years it was the home of the Leigh family who had been landholders in Aberdeenshire since the fourteenth century.

Elizabeth Byrd tells me that she and her husband knew nothing of any reputed hauntings when they moved in, nor could they drag any information out of their wing-neighbours, but it was not long before Elizabeth's English husband, Barrie Gaunt, saw his first ghost at Leith Hall. They moved into the east wing in early July 1966, and a week later Barrie was touring the historic wing of the house with a party of eight tourists when he saw the ghost of a Victorian lady in the Leith Bedroom.

Although it was to be two years before Elizabeth saw a ghost at Leith Hall, it was not long before she was conscious of repeatedly hearing the sound of soft footsteps on the third floor of their fourteen-room wing, 'sometimes a slow shuffle, at other times a scamper such as a child or a puppy might make'. And there was also a padding sound, such as a big dog might make, and a certain door that often slammed on windless summer nights.

Before long guests, television actress Isabel Bigg and airline hostess Mary Poulton among them, expressed a distinct uneasiness in the area of the huge master bedroom on the second floor, a feeling that Elizabeth herself had already had many times although she had told no one. In that room, with its 150-year-old draperies and massive four-poster bed, she had had horrible dreams and visions.

After persistently sleeping in the room for many months Elizabeth saw a ghost there. She awakened early, around dawn, and decided on a walk with her dog and a picnic breakfast by the side of the loch. She turned to get out of bed and froze — between the dressing-table and the foot of the bed stood a man with a bandaged head, so solid-looking that she took it to be a real person until, perhaps two minutes later, he took a step backwards and completely disappeared. That day Elizabeth moved to a small bedroom on the third floor.

Later, looking over the historic wing of the house which she had not yet visited, she found herself looking at a portrait resembling the ghost-man she had seen in her bedroom: Colonel Alexander Sebastien Leith-Hay (1818-1900). Subsequently she thought that the man she saw might be John Leith, the laird of Leith Hall, who had been shot in 1763, his widow being convicted of murder.

In addition to at least two other ghosts, seen by Elizabeth Byrd, her husband and other people, there was also ghostly music — pipe music, drums and a chanted Mass; ghostly smells of food and camphor; heavy footsteps and slamming doors, even on still, sunny afternoons. But for the full story of these fascinating experiences it is necessary to read Elizabeth Byrd's own account, *A Strange and Seeing Time: Life in a Haunted Scottish Castle*.

Leith Hall in Grampian
has been the scene of
several reported ghosts
and ghostly happenings.

After they left Leith Hall, Elizabeth tells me that their wing was taken by the Member of Parliament for Aberdeenshire who was ' grimly against the "rubbish" of ghosts'. The fact remains that certainly for five years strange things happened at Leith Hall: apparitions, voices, apports, footsteps, music, poltergeist phenomena — a wealth of unexplained happenings that convinced Elizabeth Byrd and her husband and many of their visitors that Leith Hall was haunted, and perhaps still is.

Other people have reported apparently paranormal experiences at Leith Hall, both before Elizabeth Byrd went there and afterwards. Alanna Knight, the Aberdeen author, found the nursery area particularly disturbing and she believes that part of Leith Hall is haunted by a ghost child and its governess.

Donella Gordon worked at Leith Hall many years ago and she has recalled an incident that took place in 1929. 'The Lady of the house allowed us to have in our boy friends one night a week. I will never forget the evening a young couple went along for a quiet spell to the Gun Room, that was situated underneath the Music Room. The rest of us were preparing to have our tea and the cakes were passed round when, most unexpectedly, the young couple returned. The boy's face was deathly white and his hair was almost standing on end. The girl was sick with fear. They said someone had walked from the Music Room to the Leith Bedroom, above them, in chains (it sounded like), moaning and groaning. I'll never forget the effect it had on them, and I do know that when we maids had duties in the Leith Bedroom we always felt that someone or something was in the room with us and we were always thinking that something would step out of the shadows.' This is the bedroom in which Barrie Gaunt saw the ghost of a Victorian lady, possibly a nanny'.

Lindisfarne Castle, Holy Island, where ghostly monks have been seen on the causeway to the island.

Lindisfarne Castle, Holy Island, Northumberland

Romantically situated on a high rock, this solid border fort was built about 1550 and transformed into a comfortable home by Sir Edwin Lutyens in 1903. A holy and sacred place even before the arrival of St Aidan in A.D.635, a saint renowned for his abstinence and divine powers, Holy Island has long been known as the cradle of Christianity. One example tells of his seeing Bamburgh being attacked by Penda and his Mercian army. Seeing the flames of fire and smoke rising above the city walls, he lifted his hands to heaven and cried: 'Behold, Lord, the great mischief wrought by Penda!' He had hardly uttered these words, says the venerable Bede, 'when the wind, immediately turning from the city, drove back the flames upon those who had kindled them' and they forebore any further attempts against the city.

St Cuthbert came here in A.D.664 and his ghost is said to haunt the rocks, making 'St Cuthbert's Beads'. These discs, from the 'stem' of an animal known as a crinoid or sea lily, are considered by those who find them as good omens for the future. They are also sold in local shops. Dread prodigies, it is said, appeared over Northumbria in A.D. 793. There were whirlwinds beyond measure and lightnings; and fiery dragons were seen flying in the sky, and in the sarpe year heathen men miserably destroyed God's church at Lindisfarne through robbery and slaughter. Lindisfarne also saw the royalist garrison of Charles I at the Castle — built on foundations made from the stones of the old priory — a garrison that was besieged and driven out by the Parliamentarians in 1644, immediately before the Battle of Marston Moor. This event may account for the reputed ghost of a Cromwellian soldier that has been seen at the castle.

Some years ago a member of the Ghost Club, the Rev. T. Wemyss Reed, introduced me to the Rev. A.W. Jackson and for several hours we talked about the ghost monks of Lindisfarne: St Cuthbert and the Brethren of the North. The case came to the attention of the Rev. A.W. Jackson when one of his choir boys revealed that he often saw a 'man with parchment, a tall man, a nice man', who sometimes disappeared through a wall. Later the boy described the monk as wearing a browny-black gown with a rope tied round the middle and having long hair that was cut away at the back leaving the head bare in a half-moon. For a long time this half-moon tonsure puzzled the Rev. A.W. Jackson until he met a man 'well versed in ecclesiastical and historical matters' who told him that this was a characteristic tonsure of the Celtic monasteries, superseded by the circular Roman tonsure in the seventh century.

The choir boy, under the guidance of the vicar, became something of a spontaneous medium and he reportedly received thousands of communications from Bishop Cuthbert. It is a fascinating story that was published, with a foreword by John D. Pearce-Higgins, at that time Vice-Provost of Southwark Cathedral, in 1968 under the title, The Celtic Church Speaks Today? The ghost of St Cuthbert has been seen by other people and similarly described.

Elliott O'Donnell stated categorically in one of his books: 'Both abbey and island are haunted by the phantom of St Cuthbert', one-time Bishop of Lindisfarne. 'On dark and gloomy nights, when the waves rise high and the wind roars, the spirit of St Cuthbert sits, veiled in mist, on a fragment of rock, on the shore of Holy Island, or on a stone in the abbey ruins. The sound of hammering, attributed to him, can be heard at times, both onshore and out at sea.' Sir Walter Scott refers to this haunting in one of his poems:

On a rock by Lindisfarne,

St Cuthbert sits, and toils to frame

The sea-born beads that bear his name;

Such tales had Whitby's fishers told,

And said they might his shape behold,

And hear his anvil sound;

A deafening clang — a huge, dim form,

Seen but, and heard, when gathering storm

And night were closing round.

O'Donnell also refers to 'another ghost that used to haunt the abbey ruins: that of a large, white hound that sometimes startled visitors by emerging from behind pillars, bounding in front of them and then disappearing in the most disconcerting and inexplicable manner'.

The ghost monks of Lindisfarne, apart from the phantom St Cuthbert, are generally seen moving in the area of the causeway which links the island to the mainland. They are thought to be the ghosts of some of the scores of monks who were cut down as they fled from Viking raids, in particular the frightful raid in A.D. 793 when the Danes ran their dragon ships on to the curving shore of golden sand and pillaged, sacked and destroyed the monastery founded almost two centuries earlier. The ghost monk most commonly seen is described as a 'grey-clad' figure and it seems to be that of a man watching with trepidation some long-ago landing on the hazy sands.

Such a report, in 1962, comes from two visitors on holiday from Worthing and they took the monk to be a real person until the figure faded away into the sand. Yet another ghost seen at Lindisfarne is that of Constance de Beverley, but detailed sightings are hard to come by.

But Lindisfarne's principal ghost is certainly that of St Cuthbert and, in addition to appearing among the rocks on the shore, his ghost has also been seen in the ruins of the Norman priory. Perhaps the most famous appearance of this ghost, if not the best authenticated, is the occasion when it was seen by Alfred the Great, who was a fugitive at the time. The ghostly saint indicated that all would be well and that Alfred would one day sit on the throne of England, and so it came to pass.

Loseley House, near Godalming, Guildford, Surrey

This magnificent house, home of the More-Molyneux family since the middle of the sixteenth century, rests serenely in its graceful setting, slumbering it seems after its heady historical associations, for it is the one house which Queen Elizabeth I undoubtedly visited and slept in — three times in fact. The bed where she slept is still there. James I slept at Loseley too and Queen Anne.

The present family are connected by marriage to Sir Thomas More, Henry VIII's Lord Chancellor of England. Major and Mrs More-Molyneux, the present owners, justly famous for their dairy products, are somewhat reticent about their ghosts: 'It's a family affair which we think should be treated as rather a personal matter,' they will tell you, although some years ago, when I approached Major James More-Molyneux about the possibility of a party of Ghost Club members visiting the house, he readily agreed but added: 'I should perhaps add that we do regard our ghosts as rather personal and would not encourage any stirring up! My wife, however, has met one of them ... an experience which was entirely amicable.'

Mrs More-Molyneux saw the ghost of a pleasant-looking lady, late-Victorian judging by her dress, outside the door of a bathroom. The form was smiling gently and had overall a most friendly expression. Other people have seen the same form. A portrait of this lady was discovered in one of the attics and it has been suggested that the removal of the picture caused the ghostly form to appear.

A few years ago a visitor to this truly delightful house noticed a woman in brown clothes standing at the foot of the stairway. In particular the visitor noticed the staring black eyes in the otherwise not unfriendly face. She mentioned the figure to her companion — who was unable to see the figure — which then faded slowly away. The visitor's companion then realized however that at the precise spot where she had been told the form had appeared, she had felt suddenly icy cold; had in fact visibly shivered and felt altogether uneasy. Both ladies then noticed for the first time a portrait hanging on the wall nearby.

The lady who had felt suddenly cold remarked that perhaps it had been on account of the staring expression of the woman portrayed in the oil painting that she had felt so cold, whereupon the visitor who had seen the ghostly form realized that the form she had seen was the woman portrayed in the painting! I am told that as many as ten other visitors, who have had no previous knowledge of the ghostly woman in brown, have remarked upon such a figure either gliding up the stairway or standing at the foot of the stairs, staring intently with piercing eyes, before slowly fading away.

An American lady visited Loseley a few years ago and joined a party of people who were exploring those parts of the house to which the public are admitted. After seeing the banqueting hall with its Minstrels' Gallery, and the drawing-room and the bedroom that had known Queen Elizabeth I, she was told a story about the house that has been handed down over the centuries.

Loseley House - where
the ghosts are as
mysterious and
shadowy as the house
itself is beautiful,
mellow and quietly
welcoming.

It is said that some 400 years ago, when the house was comparatively new, the second wife of the then owner murdered her little stepson in his father's absence so that her own son would inherit the valuable property. When her husband returned and discovered what she had done, he had her imprisoned in a small room in the upper part of the house and there she lived for the rest of her life. How long that was is not known; even the method of murder that she is said to have employed is confused, one version saying that she cut off her stepson's legs and he bled to death while another story has it that the stepmother drowned the child in the moat. Interestingly enough at one time there was a picture at Loseley showing a legless child seated on his stepmother's lap, but later a bunch of roses was painted in to alter an unpleasant picture into a pleasant one. I am not aware of any story of haunting associated with the area of the former moat although there certainly is, or was, a so-called 'haunted room'.

One reference in an American book speaks of terrible screams issuing from this room on one certain night each year, and so common and regular an occurrence was this that the family used to arrange to be away on that evening. An entirely different room at Loseley, says this authority, had the reputation of being haunted because of a feeling in the room of great evil, a feeling that was reported by scores of visitors who had no previous knowledge of the same impression being experienced and reported by other people. This is the room, it is said, where the murdering stepmother was incarcerated.

Not many years ago the young daughters of one of the occupants informed their mother that they were never lonely when there was a party downstairs and they were banished to the upper portions of the house because 'a little old lady, dressed in grey' used to come and join them. They used to look forward to her visits for she would sit and smile at them as they played together; but she never spoke. They thought perhaps she had some affliction that prevented her from conversing with them or perhaps she had instructions not to speak to them but at all events they soon took it for granted that she would not speak. She seemed to have such a kindly manner and to promote such an air of security and safety that they came to accept the presence without question although they did think it rather odd that they never saw her arrive or leave; one minute she was not there and then she was — later, she was there one minute and the next she had disappeared. The girls also sometimes wondered why they never saw her anywhere but upstairs in their playroom.

As they grew older the girls realized that the dear little lady in grey' was never seen by anyone else and her presence was never willingly discussed by the grown-ups. Gradually they sensed that there was something unusual about their friend, something inexplicable and something to be nervous about. Soon afterwards the family left the house.

At one period some temporary occupants, having heard the story of the wicked stepmother, decided to hold a party and to bring a medium to the house in the hope of making contact with the unquiet spirit of the murderess. The result, it is said, was not that which had been expected: whereas before the visit of the medium only parts of the house had seemed to be affected, during and after the seances the whole house seemed to be haunted! So many odd things happened, so many strange sounds startled the guests and so many unexpected raps and bangs sounded — sometimes accompanied by forms that disappeared in mysterious circumstances — that the guests became quite terrified and none of them dared to go to bed. As soon as dawn broke, they beat a hasty retreat from the house of ghosts! Before they left, however, the hostess called all the guests together and the servants and requested them to promise never to divulge what they had seen and heard that night.

One of the guests is supposed to have related something of what had happened to a relative who published the story. But few details were ever revealed, other than whereas before that night the ghost of the wicked stepmother had haunted one bedroom; after that memorable night ghostly forms were not infrequently to be met in many of the bedrooms, in the passageways, on the staircases and throughout the house. Whereas there had once been a single ghost or at any rate very few, now it seemed there were many!

Another ghost story told about Loseley has to do with a large dinner-party held there one winter night. Extra help brought in from outside included a waiter who was hired from Bretts, then a well-known catering establishment in Guildford. He was an elderly man, quiet and dignified in his manner, discreet and courteous. A heavy storm broke while the party was in progress and continued for many hours. The housekeeper, not wishing the old man to travel back to Guildford in such weather, made up a bed for him in a spare room.

Next morning, on being asked what sort of a night he had spent, he replied that he had slept well enough, 'but I'm afraid the gentleman who kept passing through my room in fancy dress didn't like my being there'. Needless to say none of the guests at the dinner-party had worn fancy dress, nor had any of the occupants or the servants. Oddly enough the room in which the old man had spent the night had been partitioned off from what had once been a long gallery, doubtless much frequented in its day.

The same gallery seems to affect animals and dogs in particular, rather than human beings, and there are stories of a dog suddenly becoming transfixed with fear and refusing to pass a certain spot in the old gallery and, another time, of a visitor finding, when he descended to the lower floor, that his dog had not followed him. On retracing his steps he found the normally brave and rather snappish animal cowering in the middle of the gallery, whimpering with fear at something invisible to his human companion.

And so Loseley House slumbers on, its ghosts occasionally seen, but more often sensed, from time to time; the most frequent a 'pleasant lady', less commonly an 'unpleasant lady' and very rarely now, it seems, a ghost child — perhaps the mother, the stepmother and the unfortunate little boy who was murdered. Yet some say the ghost child is that of a little girl who was murdered by her mother in a fit of jealousy. The ghosts of Loseley House are as mysterious and shadowy as the house itself is beautiful, mellow and quietly welcoming.

Lydford Gorge, Devonshire

This water-formed deep ravine in the valley of the Lyd has long been haunted, especially in the vicinity of the pool known as Kitty's Steps (or Kitt's Hole or Kitt's Pool) by the ghost of an old woman wearing a red kerchief on her head.

Elliott O'Donnell tells of two elderly ladies visiting the place and standing gazing down at the waterfall one day when they suddenly saw the shadowy figure of a woman in a red shawl, standing close beside the pool at the foot of the fall. She appeared to be holding a basket and seemingly did not mind the occasional spray of water that washed over her, but suddenly she slipped or toppled forward and fell into the pool.

Much alarmed at the still form floating in the water the two ladies hastened to get assistance, fearing the poor woman would drown and they hurriedly explained the situation to an old man they met. He replied: There is no need to fear about her being drowned. People can't be drowned twice. What you saw was the ghost of an old woman called Kitty who haunts the waterfall. The place is named after her. She was returning home from market one dark and stormy night many years ago when she fell into the pool and was drowned.' The ladies at once hurried back to Kitty's Pool but of the figure they had seen there was no sign.

Nearby, the vicinity of the 'castle' (in the care of the Department of the Environment) is haunted by a ghostly Black Hound which, according to some writers, may have once been the Lady Howard, while the gloomy castle itself, described in the sixteenth century as 'one of the most heinous, contagious and detestable places within the realm', allegedly harbours the ghost of the infamous Judge Jeffreys. He haunts the site of the old courtroom where he presided during the Civil War.

Lyme Park, Cheshire

Proud Lyme Park stands 800 feet above sea level on the borders of Cheshire, Lancashire and Derbyshire — the name Lyme being derived from the Latin limes' for border. The present appearance of the house is eighteenth-century work commissioned to alter the structure built by Sir Piers Legh VII in 1541 on the site of an even earlier building that stood here in 1465; a fact that is recorded in a manuscript of that date. Today the house that dates from Elizabethan days and contains period furniture and tapestries, Grinling Gibbons carvings and a secret panel, often seems to brood silently on its past, as it has each time that I have been there.

Granville Squiers, that mine of information on secret hiding-places, told me about the fascinating one at Lyme: an actual picture that swings out of its frame. The picture, a full-length portrait representing the Black Prince that came from St James's Palace, hangs on the north wall of the hall. It stands out from its companion portraits for it is set in a massive frame in the centre of the end wall and this frame was originally the frame of a door. During alterations in the early eighteenth century the level of this large and lofty apartment was dropped some eight or nine feet and the architect covered

Lyme Park, Cheshire, the scene of a ghostly funeral cortege - and where ghostly sounds have been heard issuing from the Ghost Room.

The imposing entrance hall at Lyme Park.

the gap on that side with this large picture. It has hinges on one side, and a cord and pulley at the top to assist in drawing it back to its frame after it has been swung out. The floor of the drawing-room on the other side of the wall is level with the bottom of the picture, and this room is lined with old panelling in which there is a well-concealed double door which opens on the back of the picture. It might be thought that there was a secret entrance here at an early date but I am told that careful examination reveals that the door is a clever copy of the original panelling.

The presence of the secret door is therefore puzzling, although on special occasions it is possible for the whole arrangement to be thrown open, giving a pleasing effect from both rooms. Granville Squiers told me that he had examined a genuine hiding-place here in an old room on the top floor, known as the Knight's Chamber; there the floorboards of a closet on the right of the fireplace can be removed to reveal an entrance to two secret compartments, one behind a chimney being eleven feet long while the other is fourteen feet square and occupies the whole of the space under the flooring of the chamber.

The ghosts of Lyme Park are said to comprise a ghostly funeral cortege. The house of Lyme' is thought to have its origin in the person of Sir Piers Legh, who in 1388 married Margaret, daughter and heiress of Sir Thomas Danyers, and he founded the family of Legh of Lyme. Sir Thomas Danyers had been granted the land, called Lyme Hanley, by the King in reward for rescuing the Black Prince's standard at Caen. The house, Lyme Park, was built by Sir Piers VII (1513-1590) but it is with Sir Piers (or Peter) II that the ghost story is associated.

History reveals that he fought at Agincourt (1415) and it seems that he had only recently married the young and beautiful Lady Joan. Sir Piers fought bravely beside the King, and when the French forces seemed about to overwhelm the

English archers and capture the King, it was largely through Sir Piers's efforts that the enemy was driven back, and the King saved from capture or possible death. But this was at the expense of his own life, for Sir Piers received multiple wounds and would not permit any attention to be paid to his injuries until all danger to the King was past. Then, it is said, he died of his wounds after the battle. History, however, says he lived until 1422 and died of wounds received at Meaux, but at all events his body was brought to England and the broken-hearted Lady Joan was not the only woman who watched the solemn, silent and slow funeral cortege bring home the body of Sir Piers. A woman named Blanche is said to have long loved Sir Piers. She never recovered from the grief of his death and it was not many weeks before her body was found beside the River Bollin. Without Sir Piers she had no reason or wish to live.

The body of the brave knight had been buried at the top of a hill which was afterwards known as 'Knight's Low' or 'Knight's Sorrow', while Blanche was buried where her body was found in a place afterwards called the 'Lady's Grove'. Ever since, when the wind howls across the moors and clouds hide the full moon, the funeral cortege of Sir Piers Legh can sometimes be seen ascending the Knight's Low, carrying the corpse to burial, while following it there is a lady, dressed completely in white and contrasting sharply with the rest of the procession. This is the ghost of the mysterious Blanche, and it has been said that the sound of her sobs and uncontrollable weeping is clearly heard above the moaning of the wind. And still the phantom funeral winds its weary way up the hill — and disappears.

Inside Lyme Hall there is a room opening out of the long gallery that is known as Mary Queen of Scots' Room and also, more ominously, as the Ghost Room. The unhappy Queen was imprisoned at Lyme for a while and occupied this room, which is supposed to be connected by a secret passage with a building in the park known as Lyme Cage. But it is not her ghost that haunts the house or causes the sound of distant bells, faintly but distinctly ringing, that has been reported here at night. Many years ago a small secret chamber was discovered under the floorboards in the Ghost Room containing the skeleton of some forgotten priest or other fugitive and it is his ghost that has given the room its name. As Christina Hole once said to me: His appalling death agony as he starved to death in those restricted quarters may well have impressed his thoughts sufficiently on the room to give rise to the haunting.'

N

Newark Park, Wotton-under-Edge, Gloucestershire

This individual house, perched on a spur of the Cotswolds with fine views over the Severn, was given to the National Trust in 1949 by Mrs C.A. Power-Clutterbuck, together with 643 acres of woods and agricultural land, in memory of her son James Edward, killed in the First World War. It is occupied by Bob Parsons, who readily agreed to a party of Ghost Club members spending a night at the house after one of his friends, a Ghost Club member, had told me about some of the strange happenings reported there. Subsequently two Ghost Club members paid a separate visit and then an extended week-long visit when Bob Parsons was away and they were completely alone in the house.

Initially I heard that for a long time there had been disturbances at Newark Park suggesting that the place was haunted: doors opening and closing by themselves; strange rustling noises, as of a person passing by in a long dress or cloak that trailed on the floor; distinct and clear footfalls along deserted corridors and stairways; disembodied voices;

inexplicable lights and bell-ringing; thumps and bangs and the sound of rattling chains that had no rational explanation and an unnatural coldness. I lost little time in preparing a visit.

The house looked forbidding in the gathering dusk as we arrived that spring afternoon — to be greeted by Bob Parsons' enormous black dog! During the time he had been there, bringing back some of the former beauty and grandeur to the place, Bob Parsons told us that he had had various people staying for short and long periods who helped in the restoration of the house. Many times he had been told that unexplained nocturnal footsteps had been heard walking down the stairway. Time after time one of the visitors would assume that their companion had awakened in the night and gone downstairs, only to find that his companion was fast asleep and that no one had in fact gone downstairs at the time the footsteps were heard. Other visitors had complained of the sound of rattling chains at dead of night, of the sound of bell-ringing and of strange lights which they had seen in the house as they approached along the drive; lights that disappeared inexplicably.

During our first visit one group was detailed to the allegedly haunted cellar, but after about fifteen minutes the female members became nervous and wanted to leave. In view of the extreme coldness, the cellars were left for the time being to themselves and the whole party moved to the slightly warmer parts of the house. Bob Parsons told us that he had chanced to mention some of the odd happenings to his friend, the author Elspeth Huxley. She was fascinated and before long, over dinner, she implored him to tell her everything he could about the supposed haunting. Bob duly recounted all the incidents he could remember and at the end, as he looked at her eager face, he added: 'Of course, its all nonsense — there are no such things as ghosts!' That night he was disturbed as he had never been before with strange noises at Newark Park; even his dog was petrified by 'something' and refused to sleep in its accustomed place and Bob heard footsteps and chain rattling: after that night he was never again quite as sceptical as he had been!

During the course of the night we spent at Newark Park several members heard (and we recorded) the sound of rustling on a landing of the stairway where such sounds had sometimes been reported previously. We satisfied ourselves that there was no natural explanation — rodents or wind for example — and then proceeded to conduct a lengthy vigil at the spot with members covering every point, recording apparatus running and a camera, fitted with infra-red film, trained on the spot where the rustling noises had been heard and the camera operator poised to press the shutter as soon as a sound was heard.

We sat for a long time with most of us hearing not a sound, except for the rattle of rain on the roof. Afterwards in the warmer and more relaxed atmosphere of the enormous kitchen with its roaring open fire, we played back the recordings that had been taken of the whole episode. There was no unexpected sound, except that halfway through the watch, when no one had spoken, we were astonished to hear two different voices recorded on the tape: one said something that sounded like 'It's looking,' and the other, 'It's looking at us.' It was almost as though whatever had spoken was referring to the camera lens pointed at them! During a second session in the same place two members of the group, separated by several yards and with other members on both sides of them who heard nothing, heard the sound of a woman's voice.

Later during a period of watching in one of the bedrooms, I heard footsteps walking down the small staircase towards the 'haunted' landing. I thought that one of the watchers in an upper room had come down for something, although I was mildly surprised that he or she would do such a thing under the arrangements we had made only minutes before; but the party was a larger one than we normally take on such an investigation and it was difficult to institute and maintain control conditions. I quickly and quietly left my post and went to meet the member and have a word with him. As I left the bedroom the footsteps ceased. There was no one on the stairs or on the landing, which was icy cold; no one had left their post upstairs and there seemed to be no explanation for the footsteps, but they were recorded on tape.

Once, when a party of six people were investigating the mysteries of Newark Park, a series of curious knockings was heard and five of the party felt suddenly very cold at the same time. Almost immediately windows in the room suddenly vibrated and rattled at an incredibly fast rate and this same thing happened on three separate occasions and was verified by everyone present.

Subsequently two Ghost Club members who took part in the original investigation visited Newark Park again one week-end and then spent an extended visit to the house when Bob Parsons was away and they were completely alone there. They were struck by the extreme coldness of the place and, usually, by the complete silence that reigned in every room and all parts of the house at all times of the day and night. But they did report a number of curious and seemingly inexplicable incidents. For example it is routine in such investigations to ring with chalk all movable objects and one such article definitely shifted outside its chalked circle without being touched by a human hand. Both watchers heard the voices of two men talking, as though in a large hall, and one wonders whether this could have been some sort of 'throw-back' to the days when Newark Park was a Tudor Hunting Lodge; later there were Jacobean, Georgian and Victorian additions, resulting in a curious mixture of architecture and atmosphere.

The two watchers also reported a strange tapping sound that seemed to originate within the room itself. A tap-tap-tap followed by a moment of silence, then tap-tap-tap again. This was repeated three times and sounded almost like a blind man tap-tapping his way round the room with his stick, except that a blind person usually taps in duplicate, not in triplicate. Once, when one of the watchers was outside the house, sitting on a stone seat, the other investigator, upstairs, was walking across the landing when he distinctly heard the voices of two women, seemingly from downstairs. He immediately thought that Bob Parsons had returned from London and the two women were picking up their youngsters whom Bob had taken with him, but this was not so. Neither Bob Parsons nor anyone else had arrived, the house was empty and the watcher outside had not heard or seen anything unusual.

It was noticed by both investigators, and it may be significant, that many of the bangs and thumps occurred when the watchers were lying down, resting; in a relaxed, receptive, and un-investigative mood. But not always; once the sound of horses' hooves and the grind of wheels on gravel was heard when both men were upstairs, but an immediate investigation revealed nothing to account for the sounds. The bangs and bumps and thumps varied in intensity: one resembling the sound of a garment being dropped to the floor outside a door, another sounding more like a heavy log being dropped.

An article about Newark Park, written in 1978, stated unequivocally, 'the house has many ghosts'. The ghostly tread that has so often been heard on the stairway is thought to be that of the Abbot of Kingswood, seeking his lost Abbey. When the house was built, stones from Kingswood Abbey were reputedly incorporated and, it is said, stone from village crosses in the neighbourhood. Newark Park has kept its secrets for centuries and perhaps when it is finally restored its ghosts will disappear forever.

Newark Park, Gloucestershire, where the Ghost Club have recorded ghostly voices.

The haunted
landing at Newark
Park, where the
author head
disembodied
footsteps.

O

Old Soar Manor, near Borough Green, Kent

This portion of a late thirteenth-century dwelling (under the guardianship of the Department of the Environment) is a remarkably unspoilt example of a dwelling belonging to a knight in the reign of Edward I and a notable survival of thirteenth-century domestic architecture. But the ghost, if ghost there is, seems to date from the eighteenth century.

Old Soar (Norman for grief) originally belonged to the famous Colpeppers of Preston, at one time the largest landowning family in Kent and Sussex — reputedly due to their habit of kidnapping heiresses and forcing them to marry a Colpepper!

Later the property passed to the Geary family and the story goes that about 200 years ago a young dairymaid became pregnant by a drunken young family priest and, in some way that has never been completely explained, was found dead in the chapel. The Geary family decided that the death had been one of suicide and the body was buried at midnight in unconsecrated ground.

Little was heard of any ghost at Old Soar until 1971 when a local resident told a new Caretaker that the building had long been haunted by the ghost of an eighteenth-century dairymaid who had committed suicide in the chapel because she was pregnant by the priest. This informant, to the continuing surprise of the Caretaker, revealed that local people often saw lights in the deserted building at night and sometimes reportedly heard the sound of music, quiet but penetrating, that seemed to emanate from the chapel. People in the adjoining eighteenth-century farm house (built on the foundations of a thirteenth-century aisled hall that disappeared in a fire 300 years ago) independently inquired about the source of the 'church music' they had heard, music that seemed to issue out of the wall. The adjoining Old Soar property was empty at the time.

In June 1972, a young couple explored Old Soar, and as they were leaving they asked the Caretaker what she could tell them about the ghost they had seen in the chapel, a vague form resembling the figure of a priest that they had both seen at the same time as they had noticed that it had suddenly become very cold. A week later another party of visitors, strangers to the area who had no knowledge of any stories associated with the place, commented in a puzzled way on the 'icy cold and ghostly feeling' in the chapel.

In 1973, again in June, the Caretaker was checking over the property and found her attention drawn to the small chapel. She was puzzled to see what appeared to be a long grey cloak hanging on the wall. Trying not to take her eyes from the object, which she knew had no business to be there, she entered the chapel, glancing down for a moment as she did so; when she looked up again the cloak or whatever it was, had vanished.

A few days later yet another visitor reported seeing a phantom priest in the chapel; this time the figure seemed to be bending over the piscina. One version of the death of the unhappy pregnant girl, 200 years before, says she had fallen against the piscina and had drowned in the few inches of holy water.

Other apparently paranormal incidents reported from Old Soar include a vision of water in the piscina; the distinct and disturbing feeling of an unhappy presence' on the spiral staircase; and the sound of inexplicable footsteps, 'light, like those of a woman'; and these strange happenings always seem to take place in the month of June.

Osterley Park, Osterley, Greater London

Originally Elizabethan but re-modelled between 1760 and 1780 by Robert Adam, impressive Osterley is reputedly haunted by a lovely lady in a white dress. Who she is, or was, nobody seems to know but over the years the attendants have not infrequently been asked about the White Lady of Osterley'.

Parapsychologist Andrew Green once told me that when he lived at Ealing he talked with two workmen who had been employed at Osterley. Both men said they had seen the mysterious phantom, independently and on different occasions, but both sightings were at the same time of day, around 4.30 p.m. in the afternoon.

In 1978 a group of schoolchildren were visiting Osterley in the charge of a couple of teachers who were puzzled by being asked by three of the children, separately, about the lovely lady in white' that they had seen as they had walked through the apartments, still furnished as Robert Adam and his craftsmen had left them.

The teachers questioned the children closely and two of them had seen the figure near an archway by the main stairs, not far from the portico on the south front; while the other had seen an identical figure in the Gobelins Tapestry Room. All the children said the figure was dressed in a white, flowing gown and that it had seemed to float out of sight although they had seen no door or exit that it could have used.

The teachers questioned the attendants and then learned for the first time that there were stories of such a figure being seen from time to time and always around 4.30 p.m. in the afternoon, the time the figure had reportedly been seen by the visiting children.

P

Pass of Killiecrankie, Pitlochry, Perthshire, Tayside

This wooded gorge, a famous beauty spot much admired by Queen Victoria and by thousands of visitors every year, was the scene of the battle in which King William's troops were routed by the Jacobite army led by 'Bonnie Dundee'. The National Trust for Scotland owns the woods on the east side of the Pass and there is a permanent exhibition in the Visitors' Centre featuring the battle. The whole area is reputedly haunted each 27 July, the date of the battle, by a red glow that hangs over the scene of the conflict and, according to some reports, the distant sounds of battle and the occasional appearance of a phantom army.

The battle of Killiecrankie took place on 27 July 1689, when William III's troops under General Mackay were routed by 3000 Highlanders under John Graham of Claverhouse, Viscount Dundee, for James II. 'Bonnie Dundee' himself fell mortally wounded almost at the moment of victory. A stone marks the spot where he fell.

The battle itself was fought on the hillside above the main road a mile north of the Pass through which King William's men advanced to engage the Jacobites, only to return shortly afterwards in retreat as they fled from the torrent of barefooted redcoats and tartans that swept down the valley.

Each 27 July, I have been told, a red glow hangs over the scene of the conflict; a phantom light that many people, but not everyone, can see in the valley through which the Highlanders charged. The mysterious glow is thought by local people to have its origin in a vision seen by Viscount Dundee on the eve of the battle.

As he slept, Dundee saw a man whose head poured with blood standing at his bedside, bidding him to get up and follow where he led. Dundee awoke, but, seeing no one, interpreted the vision as a dream and returned to sleep. But again he was awakened by the same voice and the same figure; this time the form pointed to its bloody head and seemed to implore Dundee to rise and follow. Now Dundee did get up and ascertained from the guard that no one had entered his tent. Satisfied, he once more returned to his bed, but for the third time the same form appeared to him. Pointing towards the plain of Killiecrankie it bid him arise, seeming to indicate that he would meet Dundee there.

When the figure had disappeared, Dundee got up, dressed and discussed the strange vision with a Highland chief, who agreed never to speak of the matter if the coming battle should prove unsuccessful for the Highlanders.

On the day of the battle Dundee was reluctant to descend from the high ground. Perhaps he had a premonition of his own death or maybe he wished to wait until darkness before coming to close quarters with the enemy so that his troops could find shelter in the mountains if they were defeated. At all events, it was sunset, red and glowing, before he gave the order to charge. Within minutes King William's forces were defeated and beginning to flee when, almost as if by accident, a fatal shot struck Dundee in the side.

When I was there a few years ago I talked separately with two people, one a local man from Pitlochry and the other a visitor, who both claimed to have seen phantom figures here on different years but each on 27 July. The figures were those of Scottish Highlanders, appearing from nowhere, charging down the valley to the gorge and disappearing to the accompaniment of shouting and the sound of distant battle while a mysterious red glow hung over the scene.

One late summer day some years ago a cyclist, touring Scotland, reached Pitlochry where he stopped for a few days. One evening he rode over to view the site of the historic battle. It was late when he reached the Pass and he perched himself on a rock at the foot of one of the great cliffs; but it was a warm night and he had refreshments with him so he decided to spend the night there, for the view was enchanting.

Soon he was aroused by the sound of a dull booming noise which he associated with distant musketry. He looked around him: all was now quiet and still. It was almost two o'clock. Then he heard it again: the queer booming noise that was unmistakably the report of firearms; it was the beginning of a night he would always remember.

During the course of the next few minutes — a period of time that seemed like hours — he saw the ghostly figure of a Highlander, running with huge bounds; he heard the rattle of drums accompanied by the shrill sound of fifes and flutes; he saw what appeared to be a whole army of scarlet-clad soldiers away at the far end of the Pass with a mounted officer at the head. He particularly noticed how tall the marching men seemed and, as they grew nearer, he clearly saw the white, set faces in the red glow that hung over the whole scene. He heard the sound of their steady march, watched as they passed and disappeared round the bend of the Pass and listened as the sounds slowly died away. He saw too dozens of bodies, men and horses, Highlanders and Englishmen, gory and silent. He saw too the ghost of a Highland girl robbing the corpses ... or was it all a dream?

The awesome Pass of Killiecranckie, Perthshire, where each July a red glow hangs over the scene of a battle which was fought nearly three hundred years ago.

This sighting is recorded soberly and sensibly and it could just be that the relaxed and unexpectant visitor witnessed a re-run of something of the terrible events that took place in the Pass long years ago. Bearing in mind the theory that such ghostly appearances run down like a battery, perhaps today only the ghostly red glow, the occasional sound of battle and sometimes a phantom Highlander remain here: soon even these last remnants of the event may disappear forever.

Pengersick Castle, Praa Sands, Cornwall

The National Trust has covenants over this fortified tower, part of the once great manor that existed here in the twelfth century. The family took its name from the place and one Henry de Pengersick, known as 'le Fort', was without doubt a violent character. He married Engrina Godolphin, a member of the family owning adjoining estates, and seems to have had a stormy relationship with the Church of the day, gaining for himself Greater Excommunication for attacking and wounding the Vicar of Breage and a monk from Heiles Abbey when they called to collect their dues. The present owners tell me: 'If ghosts there are, we would be inclined to think they might be those of Henry le Fort and his wife.'

In Tudor times Pengersick was rebuilt as a fortified manor, probably by John Milliton. Antony Hippisley Coxe suggests that his is one of the ghosts haunting Pengersick, for he is said to have tried to murder his wife by poisoning her, but she craftily changed goblets. I am informed that this and the other reputed ghost, as recounted by Antony Coxe, are pure legend', but Pengersick Castle, like many another Cornish location, attracts legends of the supernatural.

The other story goes back even further in history, to the time of the Crusades, and tells of an early owner of Pengersick forgetting all about his wife and son in Cornwall and marrying a foreign king's daughter. Soon he tired of her too (although she had given him a magic sword) and when he returned at length to England, she followed with their infant son. When he saw them he threw them both into the sea and she was drowned, although her spirit entered into a white hare; the child was picked up alive by a passing ship.

After the death of his legal wife, so runs the story, this evil man married a witch who was very cruel to his legitimate son. One day a ship was wrecked nearby and the only survivor was a boy who bore a striking resemblance to the heir of Pengersick. He was, of course, no other than the boy's half-brother.

One day the two boys, guided by a remarkably friendly white hare, discovered the magic sword. The wicked baron was thrown from his horse and died as a result when his mount was frightened and shied at the sudden appearance of a large white hare. The boys, having mastered the occult arts with the help of the friendly white hare, are said to have discovered the elusive elixir of life and to have lived in happiness at Pengersick for several generations.

The first John Milliton was succeeded by his son, another John, and he became involved with William Godolphin and an unnamed neighbour in the mysterious looting of the King of Portugal's carrack St Anthony, wrecked at Gunwalloe in 1526, the fabulous cargo vanishing without trace. The matter became the subject of a Royal Commission but the whereabouts of the untold riches were never discovered. However John Milliton must have somehow cleared himself of all suspicion, for in 1548 we find he is High Sheriff of Cornwall. At the time of the Reformation, after the execution of Sir Humphrey Arundell for his part in the Rebellion of 1549, Milliton became Captain of St Michael's Mount.

The present owners tell me that ghosts from the Gunwalloe wreck might well be possible as there is strong evidence to suggest that the treasure was, at one time, bricked-up within the walls or secret passages of Pengersick. There is also reputed to have been an underground connection between the castle and the beach, long since fallen in, which could have been used to store the treasure; it was almost certainly used by wreckers and smugglers in days gone by.

In 1571 the property was left to be divided between six daughters and when this became impractical the house fell into disuse. All but the fortified tower gradually became decayed; the materials were used to build neighbouring cottages and an adjoining farmhouse where the moulding from one of the original castle doorways may still be seen surrounding the front door.

Today, thanks to the labours of the present and past owners, this fascinating place has been restored, the modem wing being converted into an up-to-date house and the tower remaining in its Tudor state. And, most successfully, the main rooms have been provided with authentic furnishings, although inevitably most items date from the seventeenth century.

I am told that many visitors feel a 'presence' at Pengersick and imagination can easily create an atmosphere. But the three cats and the dog that belong to the present owners seem totally at ease wherever they are within the building; as well they may be in a place that once saw turmoil but now slumbers in peace.

Polesden Lacey in Surrey, which has two unusual ghosts; a brown hooded figure on a bridge, and a whirlwind along the Nun's Walk.

Polesden Lacey, Bookham, Surrey

When Richard Brinsley Sheridan bought the 1632 Carolean house that stood here until the second decade of the nineteenth century, as part of the marriage settlement of his second wife, Elizabeth Ogle, he wrote to her: 'We shall have the nicest place within a prudent distance of town, in England.'

Sadly no trace of that Carolean house now remains and the only visible legacy of his ownership remains in the long terraced walk. This, as a date carved in the foundation wall would seem to indicate, was begun in 1761 (Sheridan bought the place in 1797), but he greatly extended it and the terrace is now the most impressive feature of the garden. It is also one of two haunted places at Polesden Lacey.

In his People and Places, Great and Little Bookham, local historian S.E.D. Fortesque says Polesden Lacey has two unusual ghosts: a brown-hooded figure on a bridge and a whirlwind along the Nun's Walk.

West of the ornamental garden there is a wooden bridge crossing the sunken road and here, standing on this bridge, a mysterious figure has been seen on a number of occasions. The form seems to be wearing a brown cloak with a hood and the hood is pulled up so that no part of the face is visible.

Along the Nun's Walk, which runs parallel with the long terrace, just inside the wood, a strange whistle has been heard, sometimes described as resembling the sound of a whirlwind rushing along the track from the eastern direction towards the house. Such a sound has been heard many times and no satisfactory explanation has ever been discovered.

On occasions the noise has been followed, but it suddenly ceases as mysteriously as it begins and so far no one can offer any sort of explanation, either a rational one or a possibly psychic answer.

Mr Davis, a long-standing member of the staff at Polesden Lacey, tells me that he once saw a dead female figure lying on a sofa in one of the smaller rooms and another time, in the Billiards Room, something made him turn round and he saw a man in old-fashioned clothing standing behind him; then, suddenly, the figure was no longer there. Many times in the seven years he has been at Polesden Lacey Mr Davis says he has heard a shrill cry for help which has no objective reality. All the apparently paranormal activity that he has witnessed has taken place in the morning, before the house is open to the public. Mr Davis recounted some of his strange experiences at Polesden Lacey when he joined me in a BBC Radio 4 broadcast about ghosts with Bob Symes in April, 1984.

Powis Castle, Welshpool, Powys

The story of the best-known ghost of Powis Castle, that ancient and gloomy feudal stronghold also known as Castell Coch — the Red Castle — for it is built of red sandstone, has often been quoted and misquoted but a member of Lord Powis's family has asserted that there is every reason to believe that it is true.

The earliest owners of Powis were the Princes of Powe who allied themselves to the English in the thirteenth century and became Barons de la Pole. The line died out in the sixteenth century and Sir Edward Herbert bought the castle. In 1784 a Herbert heiress married Edward Clive, the son of Clive of India, and he later became the first Earl of Powis. Many relics of Clive of India are preserved at the castle and were transferred, together with the principal contents including portraits, tapestries and early Georgian furniture, to the National Trust in 1965. The fourth Earl had already given the castle to the Trust in 1952.

The best-known ghost story associated with this impressive and atmospheric castle is vouched for by an early Wesleyan Methodist minister, the Rev. John Hampson. He heard various reports of the ghostly associations of Powis Castle and, determined to ascertain the truth of the matter, he sought out an elderly inhabitant who claimed to have seen and spoken to the ghost that was long reputed to have haunted the castle.

From her he heard the full story, subsequently incorporated into the autobiography of Thomas Wright of Birkenshaw, dated 1870; an arresting event that is said to have taken place in the winter of 1780, a time of the Revolutionary War in the American colonies and a difficult time for poor people in country districts.

This poor woman obtained her living by spinning hemp and sewing. It was customary for the farmers and gentlemen of the neighbourhood to grow a little hemp in a corner of one of their fields for their own use and to employ such women as herself to visit the various houses and stay there until her work was completed. During this period it was understood that she would eat and sleep under the roof of the house then employing her.

One day she went to Powis Castle and asked whether there was any spinning or sewing that she could perform. She learned that the Earl and Countess of Powis were away in London, but the wife of the castle steward gave her some sewing and invited her to stay the night as she had some more work for her to do, enough for several days in fact. Not for one moment did the simple countrywoman suspect that she was to be the subject of an experiment. Of late a number of strange disturbances had been taking place in the castle — ghostly

Powis Castle, an imposing and atmospheric red sandstone stronghold, also known as Castell Coch (the Red Castle).

forms and figures, the sound of voices, footsteps and odd noises — which seemed to originate from one particular room, a room that had become known as 'the haunted room' and the room to which the unsuspecting visitor was shown for the night.

The working woman, whom some writers have named Gwen Morgan, found herself shown into a large and grandly furnished ground-floor room with polished board flooring and two sash windows. A good fire was burning in the hearth, there was a comfortable chair close by, a comfortable-looking bed stood in the room and a candle stood on a table. As soon as she was safely installed, the steward's wife bid the visitor 'Goodnight', and quietly closed the door behind her. She then hastened to tell her husband and the servants what she had done and they all eagerly awaited the outcome of the experiment.

Having carefully examined the apartment and the furniture and contents — for the room was far grander than she had been used to — the old lady took out the small Welsh Bible that she always carried with her and prepared to read a chapter or two before retiring for the night; this being her custom for many years.

While she was so engaged, reading in comfort by the light of the candle in front of the blazing fire, she heard the bedroom door open and, turning her head, she saw a gentleman enter, wearing a gold-laced suit and a hat. The man walked towards the window, passed to the corner of the room, then turned and returned the way he had come, stopping by the window and resting his elbow on the window-sill and his face in his palm. He so remained for some little time, partly turned towards the somewhat surprised old lady who was able to study his face. Since she did not recognize him, she supposed he must be waiting for her to speak but somehow she could not find any words. After a little while he walked out of the room, closing the door behind him.

The old lady now became thoroughly alarmed, for she concluded that the form, which she then realized had made not a sound, was an apparition and that she had been put in the room — a serious, conscientious and truthful woman — to see what she would make of such a strange occurrence; which was indeed the case.

Thoroughly startled by now, the old woman rose from her chair and knelt down by the bed to pray. While she was praying she heard the bedroom door open and when she opened her eyes she saw that the apparition had returned! It walked round the room close to the walls and then came close behind her. She tried to speak but again no words came and then the figure moved away, walked out of the room and closed the door. Praying for strength the old woman pluckily pulled herself together and resolved to speak to the figure if it returned yet again.

Presently the bedroom door opened — and once more the figure entered, walked round the room and then came up close behind the old woman. Summoning all her strength and courage, she spoke, in a voice that she hardly recognized as her own: 'Pray sir, who are you and what do you want?' The figure raised a forefinger and said: 'Take up the candle and follow me, and I will tell you.'

On shaking legs the old woman got up, picked up the candle and followed the figure out of the bedroom, along a passage, through a long, boarded chamber and into a small room or closet. As the room was so small and she believed herself to be in the presence of a ghost, she stopped just outside the doorway. Turning, the figure said: 'Walk in, I will not harm you,' and so she walked inside the little room.

Then the figure said: 'Observe what I do,' and he stopped and tugged up a floorboard, revealing what appeared to be a box with an iron handle in the lid. Having shown her the box the figure next made its way to a comer of the small room where it revealed a crevice in the wall, saying a key was hidden there that would open the box hidden under the floorboards. That box', said the ghost, and the key must be sent to the Earl in London; will you see that it is done?' The old woman said she would do her best and the ghost then said that if this was done he would 'trouble the house no more'. He then walked out of the room and disappeared.

The old woman went to the door and shouted, bringing the steward, his wife and other servants — all apprehensive as to the outcome of her encounter with the ghost. When they learned what had transpired, the steward and his wife pulled out the box, found the key and said they would see that the matter was dealt with first thing in the morning. The old woman returned to her room, retired to bed and slept peacefully until morning.

The box was duly sent to the Earl and when he returned to the castle he sent a message to the old woman, then back home in her own cottage, to say that he was grateful for what she had done and he would like her to come to the castle and there reside for the rest of her days or, if she wished to reside elsewhere, she would be looked after. Such is the story of one of the ghosts of Powis. Whatever the truth of the story, it is a fact, well known in the neighbourhood, that the old woman was provided for by the Earl's family after she had spent a few nights at the castle. Some people maintain that the ghost still walks on occasions and that the haunted room, the one in which the box was found, may be seen by visitors to the castle.

Other stones of ghostly happenings at Powis Castle that I heard when I was there in June 1978 include the spectre of an unidentified man in one of the ground-floor rooms, a woman in white in one of the bedrooms, and a man on horseback in the beautiful garden. But few, if any, ghostly associations remain today at Powis Castle, I believe, and quite recently Lord Powis told me that there is now no area of the castle which can be regarded as haunted. And yet, I wonder. If tragic and violent happenings can leave something behind, if concentrated thought can leave its mark upon the atmosphere, may there not yet be ghosts at Powis Castle with all its history and varied inhabitants — for those with eyes to see? In 1981 I was told that the ghost of the second Marquess of Powis haunted the Duke's Room in Lord Powis's private quarters.

Priest's House, Muchelney, Somerset

This late medieval house was originally the residence of the secular priests who served the parish church and perhaps it was such a man who figures in the local legend associated with the Priest's House, an age-old legend perpetuated in a long narrative poem called The Abbot of Muchelnaye and containing the lines:

And often, down that dark and narrow way,

Along the windings of the hidden stair,

Sweeps a dim figure, as the rustics say,

And tracks the path even to the House of Prayer...

One version of the legend tells of a nun and a priest who love one another and devise a scheme for breaking their vows and fleeing away together. The girl is temporarily locked up for safety in a secret room (presumably in the haunted part of the house), the existence of which is known only to one or two of the inhabitants. In the midst of enjoying a few stolen hours of marital bliss, the priest is called away on some pious duty and he returns to find his beloved dead.

The present occupant of the Priest's House tells me she thinks the local belief that the house is haunted is based mainly on stories told by a former tenant, now deceased; stories of a monk and buried treasure, of a woman, and of a banging door; but no details seem to be available. However, since I am told that the unfortunate man had a drink problem, it is hard to know whether these stories were imagined or real experiences. The fact remains that for centuries the Muchelney legend pointed to the house being haunted and as the present occupant says: In over 600 years who can doubt it?'

R

Rainham Hall, Rainham, Essex

The present tenant of Rainham Hall, Mr Adrian Sansom, tells me that he and his wife have 'regrettably seen no ghosts since we arrived here in 1973' but a previous occupant, Mr Anthony Denney, described the comparatively modern ghost as an unglamorous type'.

The phantom form is thought to be that of Colonel Mulliner, a former resident of this eighteenth-century red-brick house, whose great love of the place prevented his ever leaving. The figure of a tall man, dressed in grey tweeds and sporting a dandified collar, has been seen in various parts of the house; a friendly ghost who only ever appeared in daylight, in typical Edwardian costume, the very image of the friendly Colonel who lived there seventy or so years ago.

Mr Sansom tells me there was a reported sighting of 'the Colonel' by a carpenter working at the Hall in 1968, but that is the only one he has heard of. It must be within the realm of possibility that, as has been suggested, Colonel Mulliner 'so liked the house that he decided to stay there, even when he died'.

Ramsey Island, off St David's Head, Dyfed

The National Trust has covenants over 625 acres of Ramsey Island, uninhabited apart from Robin Pratt and his family and Tom Sutton, warden and farm manager; and the grey Atlantic seals, the chough, peregrine, guillemot, razorbill, the thousands of rabbits and a ghost.

On the island — where one spring day can be so absolutely lovely, enough to make up for all the weeks through winter when sometimes the wind is so strong that you can't go outdoors for days on end — St Justinian is supposed to have been murdered by his followers when he settled here briefly during the sixth century. His ghost is said to walk right through the main house and across the sea to his chapel on the mainland, restored in the sixteenth century. Many people claim to have seen the ghost and many more claim to have heard the saint's footsteps.

Tom Sutton said in 1981, when he had been the island's only inhabitant for two years, that he had never seen or heard the ghost but his bungalow is about half a mile from the big farmhouse, now inhabited again. Perhaps the presence of human beings will bring St Justinian back to lonely Ramsey Island.

Ray Island, Essex

This stretch of unspoilt salting in the tidal creek between the mainland beaches and West Mersea is full of mounds of Roman and Saxon origin — mounds of charcoal, clinkers of fused sand, Samian pottery. Caves have been discovered hereabouts with Roman pavements, perhaps the burial places of forgotten centurions who ruled this wild place when eagles swung across the salty Strood; one centurion, perhaps tired of his musty tomb, walks again on nights of the spring-tide moons.

Years ago I talked with Mrs Jane Pullen, then the elderly but spry landlady of the nearby Peldon Rose, a lady who remembered clergyman and author Sabine Baring-Gould (1834-1924): 'a tall, thin man, who walked along the marsh roads singing, and was forever writing books.' Mrs Pullen told me of the time she walked the best part of a couple of miles accompanied by a ghostly Roman centurion and met a friend who joined her and had the same experience.

In the 1920s Mrs Pullen's grandson, Ivan Pullen, on a visit from London, camped one night on Ray Island, alone in a tent. It was a night of the full moon and as bright as day. 'You could see from one end of the island to the other,' Ivan said afterwards. 'I could hear wigeon and mallard and I had my gun with me and I told myself that at dawn I would be out and get one or two on their morning flights.' In the middle of the night he was awakened by loud and thumping footsteps that seemed to walk right up to the tent; then they stopped for a moment as though someone was listening; then they went right round the tent; and then they seemed to enter the tent itself: 'I lay there petrified,' Ivan continued. They made the ground shake within an inch or two of where I lay. Then the footsteps went out of the tent, although the flaps were tightly laced, and faded away towards the path. I was shaking with fright but I hopped up smartly, grabbed my gun and looked out. The moon was bright as ever but there was not a thing in sight, anywhere. I couldn't pack up my things fast enough. I'll never camp on Ray Island again, not for all the money in the world.'

The great hall at Rufford Old Hall where Shakespeare is thought to have performed.

Rufford Old Hall, near Ormskirk, Lancashire

Here there is a well-authenticated Grey Lady ghost haunting the house and grounds; the ghost of a man in Elizabethan costume and the ghost of Queen Elizabeth I herself.

A persistent tradition asserts that Shakespeare once performed in the medieval great hall with its hammer-beam roof and massive movable screen, and there exists evidence that a 'William Shakeshaft' (an alternative version of his name) visited Rufford about 1585, the opening date for a gap of about seven years in our knowledge of the actor-dramatist's life. Certainly he was absent from his wife and three children at Stratford during this period. Rufford Old Hall belonged to the Hesketh family from the thirteenth century until 1936 and the young William Shakeshaft was a member of the Hesketh Company of Players. Shakespeare would have been twenty-one in 1585. The ghostly figure of a young man in Elizabethan long hose and full-sleeved jacket with a high collar has been seen from time to time standing beside the big fireplace in the great hall that has hardly changed for 500 years and where a secret chamber was discovered in 1949.

The dining-room, I was reliably informed when I was there in 1977, has been visited by the ghost of Queen Elizabeth I. One witness saw the colourful figure of the stately queen through one of the windows. He hastened into the Hall and reached the dining-room in time to see the regal figure still standing in the same position but now seen from a different viewpoint. He stood and looked at the motionless figure for a moment and then, as he quietly approached the form that showed no indication of being aware of his presence, the seemingly solid figure became less distinct and then slowly disappeared and within seconds it had completely disappeared.

The best-known and commonest ghost at picturesque, half-timbered Rufford is a Grey Lady that haunts the house and grounds and has been reportedly seen many times over the years. This ghostly form is very clear and appears to be solid and life-like but it throws no shadow. Most often the Grey Lady is seen near the main entrance, in the grounds near the house, or in the drive leading to the church. She has also been seen in one of the rooms on the ground floor — apparently enjoying a piano recital given by a mere mortal! Not so long ago the late Mr Philip Ashcroft, who donated the Rufford Village Museum collection displayed in the Hall, asserted that he saw the Grey Lady several times. Once he was by himself, playing the piano in the dining-room one evening when he chanced to turn round and he saw her standing behind him.

He turned back to the piano and continued playing until his fingers ached and he had plucked up enough courage to look round again; but when he did so the shy Grey Lady had disappeared.

The original Grey Lady is thought to be a former Lady of Rufford, a Hesketh, who waits for her husband, or lover, to return from some forgotten escapade or skirmish. In 1948 a local museum curator reported that he had located evidence that the Grey Lady was a sad and lonely woman, Elizabeth Hesketh, whose husband had been summoned to a Scottish war in the middle of their wedding celebrations, by bonfires lit on Ashers Beacon. Some time later an old warrior, passing through the village on his return from the same conflict, gave her the news that her husband was on his way home. Immediately a great feast was prepared in his honour and the whole village and many of the surrounding local people gathered at the Hall; but the hours passed and then the days and the Lord of Rufford failed to arrive. The young bride vowed that she would wear her wedding gown until he came, saying: 'I know he will return tomorrow.' Tomorrow came and went, the distressed girl refused to eat, she slowly lost her strength and on her deathbed declared that her ghost would wait on at the Hall until her beloved did return, forever if necessary.

At one time the Custodian of Rufford Old hall declared: 'I have known this building intimately all my life and I have seen the ghostly Grey Lady.' An authority on Rufford and its history has stated: 'I never saw the Grey Lady myself although I was present when she was reported to have walked and I have known many people who have seen her.' In 1981 the Administrator himself claimed that he saw the Grey Lady on his return to the Hall one night, but by his own admission his critical faculties may have been somewhat blunted by a jolly evening! Kathleen Eyre, in her Lancashire Ghosts, refers to the Rufford Grey Lady as 'well-authenticated', saying: 'She has been clearly sighted in the grounds and along the drive leading to the church.'

S

St Michael's Mount, Cornwall

The castle dates from the fourteenth century. Edward the Confessor founded a chapel here in 1044 under the Benedictine Abbey of Mont St Michel in Brittany. Richard I was here at the time of the Crusades. King John's partisans seized and held the Mount as a fortress. After a period of reverting to monastic use it became a stronghold during the Wars of the Roses, during the Cornish rebellion against Edward VI and during the Civil War. Small wonder that ghosts and legends abound here.

The romantic and imposing St. Michael's Mount, a granite mass rising out of the sea.

[Image previously spread across two pages]

Tradition has it that in the days when Cornwall was notorious for its giants (an idea perpetuated in the many giants' chairs, cradles, graves, castles and pulpits), St Michael's Mount was the home of Cormelian or Cormoran, an evil, one-eyed monster who, when the tide was low, was in the habit of wandering across to Marazion where he would invariably seek out the best cow in the area, sling it over his shoulder and return to his island home.

The place the Cornish call 'Cara dowse in cowse' — 'the hoar rock in the wood' (dating from the days when the island was surrounded by a forest and in fact trunks of trees have been discovered from time to time) has been the scene of many strange happenings and events.

One night in the year A.D. 495 fishermen saw a vision of St Michael standing suffused in light upon a ledge of rock. This projecting pinnacle is pointed out by the guides to this day and it does seem to be a very convenient spot for such an appearance.

In the eleventh century, when Gregory IV proclaimed an indulgence to all pilgrims to the Mount of a third of their penances, it is likely that there were hermits and mystics who were believed to be able to affect the devout by their prayers; indeed a rock chamber beneath the existing choir, discovered about 1720 with a skeleton immured inside, may have been the original cell of such a hermit.

Sir John St Aubyn bought St Michael's Mount in 1660, and it is still a romantic sight and a splendid one, as it was countless centuries ago — a granite mass of an island rising out of the sea at high tide; at low tide it is approachable on foot over the causeway. Today Lord St Levan tells me that inside the castle there is a four-poster bedstead dating from the seventeenth century with figureheads of Spanish ships that were wrecked off the treacherous Cornish coast; and figureheads depicting Spanish admirals. There is a curious atmosphere surrounding the bed which has been remarked upon by many people and, I am told, no child has been able to survive a night in the bed.

Scotney Castle, Lamberhurst, Kent

On the invitation of Mrs Christopher Hussey I took a party of Ghost Club members to Scotney a few years ago and we were treated to a brief tour of the private house before we explored the romantic castle and, what we had come to see, the wonderful — and haunted — gardens. In 1970 Mr Christopher Hussey bequeathed a large part of this picturesque landscape garden, which surrounds the remains of the moated fourteenth-century castle, to the National Trust, while Mrs Hussey continued to live in the house, built by Salvin in 1837, which overlooks the garden where ghosts walk.

Scotney was the home of a branch of the Kentish Darell family for 350 years, and among the curious episodes during the long occupation is one that may have some bearing on the ghost story. Arthur Darell, whose mother Elizabeth Darell was said to have kept her door locked and the castle gates manned with guns, seemingly died in 1720. It is said that, as his coffin was being lowered into the grave, a tall figure in a black cloak, whom nobody recognized, remarked to his neighbour among the mourners: 'That is me they think they are burying,' after which he was not seen again.

In his History of Scotney Castle, Christopher Hussey suggests that some confirmation of this story is to be found in a macabre anecdote that took place about the middle of the nineteenth century. The sexton, John Bailey, who died in 1867, discovered a massive iron-studded coffin in the Scotney Chapel of Lamberhurst Church and on raising the lid, found that it contained only heavy stones. If there is any truth in the story a possible motive for Arthur's 'disappearance' may have been the attitude of his four sisters; no love was lost between them and their brother and the girls bitterly resented the disposition of Scotney in their late brother Thomas's Will. Thomas, who died in 1710, had left their home Scotney, to Arthur.

There have been suggestions that following his mock funeral Arthur Darell turned to smuggling and that he more than once narrowly escaped detection by making use of one of the secret hiding-places at Scotney. This could have been either the cleverly-masked one within the thickness of the Tudor tower or that entered by a horizontal sliding trap-door in the old house. It is possible that he also utilized the narrow passageway that once 'threaded its way to other mysteries in quarters long since pulled down', as Allan Fea puts it. It is known that one hide here successfully sheltered two men for a week.

However, later a skirmish with revenue authorities became a desperate life-or-death struggle and in the event Darell is said to have killed one of the officers and to have thrown the body into the moat — a moat that is more of a lake and contains two islands. It is said to be the ghost of this murdered man that emerges from his watery grave, dripping with dark and stagnant water, that makes his way to the great door where he repeatedly hammers with his fists, seeking retribution. This gruesome form has been seen many times, but whenever the door of Scotney is opened, all trace of the figure has disappeared and all is quiet in this outstandingly beautiful garden. 'The grey and rust-coloured castle tower ... the lily-moat reflecting sky, trees and mined mansion ... make an exquisite picture,' says Rose Macauley. Even without its ghost romantic Scotney is well worth a visit.

Selborne, Hampshire

Selborne Hill, some 250 acres of common and freehold land, is part of the village that saw the birth and death of Gilbert White, the naturalist who produced one book and made this still largely unspoilt village a place of pilgrimage. Here the ghost has been seen of the man who loved this countryside and made innumerable minute observations here that he subsequently recorded in his immortal Natural History of Selborne, first published by his brother Benjamin White in 1789.

Gilbert White, that quietly content and intelligent mid-eighteenth-century country parson, so knew and loved every part of Selborne that it would be truly remarkable if something of him had not lingered for more than two centuries in this unique Hampshire village. Be it the old village green and White's church where his memorial window shows St Francis surrounded by the birds White mentions in his classic; or beside his modest grave; or along one of his favourite walks into the sloping meadows; or across the footbridge to the wooded slopes; or through the wood into Coombe meadow; or in Dorton's Wood; or between the high banks of Hucker's Lane; or even at the Wakes itself, White's old home and now a museum — the spirit of Gilbert White lingers everywhere in Selborne. In fact his unmistakable ghost has been seen in several parts of the village, especially in those parts that have changed hardly at all since he knew them and wrote about them with love and rare understanding.

One of Gilbert White's gifts to generations of visitors to Selborne is the Zig Zag, a tortuous climb of steps up his beloved Hanger, the steep hill behind the village where, at the top, you will find a wishing stone. But if you would have your wish come true you must walk blindfold backwards round the stone three times and then sit on the stone and silently wish.

Selborne - the
old monk's
road where a
ghost monk in
black habit
walks.

And, if we are to believe generations of local people and visitors, the Hanger is a haunted place.

Up here, amid the tall trees and ferns and fungi and wild flowers, there have been many reports from responsible people who say they have seen non-human forms and figures. Sometimes these forms are human in size, sometimes, especially it seems when they are seen by children, they are smaller than human beings.

Mrs Brian Vesey-FitzGerald told my friend Dorothea St Hill Bourne that she had a maid who had been brought up at Selborne. One day Mrs Vesey-FitzGerald brought home a large, quaint figure of a gnome in a pointed cap. The maid saw it and said immediately: 'Oh madam, that's just like the little men we used to see on Selborne Hanger when we were children. Mother said we told stories because she could not see them, but we children could.'

Selborne Priory had a brief and inglorious history, being dissolved in 1484. The last but one Prior of Selborne was named John Sharpe and the priory was dissolved only a couple of years after his death. In 1525 the priory lands were leased to another John Sharpe and he and his successors (all Sharpes) farmed the land for over a hundred years. There are many stories of ghost monks being seen in the vicinity of the long-vanished priory and along the old road that the monks built, which is still in remarkably good repair. When excavations were taking place at the priory there were many reports of the ghostly figure of a monk, a thin man with dark hair, large eyes, a sallow skin, small oval face and a long nose. The figure often had its head bowed, its chin on its chest, and most of the witnesses said there seemed to be a greyish mist around the figure that wore a black monk's habit with the cowl thrown back off the head. A Brighton woman, named Sharpe by coincidence, told the Rev. G. Knapp that in 1962 she saw a ghost monk who she believed was the old Prior Sharpe of Selbome.

A fifteenth-century farm that once formed part of the old priory estate has or had a phantom dog that used to appear on the site of the original entrance to the priory farm. Although the people at the farm say they have hot seen the ghost dog, former occupants and local people have been more fortunate, or unfortunate. Mr Edward Lucas always maintained that he saw the ghostly animal on two occasions. Each time it was about nine o'clock in the evening and he would be taking a horse to the old harness room when, twice, he suddenly saw a strange black dog with long hair, about the size of a collie. It seemed to appear from nowhere and it walked beside Lucas and the horse for perhaps a hundred yards before suddenly and completely vanishing, not far from the old farm entrance. What surprised Edward Lucas was the fact that if it was a ghost, the horse and his own dog were completely unaffected by the presence of the ghost; indeed they seemed not to be aware of the phantom dog.

Many years ago a number of bones were dug up in the area of the farm and the old priory and most of them seemed to be human bones and very ancient. A persistent local story concerning the ghost dog says it was the constant companion of one of the race horses that used to be bred there in the nineteenth century and was killed in an accident at the farm.

The ghost monk is still encountered occasionally. I was told in 1976 that it had been seen by three walkers who were strolling along the old priory road. As the figure passed them, seemingly deep in thought, they murmured a casual greeting but received no reply and indeed the figure seemed not to notice them. As soon as it had passed they turned to look at the oddly quiet and preoccupied form that they had seen, only to find the old roadway completely deserted. Afterwards they realized that the figure had made no sound as it had passed them.

Some years before, Raymond Osborne, a great admirer of Gilbert White, visited Selbome and then took the little road out of the village and walked through the woods along the old priory road. There he saw, as he rounded a comer, the figure of a monk in a black habit about a hundred yards ahead of him. After a little while he quickened his pace, thinking he would have a word with the monk; but he found that however fast he walked, the monk seemed still to be the same distance ahead and then, where the wood ended with a gate into the fields leading to the site of the priory, the figure suddenly vanished. Raymond Osborne, the most practical and level-headed of men, was completely mystified, for there seemed to be no possible path the monk could have taken without being visible. Raymond Osborne never saw another ghost in the whole of his life, but that sighting puzzled him for the rest of his days.

Some fascinating information and physical records are preserved in Gilbert White's old home. It seems there are occasionally psychic manifestations hereabouts for the ghost of the great naturalist and unrivalled observer of nature has been seen here — a fact and figure of considerable interest since no portrait of him appears to be extant. According to reports his ghost has been encountered most frequently in the beautiful garden he created, but he has also been glimpsed within the house he knew and in the vicinity of the haunted Hanger.

Shaw's Corner, Ayot St Lawrence, Hertfordshire

There are occasional stories of a ghost at Shaw's Comer, the home of George Bernard Shaw, whom I met before the Second World War when I lived in Hertfordshire. Shaw always believed that he belonged in the company of immortals, although he disbelieved in personal immortality. It is not his ghost that is said to haunt the house but that of Lawrence of Arabia, who certainly visited Shaw many times (indeed Shaw drew from Lawrence of Arabia for his brilliant characterization of Private Meek in Too Good to be True). But there really does seem to be little substance in these sporadic reports of the ghost of the complex Lawrence at Shaw's Corner — even if he did take the name of Shaw.

The present Administrator suspects that it is pure guesswork that there is a ghost here at all and has yet to meet anyone who has actually encountered it. The only printed reference I have come across is in Andrew Green's Our Haunted Kingdom (1973) where the author states: 'Shaw's home, incidentally, is rumoured to be haunted by Lawrence of Arabia who used to visit the family when on leave, but there seems little evidence to support the idea.'

My friend and Ghost Club member Tony Broughall compiled an exhaustive study of reported ghosts and ghostly phenomena in Hertfordshire and neighbouring Bedfordshire and he says, of Shaw's Comer: It is rumoured that the house is haunted, not as one might expect by the great man himself, but by the ghost of Lawrence of Arabia. Apparently Lawrence visited the house frequently and often spent his leaves there during his time in the army. Unfortunately careful inquiries have failed to substantiate the story in any way.' There seems little more to say about ghosts at Shaw's Corner, although many people have found that something of the spell of the six-foot, inexhaustible, highly-spirited and wild orator and playwright does still linger at the house he lived in from 1906 until his death in 1950; a man who from the coffers of his genius enriched the world.

Shaw's Corner, George Bernard Shaw's home.

Shute Barton, near Axminster, Devonshire

This medieval manor house, partly fourteenth century, partly fifteenth century and partly sixteenth century, was acquired by the de la Pole family in the latter part of the sixteenth century. It was a family that had links with the Petre family and Shute was granted to Sir William Petre, Secretary of State, by his Queen, Mary Tudor. Earlier, Henry, Duke of Suffolk, owned Shute and his daughter Lady Jane Grey probably visited the grey-stone property with its battlemented tower and late Gothic windows; it may even be the ghost of the nine days' queen that has been seen here on sunny afternoons but it is more likely to be a forgotten member of the de la Pole family who lived at Shute Barton for so many centuries.

There is said to be a phantom white cat here and a poltergeist, but the ghostly 'Grey Lady' is the best-authenticated paranormal manifestation. The ghost is thought to date probably from the days of the Civil War when Shute was staunchly Royalist. Details are few and we have no name, no date and no coherent story, but it seems that this Lady de la Pole had certain enemies, although whether they were against her on political or personal grounds is not known. In any case, one afternoon — so goes this fragment of a story — these enemies waited for her and captured her in a grove of trees not far from the house and promptly hanged her from one of the trees. That tree, according to the story, never thrived again and gradually withered and died. Exactly where it stood is no longer known, but the tragic event gave the name of The Lady Walk to a group of trees within sight of the present house, a grove reputedly haunted to this day by the ghost of the murdered Lady of Shute.

There used to be a girls' school at Shute, and a former mistress is among those who have related their experiences of the ghost of Shute Barton. This young lady had only been at the school a couple of weeks; she didn't know there was reputed to be a ghost and had never heard of any Lady de la Pole. One Saturday afternoon another member of the school staff came into the house from the playing-field that was situated in front of the house and bordered the Lady Walk. Idly she said; 'I wonder who that woman in grey is who's walking up and down as though she owns the place.' Another member of the school staff went to find out, but she didn't return to report what she had found which was, doubtless, nothing.

Some time later one of the older girls at the school told the same mistress that she had been looking out of the dormitory window and had seen 'a woman in grey' walking in the Lady Walk. She too, as far as could be established, had never heard of the Shute Grey Lady; certainly she reported the incident simply as a matter of routine and did not seem in the least troubled, puzzled or excited by what she had seen.

At this period one member of the school staff had a very old pet dog, stone-deaf and mostly asleep, but some afternoons it would be found sitting outside the house, looking towards The Lady Walk and barking its head off ... perhaps it could see or sense the Grey Lady.

As might be expected the poltergeist at Shute manifested at the time of the girls' school; there were repeated reports of movement of objects, including furniture and a heavy piano, without a sound being heard; doors that locked and unlocked by themselves and lights that switch themselves on and off.

The phantom white cat has been seen many times, usually outside the house; it has been described as very white, almost translucent and shining, but otherwise just an ordinary cat, except that there is no such animal at Shute and an ordinary cat can't walk through walls.

One April afternoon in 1979 two National Trust members visited Shute Barton. Inside the house they enjoyed such treasures as the newel stair, the great open fireplace, the collar-beam hall roof and the fine panelled room that has survived 300 years; while outside they equally enjoyed the quiet of the peaceful surrounds of Shute Barton.

They had explored the detached gatehouse and had then wandered off towards a group of trees when they were rather surprised to see a woman walking among the trees, for they had not seen her approach the grove and it had appeared to be quite deserted when they set out for it. The figure was that of a slim female. They caught a glimpse of a determined face and she certainly walked with an air of familiarity, which made them wonder whether this could be a present-day member of the de la Pole family that had been connected with the ancient house for so long. On the other hand the figure seemed to be dressed so oddly, almost like a nun, except that her head was bare, and the wife of my informant whispered to him? 'Perhaps it's a ghost!' A moment later they entered the grove of trees and suddenly they were aware that the figure they had both seen seconds before had completely disappeared. Puzzled, they searched here and there but found no trace of the woman they had seen. Back at the house their story caused glances to pass between the people to whom they related their experience, and then they learned for the first time about the Grey Lady of Shute Barton.

Sissinghurst Castle, Sissinghurst, Kent

Percival (Felix) Seward, who helped to revive the Ghost Club in 1954 and was Chairman until his death in 1960, knew Harold Nicolson and his wife Vita Sackville-West. Knowing of Felix's great interest in such matters they talked to him of ghosts: the ghost priest, thought to have been walled-up alive long ago for some forgotten crime and other mysterious happenings including distinct footsteps which certainly had no natural explanation. Examples of these and other exhibitions of possible paranormal activity have been reported from Sissinghurst in recent years.

The very beautiful garden, amid the dramatic fragments of Elizabethan Sissinghurst Castle, might almost be as ancient, with its great yew hedges, but in fact in 1930 this place was a wilderness without a worthwhile plant. Today the long axial walks; the small enclosures, each at its best at a different season; the old roses, famous a hundred years ago; the herb garden; the thyme lawn and the stone paths, grass, beds under walls and old shallow containers filled with flowers — it is all indescribably beautiful, calm and peaceful and just the magic place for a gentle ghost.

Until 1930 Harold Nicolson was a professional diplomat who wrote elegant biographies in his spare time. Then he resigned because he wanted to see more of his wife, or so he said. 'Both he and his wife were predominantly homosexual but they were bound together by a deep love which seems to have increased with the passing of the years,' as A.J.P. Taylor told me when he and I once shared a railway compartment on an Intercity 125 train.

Some years before his death in 1968 Sir Harold Nicolson invited me to lunch at his London club in Pall Mall, the non-political Traveller's founded in 1819. I was a little surprised to find this diplomat, author and critic, no cynic where psychic matters were concerned. I learned that he had had experiences that left him in no doubt as to the possibility that those who slept the sleep of death were sometimes able to return and be visible to those still in the land of the living: a view that may have influenced his naming one of his books Another World Than This.

Sir Harold told me that he had had personal and, to him, irrefutable evidence of such happenings on occasions, and in particular he referred to the ghost priest that haunted the
[...text continues on page 292]

Sissinghurst Castle, where at least one ghost has been seen many times, both by people living in the house and by visitors.

gardens that he and his wife had created at Sissinghurst. He told me how excited they had been when they had come across a story about a priest having been walled-up long long years ago. Sir Harold felt that perhaps the restful and timeless quality that the gardens had acquired had possibly tempted the unquiet spirit of the priest to seek peace there and he felt happy about that. The figure has also reportedly been seen by reliable Mrs Hayter, Sir Harold's housekeeper, and by a number of visitors who have sometimes asked about the identity of the 'reverend gentleman' who walked by himself and didn't seem to make any sound. Visitors also sometimes ask about the sound of footsteps that seem to come from close beside them, although nothing is visible that might account for such sounds.

Sir Harold, I have been told, occasionally had a curious habit of clicking his teeth or his tongue — a peculiarity that was well-known among his sophisticated young men friends. After his death a mysterious clicking noise' was heard from time to time in various parts of the property, usually by young men, among them Peter South who, at the time, was living on the estate.

Although they are reluctant to talk about ghosts at Sissinghurst there can be no doubt that at least one ghost has been seen there many times, both by people living in the house and by visitors. Unexplained sounds have also been repeatedly reported, and it has been suggested that the gentle air of magic and enchantment at Sissinghurst may have been created by Sir Harold and Lady Nicolson who have, unknowingly and unconsciously, left behind something of themselves.

Sizergh Castle, Kendal, Cumbria

The Strickland family acquired this lakeland castle by marriage in 1239 and it continued to be the main home of this historic family for over 700 years, until Mr and the Hon. Mrs

H. Homyold-Strickland and Lt.-Com. T. Homyold-Strickland gave the castle and its contents to the National Trust in 1950.

A Strickland fought with Henry V at the Battle of Agincourt; another became Bishop of Carlisle; another was knighted by Charles I at the Battle of Edgehill; and Stricklands fought in the Wars of the Roses. A Strickland married Robert de Wessington and one of their descendants was George Washington.

Sizergh was the scene of many border clashes, and doubtless Catherine Parr, that luckiest of Henry VIII's wives, who was born at Kendal, heard stories of those troubled times during the many visits she made to Sizergh Castle. The tapestried room in the pele tower in which she slept — now the oldest part of the castle — is reputedly haunted by her ghost, as well it might be, but hers is a quiet ghost whose presence is more often felt than seen.

The room above the Queen's Room is said to be haunted by the ghost of the wife of one of the wild Stricklands of the Border Wars. Whenever he went off to war he locked his wife in this room and forbade the servants, under pain of death, to release her before his return. The terrified servants obeyed their master's instructions, even when he was away for weeks at a time. Came the time when his absence stretched into months and although everyone knew that now he would never return, no one dared to release his frantic and beseeching wife. Eventually she went mad and died in the room that was haunted ever after by her cries and sobs, her wails of anguish and occasionally by her demented form, struggling to escape.

There is another haunting here, a kind of poltergeist disturbance. In one room the floorboards have repeatedly been found pulled up. They have been replaced time without number, but are always disturbed again. No logical explanation has ever been discovered and there is no known story that might explain this curious phenomenon.

Snowshill Manor near Broadway, Gloucestershire

This practically untouched Tudor house, with a facade of about 1700 and collections of musical instruments, clocks, toys, and craftsmen's tools, was given to the National Trust in 1951 by the enigmatic owner and occupier Charles Wade.

This strange and fascinating man, born out of his time, loved period costume, furniture and architecture of a haunting quality. He was a man who rejected motor cars, electricity and other necessities' of modem life. There is no doubt that the darker side of mankind appealed to him for he amassed a truly remarkable collection of strange and macabre objects, including a preserved bat which he kept in his sleeping chamber — a fact that suggested vampiric associations to some people, including Robert Fordyce Aickman, something of an authority on the subject; L.T.C. Rolt, who resided for many years near Winchcombe; and Lady Cynthia Asquith, who also believed that Wade was the original of Lob in Sir James Barrie's Dear Brutus with its theme that each man carries his destiny within himself and takes us from reality into ghostland.

A recent Administrator of Snowshill (once occupied by Catherine Parr) and J.A. Brooks, the author of a recent book about the folklore of the Cotswolds, regard such vampiric aspersions as complete nonsense and I am sure they are right.

Nevertheless Charles Wade, whose gifts included artistic imagination (he illustrated Kate Murray's The Spirit of the House), was seriously interested in such subjects as magic. One room at Snowshill, not usually shown to the public, has a pentagram painted on the floor and a wall decorated with mystic symbols; it is a room at the top of the house that contained, in Wade's day, a quite remarkable collection of objects connected with magic, alchemy and the black arts.

A recent Administrator who had been there for more than eight years, working in the house summer and winter, day and night, told me that he had never seen a ghost, adding this does not mean there is none, but I have just not seen any'. Other visitors to Snowshill are not so sure. Some immediately comment on the odd and perhaps even frightening atmosphere or feeling of the place; others, having reached the threshold, have even refused to enter the house. Still others, to whom I have spoken, have no doubt that the place is haunted; but perhaps that is a moot point, although it is possible to find stories that suggest that the place was haunted at one time if it is not today.

Years ago Charles Wade sent a small piece of old timber from the manor to a celebrated psychometrist who simply by handling the fragment obtained several curious reactions including a feeling that in an upper room, late at night, there was a seventeenth-century girl in a green dress, pacing up and down in an agitated way, a girl who did not live there and who would leave the house before dawn. Intrigued and interested in these random reactions Charles Wade made exhaustive inquiries and discovered that a secret marriage had taken place in an upper room of the house in 1604 when Anne Parsons, a sixteen-year old heiress, was forcibly married to a fortune-seeker late one St Valentine's Eve. She apparently refused to stay a night in the house and the unhappy girl and her rascally husband made a cold and dangerous journey to Chipping Campden. Could something of that traumatic event still linger on at Snowshill?

In the room named Zenith a duel once took place, with one of the participants dead at the end of the desperate

The eccentric Charles Wade, a man born out of his time and Snowshill - his home in the Cotswolds, reflects his love of period costume and furniture and architecture of a haunting quality. Small wonder that his ghost reputedly walks here.

Anne's Room at Snowshill Manor.

contest. Could something of this bitter misadventure remain within the walls of Snowshill?

And then there is the story of Charles Marshall. When he lived here a hundred years ago he held leases, or something like them, over 1000 acres of land, and after his death his widow continued to live at Snowshill and farmed the lands, with the help of one Richard Carter. One wintry night, after working at remote Hill Barn, Carter encountered the ghost of his dead master, Charles Marshall, who rode beside him along a lonely track-way, mounted on a black pony.

When the same thing happened another night and then yet again, Carter consulted the local rector who advised him to address the phantom form and try to discover why he was putting in an appearance.

When he did so the ghost seemed to intimate that he wanted Carter to meet him at midnight in the chaff-house. Carter kept the rendezvous and received a secret message for Mrs Marshall, the contents of which have never been revealed. However the fact that soon afterwards Mrs Marshall was able to start building extensions to the manor support the rumour that the message resulted in the discovery of hidden gold. This story was related to Charles Wade in 1919 by Richard Dark, son-in-law of the Richard Carter who saw the ghost of a former owner of Snowshill.

More recent possibly ghostly episodes at Snowshill include the experience of Mrs N. Sayer, who consulted the costume collection at the manor when she was engaged in writing a book on the subject. She speaks of hearing Charles Wade's footsteps; and later Mrs West, who helped in cleaning the house early in 1981, also claimed that she heard inexplicable footsteps. I am authoritatively told that there is a persistent rumour of a ghost monk walking up and down the old stairs, built after the Dissolution of the Monasteries; and although it has been suggested (since there is a monk's habit among the costumes at the house) that the story may have originated in Charles Wade entertaining some of his visitors in his own inimitable way, it is interesting to learn that the lane running past the manor has long been regarded as being haunted by an unhappy monk. Why he is unhappy and why he haunts has never been discovered, but in medieval times a priory stood on the site of Snowshill Manor so the visitations of a monk are neither unlikely nor improbable in the vicinity of atmospheric and mysterious Snowshill.

Speke Hall, Liverpool, Merseyside

Parts of this interesting — and haunted — black-and-white house, built round a square courtyard and formerly moated, date from the fifteenth century. The rich, half-timbered exterior is a joy to behold and if only the atmospheric great hall, with its elaborate plasterwork, could talk....

The ghost here, a White Lady, is thought to be the unhappy Mary Norris, a descendant of Sir William Norreys who started to build the Hall in 1490. In 1731 Mary had inherited Speke Hall and its estates from her uncle, Richard Norris; she thus became an attractive heiress and in 1736 she married Lord Sidney Beauclerk, fifth son of the Duke of St Albans, an inveterate gambler, descended from Charles II and Nell Gwyn, and variously described as 'Worthless Sidney' and as 'Nell Gwyn in person with the sex altered'.

He had already persuaded a Member of Parliament to bequeath him his estates and had narrowly failed to marry an ageing heiress, who had finally bought him off with £1000. He undoubtedly enjoyed high living and indulged himself much in the London society of the day. According to tradition the Lady Beauclerk had not long given birth when her husband,

A White Lady, thought to be the unhappy Mary Norris, haunts beautiful, half-timbered, Speke Hall.

returning to Speke from one of his sprees in London, announced that his recklessness had resulted in financial ruin and they faced poverty and disgrace. In her over-wrought state, overcome with grief and despair, the anguished lady picked up her infant son and threw him out of the window of the Tapestry Room to his death in the moat below, before rushing down to the great hall and there committing suicide. Her ghost is said to haunt the Tapestry Room and a small cross may mark the place where the child died, although the angle makes this unlikely.

A few years ago the Curator of Speke Hall, Mr P.W.G. Lawson, told me that the Tapestry or Haunted Bedroom is in the northern range of the house, built in 1598, and has been reputed to be haunted by a White Lady since at least the middle years of the nineteenth century; and many visitors say they either sense or see a presence in the room. The Watt family, who owned the house from about 1795 to 1921, seem to have been sufficiently impressed with the story of the distraught Lady Beauclerk to have acquired, in the nineteenth century, a large cradle which still stands in the Tapestry Room: a silent reminder of a long-past tragedy associated with the house.

Known historical facts however do not support the story. Not only do the Beauclerks seem to have only visited Speke occasionally, but Lady Mary Beauclerk died in 1766 in the parish of St George's, Hanover Square — some twenty-two years after Lord Sidney (1703-44). Their only child, Topham Beauclerk (1739-80) survived to inherit the property.

However, the Curator added, the tradition of a ghost at Speke is of long standing, and the fact that recorded history does not support the popular story associated with Speke Hall does not necessarily mean that there is not some presence in the Tapestry Room. There certainly are references to a haunted chamber and a ghostly lady in white that date back more than a century. There have been many people, over the years, who are interested in such phenomena who have maintained that they have experienced disconcerting sensations in the room, including Miss Adelaide Watt who, as reported by my old friend Alasdair Alpin MacGregor, observed a ghost in the Tapestry Room — a ghost that, as she watched it, disappeared into the wall close to a window. Here, later investigation revealed a secret passage that led down through an outer wall into the grounds.

There is a report too that on one occasion the ghost appeared at a dinner party given by Miss Watt, the last private owner of Speke. She and her guests saw it, spoke to it and watched it disappear through a wall.

Sceptics have pointed to the fact that Speke Hall in Tudor times was a clearing house for priests coming into England from the Continent and a departure point for those leaving England. Behind the much-admired exterior, behind the panelled walls and old oak beams, there was once a maze.of priests' hiding-places, escape tunnels, concealed staircases, secret doors, listening holes and look-outs; while, at the back of the house, boats came up the Mersey to tie up at a private landing stage. Any of these passing priests who happened to be seen accidentally, emerging through a concealed door or stealing out of a hide to take some exercise at night, were explained away as ghosts. By the same token, strange noises, footsteps, bangs and thumps and whisperings from apparently empty rooms, were all dismissed as ghosts. But, likely as this may have been — almost certain in fact at periods — nevertheless it would appear that ghosts and ghostly happenings do take place at this most beautiful of all timbered houses: Speke Hall.

In 1981 I received full details of the ghost at Speke Hall, a report that closed with the following words: 'The ghost is not particularly active and seems to be benevolent. Odd things do happen from time to time — there are footsteps in an empty corridor, voices in empty rooms. It would be a presumptuous person who dismissed the story entirely.'

Springhill, Moneymore, Co. Londonderry

This manor house (originally a fortified dwelling) dating from the latter half of the seventeenth century, boasts a costume museum and a tradition of authenticated ghosts.

Mina Lenox-Conyngham, the mother of Captain W.L. Lenox-Conyngham, under whose will the property passed to the National Trust in 1957, always maintained that the place was haunted, especially an upstairs bed-chamber that was probably the scene of a tragedy and was certainly the centre in later years of some curious effects. As Mina Lenox-Conyngham points out, this would seem to confirm the theory that any strong outburst of anguish lingers for a long period in the place where it leads to a tragic happening, and under special conditions, causes some people to see a vision of the event and of those who took part in it.

In discussing this room Mina Lenox-Conyngham relates that the Hon. Andrew Stuart, the husband of one of the daughters of the family, when sleeping in the room used to find his belongings were mysteriously moved in the night. Two small great-grandsons, who on one occasion were sleeping in the large four-poster bedstead in the room, were heard by their governess, who occupied the adjoining room, to be talking of a strange lady whom they both saw standing by the fireplace. 'She must be a ghost,' one of the children said calmly and without any fear in his voice.

A lady named Miss Wilson stayed at Springhill towards the end of the last century and she had a vivid experience. One night the visitor sat up very late, reading, in the Cedar Room. After her host Milly Conyngham had finally said 'Goodnight' and had gone to her room on the top storey, Miss Wilson found her friend's private diary which had been accidentally left behind. She decided to return the diary to its owner at once and leaving her room, paused for a moment when her eye caught a shaft of moonlight streaming down on the broad oak staircase. A second later she saw the tall figure of a lady appear at the head of the stairs and pass rapidly to the door of a nearby room where the figure stopped, flung up her hands as though in despair — and vanished.

Miss Wilson was most disturbed by what she had seen and afterwards ascertained that all the rest of the house had been in bed and asleep at that hour and that no living person in the house had been astir.

Some years later, related Mina Lenox-Conyngham, an even more remarkable occurrence happened'. A certain Miss Hamilton visited the house for the first time and she was occupying the room where the ghost had vanished at the door. The morning after her first night in the room she came downstairs looking rather shaken and related to Charlotte Lenox-Conyngham the following experience, which is in her own words:

'I had gone to bed in the great four-poster and the fire had died down and I had begun to grow drowsy, when it suddenly seemed as if the room was filled with excited people — servants, I thought — who were pushing, and wrangling in whispers. I felt overcome with fear, but just then I heard a clicking sound behind me, as though a door had been opened, and then a light shone at my back, and someone seemed to come out through this light and stilled the commotion, so that all fear left me, and after a while I fell asleep. It was strange that I fancied a door had opened behind me, as the head of the bed is against the wall where there is no door.'

'But there is a door behind the bed,' Charlotte told her, 'though quite hidden by the tester of the bed, and it has been papered over for quite a long time.'

A few years later, when the lady of the house decided to alter the position of the bedstead and re-open the papered-over door, a small room was disclosed behind the door with a bricked-up window and bricked-up fireplace and the ceiling higher than that of the adjoining bedroom. The closet was empty except for a pair of ancient gloves and a small bag which contained a few bullets.

In 1981 I was informed that Mina Lenox-Conyngham's daughter was still alive and authenticated these stories. Furthermore Mr E.W. 'Teddy' Butler, a former National Trust Custodian, himself saw the ghost of 'a small, squat woman dressed in black, at the foot of the stairs', and he experienced other manifestations including the sounds of constant stamping and marching that other people have also reported — perhaps a psychic echo from the days of Oliver Cromwell. Mr Butler was good enough to tell me about his experiences in 1982. He writes: While I was Administrator from 1964 to 1977, my wife and I often heard the unmistakable sound of footsteps on the stairs and landing. These are made of solid oak and it sounded as if it was someone wearing heavy shoes. One day in March, about four o'clock in the afternoon, we had been working in the garden. We came down to the house for a cup of tea. I went in through a door to the back hall and my wife went straight on to the cloakroom under the stairs. As I came back through the door I nearly ran into a figure which at first I took to be my wife. As I stepped back so as not to collide with her, the figure vanished. It all happened very quickly but I had time to notice that she was small, thick-set, and had grey hair. My wife has black hair. I shouted to my wife: "Are you there?" and she said: "In the cloakroom." I said: "Well I have just seen the ghost".'

Teddy Butler tells me the ghost is supposed to be that of a Mrs Conyngham, wife of Colonel Conyngham of the Black Horse. Her children had smallpox while he was serving in the Crimea; they did not die and it is not known why her ghost walks but she was known as "the anxious mother". A miniature of Colonel and Mrs Conyngham was preserved in the house but I believe it was stolen last year.'

The present Administrator tells me that a miniature of the ghost, the only portrait of her, mysteriously disappeared about nine years ago, to be returned later in a brown paper cover. Later, it disappeared again and hasn't been seen since!

Stourhead, Stourton, Mere, Wiltshire

Stourhead is perhaps best known for its magnificent landscape garden with its temples to the Sun and to Flora, its Paradise Well, Grotto with statues of a nymph and of Neptune, its Rustic Cottage and Rustic Convent; but the house itself is a splendid structure, containing an important collection of works of art and furniture, some designed by Thomas Chippendale the younger. The present house, built between 1721 and 1724, superseded a much earlier house, pulled down by Henry Hoare, that once stood on a knoll between the present house and the road from Zeals to Kilmington. It was a house that knew ill-will, violence and murder, a house that was haunted; and the ghosts did not go away when the house disappeared.

Old Stourton House, a low, rambling gothique' building, as John Aubrey described it, probably dated back before the Conquest, and the family of Stourton were well established here by the fifteenth century; but it is with Charles, the eighth Lord Stourton (d. 1557) that the ghosts and hauntings would appear to be connected, for he was publicly hanged for murder.

Stourhead, where the site of the old house is often the scene of curious incidents.

Charles, Lord Stourton, had a bitter feud with his neighbour, William Hartgill, for many years. By all accounts William and his son John received no more than their deserts for the ruthless private war against the neighbourhood in general and the Stourtons in particular became the talk of the county and the Hartgill's neighbours lived in perpetual fear of what the madmen would get up to next.

When Charles's father died it was discovered that the Hartgills had been systematically robbing the estate for years and terrifying everyone in the vicinity with their cruelty, brutality and savage maliciousness. They stole their neighbours' pigs in such numbers that 'they had more bacon and brawn in their houses than the next three parishes could eat in one meal'; William Hartgill, while acting as agent for Charles's father, destroyed title deeds to houses on the estate and turned the real owners out; there were numerous skirmishes with the Hartgills but they always seemed to be one step ahead and invariably they came out the winners, whether the argument resulted in physical violence or whether it was settled by litigation. At one time Charles, Lord Stourton, who put himself at the head of the opponents of the Hartgills, was sent to Fleet Prison in London till he paid a fine to the Hartgills of £2000.

This must have been the final straw because as soon as he had raised the money and returned home, Lord Stourton sent a message to the Hartgills and on some pretext urged them to meet him at Kilmington Church. Accompanied by a hundred sympathizers he waited for them in the nearby Church house.

Although suspicious, the Hartgills felt they had little to fear in the neighbourhood where they did more or less as they liked and accordingly they went to Kilmington Church.

There they were roughly seized, quickly overpowered and left in the Church house for the night. Next morning they were taken to Lord Stourton's house and there they were beaten to death and secretly buried in the dungeon, a great dank cellar without steps or ventilation, into which the bodies and the burial party were let down with ropes. It is said that, as Lord Stourton helped with the grim interment, the corpse of John Hartgill moved and cried out to him: 'You will die in agony, as I have done!' It was a prophecy that came true.

Another printed version of the matter has it that the Hartgills' only offence was to champion Lord Stourton's mother who, on the death of her husband, the seventh Baron, was anxious either to marry again or else to be provided by her son with independent means, she did not mind which. He however, took it upon himself to do away with the two Hartgills, giving orders for the assassinations and 'himself bidding their throats to be cut' and their bodies thrown into a vault at the front of the house.

Whatever the truth of the matter Charles, Lord Stourton, came to an untimely and painful enfl. He was hanged in the market place in Salisbury in 1557, with a silken rope instead of a hempen one, which, as a contemporary puts it 'must needs have been a great consolation at such a melancholy moment'.

The ghost of Lord Stourton and his victims now haunt the church at Kilmington and both the fields and roads near Stourhead House — so says historian Margaret M. Pearson, writing in 1956. Sometimes Lord Stourton is seen on foot, sometimes riding a mettlesome horse followed by a wild 'army' of followers in sixteenth-century costume. They have been seen galloping madly along the road to Kilmington where they all disappear through the oak doors of the church.

When I was at Stourhead in 1980 I was told that the area where the old house stood is often the scene of curious incidents. Children are reluctant to play there; visitors ask about people' they have seen in period costume; presences' have been felt; and 'an atmosphere' is often remarked upon. There are even those who ask what film is being shot for they say they have seen several men in old-fashioned clothes struggling and fighting, although they have heard no sound; while others again, looking very puzzled, say they have heard the sound of rough voices and the noise of muttering and skirmishing, although they have seen nothing to account for the sounds. Some of the happenings that once took place at Stourhead seem to have left an echo, either visual or audible, that to some people is still acutely discernible.

T

Tatton Park, near Knutsford, Cheshire

Just north of Knutsford a whole area of country bears the name of Tatton: Tatton Park, extending for more than 2000 acres and including Tatton Mere, the large lake that is the haunt of many varieties of wildfowl and, crowning the park and the terraced garden, the beautifully sited and imposing stone-built mansion, Tatton Park itself, described as 'of a severely classical design with little external ornamentation'.

It is a grand place by any standards, with an impressive and varied choice of interests and several ghosts. On the practical side there are paintings and furniture and silver collected by the Egerton family over more than four centuries. The last Lord Egerton bought a Benz car in 1900 that bears Cheshire's first registration number, Ml. That car is here, housed in a huge room which he built to display the fascinating curiosities and big game trophies which he brought back from his extensive travels.

There is a wonderful library, collected in the nineteenth century and earlier and here, as elsewhere in this imposing house, there have been reports of supernatural happenings over the years. Maurice Egerton, it is said, frequently saw and spoke to a ghostly 'lady in blue — Elizabeth Egerton' both here and in the garden. A portrait of this ancestor hangs in the office corridor.

In August 1981, the Director of Tatton Park, Commander Peter A.C. Neate and his wife Pat, revealed that they had had 'one or two mild visitations within their flat'. These included some curious interference with the television set and, in parenthesis, it is odd that so often electrical appliances and switches seem to be affected by ghosts or by something that we have never been able to discover.

At Tatton Park the television set repeatedly went 'on the blink' at 9.20 in the evenings and the aerial kept falling out. Once the Commander became annoyed and jammed the aerial in hard, just before 9.20 p.m. As he sat down his anglepoise light clicked on and off by itself! When this event was being related to a friend later in the week, a candle fell off the holder on to his plate and, as he looked at his watch, he found that it was 9.20 p.m.!

Some time later a male figure in sports coat and flannel trousers, and taken at first to be the Commander, was seen to disappear into a bathroom. In fact the Commander turned up an hour and a half later!

Thorington Hall, Stoke-by-Nayland, Suffolk

Thorington Hall is only open to the public through written application, but I was fortunate in being shown over this oak-framed, plastered and gabled house some years ago by the National Trust Caretakers. I was accompanied by my wife and Dr Peter Hilton-Rowe and we spent some time exploring this fascinating seventeenth-century house set within retaining walls. Some time after our visit the property was converted in part into studios.

Sixteenth-century Thorington Hall, Stoke-by-Nayland, Suffolk, has a haunted attic and the ghost of a girl in a yellow dress.

The western wing of the house centred round a magnificent chimney stack, fifty feet high, with six octagonal shafts supplying fireplaces on three floors. On the ground floor the main living-room has an unusual ornamented plaster surround and it was within the walls of this room, when it was being repaired in 1937, that a sixteenth-century woman's shoe, now in Colchester Museum, was found behind the plaster.

We were told that originally the upper floors of the house were probably reached by ladders in the passageway beside the chimney. But, about 1650, a remarkable staircase was substituted, a staircase consisting of unstained oak and elaborately carved newels with a curious builder's mark, three interlacing circles, on the third newel from the bottom — a staircase where, on the dark landing, the ghost of a little girl has been seen and heard.

Inside a partly panelled room on the first floor hung one of the two portraits of the Umfrevilies family who once lived here and one wonders whether the ghost child is connected with this family. Another portrait hangs in the adjoining passage.

A dim upstairs passage is also reputedly haunted by the ghostly little girl, wearing a simple, brownish dress tied with a cord at the waist. Here and in other parts of the house, heavy and unexplained footsteps have been heard many times in the past.

The Elizabethan shoe that was found here is especially interesting from the ghost-hunter's point of view; such things were often concealed as a charm to keep ghosts from the house so perhaps there has been a ghost here for almost as long as there has been a Thorington Hall.

A few years ago some American tourists were being shown over the house when an ancient bone, a human pelvis, fell from a cupboard in front of them! My friend Eric Maple tells me there have been few if any ghostly manifestations here in recent years, but memories are long and even today there are local people who have a considerable aversion to passing Thorington Hall after darkness has fallen.

Tintagel, Cornwall

Barras Nose, the headland north of the ruins known as King Arthur's Castle (where Arthur is said to have been conceived and born), has long been regarded as haunted — by the giant figure of King Arthur himself.

Many visitors and writers have described the strange and mystic atmosphere that is to be encountered here; even on the brightest of summer days there is a sombre influence among these bleak cliffs and crumbling mins, with the sound of roaring sea ever in the background. Here it is easy to believe that the spirit or form of the legendary King returns periodically to his birthplace. There is also a local tradition that once a year the whole castle mins disappear and materialise in all their former glory in some fairy realm.

Nearby, at Bossiney Mound, legend has it that King Arthur's Round Table lies buried and that it comes to the surface at midnight on Midsummer Eve, shimmering silver in the moonlight. In 1965 my friend Michael Williams, spending his first summer in Tintagel, decided to visit the Mound at the appointed hour and a few minutes before midnight he set out with his dog, Tex, and three friends as companions. He saw no magical table but he did see a mysterious light in one of the windows of the nearby chapel: a glow rather like a patch of floodlit moorland mist. Soon it covered both windows of the little chapel.

It lasted a moment, possibly two, and then it completely disappeared. It was seen by two other independent witnesses at the same time. Yet the chapel was locked and bolted and there was nobody inside. Michael has never forgotten the eerie and unexplained experience of that Midsummer Eve glow and since sharing that eerie spectacle he has never laughed at the supernatural.

But to return to Barras Head where Michael William's dog once acted very strangely. Here, the site of earthworks far older than Tintagel Castle, a path snakes its way along the cliffs and out to the headland and at one point, Tex always halted. Nothing would induce him to go on, not even the bribery of a biscuit,' Michael tells me. 'Foxes, somebody said, but I was less sure for he acted in exactly the same way at exactly the same spot in all seasons of the year. Sometimes he would permit me to pick him up and carry him for ten yards or so, then he would struggle to get down and continue on his own, quite happily. On every return journey he repeated the same performance, always halting at precisely the same spot .... There is something very odd about Barras Head.'

The Tower of London, Greater London

For nearly 1000 years prisoners of state have been confined, tortured and executed in this ancient and sombre collection of buildings; there have been murders here too and suicides and, if violent happenings and tragic deaths can contribute to hauntings, then surely the Tower of London should be as ghost-ridden as anywhere, and so it is.

From the reported ghost of Thomas a Becket in 1241 (mentioned by Matthew Paris) to the 'long-haired lady' seen in the Bloody Tower in 1970 and the man in a utility suit of the 1940s era, seen by a yeoman warder not far from Traitors' Gate in 1977, there have been literally scores of well-attested ghost sightings at Her Majesty's Tower of London. Field Marshall Sir Geoffrey Baker, Constable of the Tower since 1975 stated, unequivocally, in 1979: 'Over the centuries, and indeed in recent times, people have reported inexplicable sights and sounds in the Tower.' Let us make a brief tour of the chief buildings within the Tower precincts and look at some of the reported ghosts and ghostly happenings.

Anne Askew's body was almost torn apart on the rack in the torture chamber of the White Tower and perhaps it is her agonized screams and groans that have occasionally been heard issuing from these impregnated walls. In 1954 what appeared to be a puff of smoke was seen to emerge from the mouth of one of the age-old cannons outside the White Tower; it was seen by a responsible officer of the Tower known personally to Mrs Jerrad Tickell, a Vice-President of the Society for Psychical Research. At a distance of some twenty-five yards the puff of smoke hovered, formed into a cube and moved along some railings towards the watching officer. He called a nearby sentry and they both watched the 'smoke'[1] dangle on the side of some steps leading to the top of the wall. The alarm bell was sounded, but by the time the guard turned out there was nothing unusual to be seen.

This extremely curious but well-attested incident is reminiscent of the equally strange manifestations that occurred in 1817 in the Martin Tower when Edmund Lenthal Swifte, Keeper of the Crown Jewels, and his wife saw a cylindrical object, like a glass tube, hover between the ceiling and the table as they were at supper. There appeared to be two dense fluids, one white and the other pale blue, within the cylinder, and the two fluids incessantly mixed and separated while the cylinder moved slowly round the table and then touched Mrs Swifte. She screamed, whereupon her husband picked up a chair and struck out at whatever it was; immediately the manifestation vanished.

My friend, Yeoman Warder Geoffrey Abbott, tells me that there have been several instances of night patrols hearing screams and stifled cries of pain apparently emanating through the heavy doors at the base of the White Tower and not many years ago some soldiers reported seeing the huge shadow of an axe spread across Tower Green before becoming stationary, silhouetted in considerable clarity against the walls of the massive tower.

A room in Martin Tower (which is not open to the public) was for a time the 'doleful' prison of Anne Boleyn, and the upper room has reportedly been visited by her sad and silent ghost which appears and disappears for a few moments at a time, seated in a dark comer and usually on wild autumn evenings.

It was near a door in the Martin Tower that a sentry in 1815 encountered the figure of a huge bear — which is not as unlikely as it may seem as a menagerie of wild beasts was kept at the Tower from a very early date and the last animals were only removed to the Zoological Gardens in Regents Park in 1834. Marshalling his courage the soldier promptly thrust at the enormous form with his bayonet, but the blade went clear through the phantom creature and stuck fast in the door! As the hairy form began to advance towards him, the soldier collapsed and only lived for two days, repeating over and over again in his lucid moments the awful ordeal that he had undergone.

When he addressed the Ghost Club on the subject of 'Ghosts in the Tower of London', Yeoman Warder Abbott revealed that at the turn of the century it was reported that a figure in white walked the upper room of the Martin Tower, to the great alarm of the resident warders. In 1973 the occupants of a residence in the nearby Constable Tower first became aware of a presence that is heralded by a strong 'horsey' smell, a compounded odour of leather and sweaty horseflesh; a presence that has touched at last one of the occupants — who are certain, however, that the manifestation is a friendly one.

Northumberland's Walk, on each side of Martin Tower, gets its name from the fact that it was used for exercise by the elderly and learned ninth Earl of Northumberland who was confined in the Martin Tower for sixteen years. His ghost was seen by many of the Tower sentries towards the end of the last century and that particular sentry duty was accordingly undertaken by pairs of sentries.

Another, earlier, Earl of Northumberland was almost certainly murdered in the Bloody Tower and for years his ghost is reputed to have walked almost nightly! The two young princes were murdered in the Bloody Tower (although their bodies were buried at the foot of the stairway in the White Tower) and the ghosts of the young brothers have been reportedly seen occasionally, walking hand in hand; silent and pathetic reminders of a never to be forgotten crime. Here too a guardsman on night duty was startled to see a white form appear suddenly before him. It seemed to rise out of the ground at his feet and although shadowy and indistinct he had the impression of a headless woman; but he challenged the strange form and then thrust his bayonet towards it, whereupon the form vanished.

In 1933 another guardsman reported seeing the white form of a headless woman near the Bloody Tower. The form seemed to float towards him and then suddenly it disappeared. Years later a Guards officer, during training for the British Olympic Games, encountered a 'most queer and utterly distasteful atmosphere' near the Bloody Tower archway. He saw nothing but was completely overcome by the experience although he was thoroughly familiar with the area and had previously passed that way at all hours of the day and night without any ill effects.

In 1978 two sentries were patrolling beneath the Bloody Tower arch when they too encountered 'something' that caused them to pause, both experiencing an eerie, unpleasant sensation. Then suddenly the hair on the back of their necks bristled and their short capes billowed up, almost covering their faces, as an icy draught of air suddenly blew towards them out of the archway; a whirl of icy air which died away as rapidly as it had approached.

I have a letter from John Howden of Solihull describing two experiences he had at the Tower of London when he was serving as a young soldier in the Second Battalion of Scots Guards. 'As I stood guard at No.3 Post situated near the Traitors' Gate one night in January 1966, I distinctly heard the sound of marching feet. The sounds were so clear and distinct that I could hear the sharp crack as the studs of the boots were brought into contact with the old cobbled roadway, and this made me feel uneasy and very alert for I knew that no soldiers were allowed to wear studded boots after 22.00 hours. I remember raising my rifle and taking up an "on guard" position and I could see my bayonet shining in the moonlight as I turned to face the direction of the sounds. I could see nothing but the sound of the approaching patrol continued and it seemed to me that the patrol was coming through the Tower archway. I approached the archway cautiously and called a challenge ... there was no reply. I shouted again, louder, but still there was no reply. I then approached to within about fifteen yards of the archway and I remember feeling suddenly icy cold; in fact I began to shiver, but I plucked up my courage and entered the archway and there I could still see nothing but the atmosphere seemed positively alive and I knew that I was not alone. The hair at the back of my head stood up and I was very frightened. I listened intently but all was quiet now and I proceeded through the archway still keeping my rifle at the "on guard" position. I could feel my palms perspiring and I had to keep moving my hands on my rifle to get a better grip. Eventually I reached the other side of the archway and there I looked for the sentry of No. I Post who should have been standing outside the old oak door leading into the Bloody Tower, but of him there was no sign. I stood for a moment trying to decide what I should do when I heard the sound of footsteps coming from the direction of

Tower Green and I was relieved when the sentry of No. 1 Post came into view. He then said that he thought he had heard the sound of a patrol from the direction of the archway and he had decided to go as far as Tower Green and see whether anyone was about.

'Later, in the guardroom, I spoke to the Sergeant of the Guard about my experience and asked him whether a patrol had been out that night. "No, everything has been quiet," he replied. "But don't worry, you have only heard the phantom patrol going its rounds from the Bloody Tower to Traitors' Gate!" Next day I spoke to one of the resident Tower warders and he told me that he knew; all about the phantom patrol; it was heard and never seen, and he added that once heard it was never forgotten — how right he was!'

John Howden's second experience at the Tower took place during the summer of 1967, when he was carrying out guard duty at No. 1 Post at the Bloody Tower. 'My duty began at 01.00 hours and lasted until 03.00 hours. I remember it was a lovely night with stars shining out of a bright sky. From time to time I would do a patrol from the Post as far as Tower Green, and while there I would stop and admire the lovely old buildings casting their shadows across the Green. It was while I was carrying out a patrol past the White Tower that I noticed a very bright and shimmering light in one of the windows high up in the Tower. At first I thought that someone must have left a light on but then I found that this could not be the answer. I left the roadway, stepping over the small wire fence, walked across the neatly cut lawn of the moat and stopped about twenty yards from the Tower; altogether I must have watched the light for the best part of ten minutes, but since there appeared to be no movement and no sign of any shadow or form in the lighted room, I decided not to report the matter and I returned to my post outside the Bloody Tower.

The Martin Tower, where the Keeper of the Crown Jewels had a very strange experience in 1817, and where Anne Boleyn's sad and silent ghost has often been seen.

The Bloody
Tower which is
haunted by a
ghostly headless
woman.

The Chapel of St Peter and Vincula, where an officer of the guard saw a procession of knights and ladies in ancient costume.

After about twenty minutes I thought I would have another look but when I looked up at the windows of the White Tower all was in darkness. I was returning along the cobbled roadway from Tower Green when I looked up and saw a light again but this time it was slowly moving, from window to window, and furthermore I could make out some sort of shape, which could have been a human figure of some sort; but the light was very bright and lit up whole windows, one after the other as it passed. I watched more closely and saw it eventually move back, away from the windows, as if making its way to the other side of the Tower; I hurried round but could see no light at the windows on the other side and now that there was no sign of any light I resumed my post until relieved by the new guard. Later that morning I spoke to a Tower warder about my experience and he did not seem the least surprised and said I had probably seen the ghost of Anne Boleyn who was supposed to haunt the White Tower and also the Bloody Tower and many of the warders had seen or heard her but they didn't usually discuss such experiences with anyone outside the Tower.'

Sir Walter Raleigh was lodged in a cell ten feet by eight feet within the wall of the Bloody Tower and for exercise he traversed the ramparts between the Bloody Tower and the timber-framed Lieutenant's Lodgings, now the Queen's House, and here the popular Raleigh would show himself and converse with passers-by; it is a path known to this day as Raleigh's Walk and it is said to be haunted by his ghost on moonlit nights.

In 1970 a visitor to the Bloody Tower saw a form that she at first took to be a real person, a woman with long hair standing by an open window. As she looked with some interest at the figure she noticed the ankle-length black velvet dress, the white cap and a large, gold medallion that the figure wore around her neck; then, as she watched the figure faded and disappeared. Intrigued by the experience, the visitor returned to the Bloody Tower a few weeks later and was astonished to see the same apparition, in the same place!

The Queen's House has been the scene of many strange experiences. Here the most persistent phantom is the mysterious Grey Lady, a ghost that is only seen by the fair sex, but who she is and why she walks we have yet to learn. Within the last decade the figure of a man in medieval dress has been seen drifting along an upper corridor and firm footsteps have been heard ascending a stairway at the rear of the building. In 1978 an American guest staying at the Queen's House heard the sound of what she described as 'religious chanting'. It was past midnight and she lay awake for some time listening to the faint music and voices, assuming that the sounds emanated from a radio or that there was some other pefectly normal explanation. In the morning she was unable to discover any explanation for the sounds and she learned that on at least one previous occasion the same slow religious chanting had been heard by a resident at the Queen's House.

It was in a room at the Queen's House that Guido Fawkes and his accomplices were 'examined' and here the harrowing sounds of the eerie screech and grind of instruments of torture and unexplained groans and cries have been heard from time to time. There is also a room with wall paintings depicting men inflicting and suffering torture that has long been reputed to be badly haunted but I have no precise details.

Yeoman Warder Geoffrey Abbott recounts in his book, Ghosts at the Tower of London, that a room in the Queen's House adjoining that in which Anne Boleyn passed her last days has a particularly strange and unpleasant atmosphere and is unquestionably colder than other rooms in the house. A peculiar perfume lingers in the air and such is the apparent menace of the room that no unaccompanied girl or young child is ever permitted to sleep there. Two of those who have done so in the past have awakened with the overwhelming impression that they were about to be suffocated!

One evening in 1864 a guardsman of the Sixtieth Rifles saw a white figure materialize in a dark doorway of the Queen's House and float silently towards him. When his challenge was ignored he stabbed at the figure with his bayonet. He found no resistance and his bayonet went clean through the figure which still advanced towards him! He realized that he was face to face with a ghost and he collapsed in a faint. The Captain of the Guard found him unconscious on the ground and put him on a charge. At the subsequent court-martial for sleeping on duty (or being drunk) several other guardsmen swore that they had seen a similar figure at the same spot while on guard duty themselves, and furthermore two witnesses maintained that they had seen the same figure at the same time as the accused. They had seen him thrust his bayonet through the figure and had heard his scream of terror before he collapsed. In the circumstances the court took a lenient view and the charged man was acquitted.

Another sentry saw a woman in white appear from the direction of the Queen's House one evening a little after midnight. He could not see her head in the darkness but he distinctly heard the clicking of her heels on the hard ground. Puzzled, he watched the figure move towards Tower Green and then, when the form entered the patch of moonlight, he saw to his horror that she was headless. He fled his post but again the authorities were lenient.

Anne Boleyn spent her last night on earth at the Queen's House and her ghost has been seen to emerge from the doorway under her room and glide towards Tower Green where she was executed on 19 May 1536. In fact the ghost of Anne Boleyn has been reported many times from many different parts of the Tower. At a meeting of the Ghost Club in 1899 Lady Biddolph related that a phantom lady with a red carnation had been observed looking out of a window at the Tower. She added that the description tallied with that of Anne Boleyn herself and it was at the window of Anne's room that the figure was seen.

Tower Green is a spot of poignant and hallowed memory and the place of execution was marked off and railed by command of Queen Victoria. Those who were 'untopped' (as Anne Boleyn's daughter put it) on Tower Green — others were executed on Tower Hill under the authority of the government of the city — included Lord Hastings in 1483, Jane, Countess Rochford (sister-in-law of Anne Boleyn) in 1542, Lady Jane Grey in 1554, and Margaret Pole, Countess of Salisbury, daughter of the Duke of Clarence, in 1541. And the latter execution is said to be re-enacted on the anniversary of the truly awful event. Over seventy years of age and innocent of any crime (her death was an act of vengeance by Henry VIII) the Countess was understandably a reluctant victim and she was forcibly carried to the scaffold, screaming and fighting to escape. Stoutly protesting her innocence to the end, she refused to kneel over the block and challenged the axeman to remove her head 'as best he could', and so her masked executioner pursued her around the block, literally hacking her to death in a welter of blood. It is this ghastly scene that has reputedly been re-enacted in all its harrowing detail annually every since.

Lady Jane Grey paid her first visit to the Tower as the sixteen-year-old Queen of England, but less than three weeks later she was taken there again, this time as a prisoner, together with her young husband. She saw his headless body carried past her on the morning that she knew she too must die — is it unlikely then that her ghost returns to this storehouse of memories? Her ghost was last seen in 1957, on 12 February to be exact, the 403rd anniversary of her execution.

Guardsman Johns, a young Welshman on duty at the Tower, stamped his feet that cold and wintry morning as a nearby clock chimed the hour of three. Suddenly a rattling noise alerted his attention and as he looked up towards the battlements of the Salt Tower, forty feet above him, he saw silhouetted against the dark sky, a white shapeless form' that moulded itself into the likeness of Lady Jane Grey. As the startled soldier shouted for assistance, another guardsman saw a strange white apparition' at the same spot, a hundred yards or so from the red-brick, seventeenth-century Gentleman Jailer's House which stands on the site of a previous structure where Lady Jane Grey was imprisoned and where she saw her husband, Lord Guildford Dudley, go to his execution.

'The ghost stood between the battlements,' Guardsman Johns said afterwards. 'At first I thought I was seeing things, but when I told the other guard and pointed, the figure appeared again.' An officer of the regiment stated: 'Guardsman Johns is convinced that he saw a ghost. Speaking for the regiment, our attitude is "All right, so you say you have seen a ghost. Let's leave it at that".'

The Chapel of St Peter ad Vincula (Peter in Chains) has been the scene of several unexplained incidents and in particular a spectacular ghostly procession. Some years ago an officer of the Guard decided to investigate a light he saw burning inside the chapel after he had been unable to get any satisfactory explanation from a sentry. He peered in through a window and could hardly believe his eyes. Along the aisle, between the tombs, moved a procession of knights and ladies in ancient costume, led by an elegant female whose face and dress resembled reputed portraits of Queen Anne Boleyn. After pacing the chapel the entire procession vanished and with it the light that had first attracted the attention of the officer.

Then there is the unidentified male figure in Elizabethan costume seen one afternoon by a Tower guide in a passageway that formerly led to the Bell Tower and was used as a promenade for prisoners; the wan form of the ghost of Henry VI outside the chamber in the Wakefield Tower where he was stabbed to death as he knelt in prayer; the ghostly stretcher bearer party seen by a sentry near the Spur Tower; the headless man in a black cloak in Water Lane; the ghost of a monk in a brown habit seen inside St Thomas's Tower; the strange glow that suddenly lights up the prison chamber in the Salt Tower; the 'bluish hovering form' seen near the Bell Tower; the piercing screams that echo from the Byward Tower and the unknown cavalier who haunts Elizabeth's Walk.

The Tower of London is indeed full of reported ghosts; indeed it is probably the most haunted collection of buildings on earth.

Treasurer's House, York, North Yorkshire

I had the pleasure of presiding at the original Ghost Week-end held at York in 1974; since then thousands of visitors have been attending similar week-ends laid on for tourists; there have been major television programmes about the ghosts of York; many countries have featured York's ghosts in radio programmes and magazine articles; they even feature in the Guinness Book of Records where York is called 'the most haunted city in Europe' — a claim that is certainly open to argument.

Among the haunted places I visited during that interesting weekend was Treasurer's House, at the north-east corner of the Minster. The site of Treasurer's House has been built on from earliest times, and remains of a Roman column, believed to be in its original position and twelve feet lower than the existing ground-floor level, have been uncovered in the basement. It is thought to have probably formed part of a colonnade lining the *Via Decumana*. It is known that the Romans had a building on the site (a fact that may be significant in view of the reported ghost sightings), but there is no evidence to show exactly what purpose the building fulfilled and Treasurer's House, as an official residence for the Treasurer of the See of York, begins in the days of William the Conqueror and ends with Henry VIII. The present structure is mainly seventeenth and eighteenth century with thirteenth-century work in the undercroft and Roman remains in the cellars. From a psychic point of view Treasurer's House has provided, at least in numbers, the most exciting activity of supernormal activity in York. Indeed Treasurer's House is said to provide not only numbers but also variety in its ghosts.

Among the many owners of Treasurer's House over the years are the Aislabie family, who also owned Fountains Hall, and it is a member of this family that is reputed to have haunted Treasurer's House for more than 300 years.

It seems that Miss Mary Mallorie, a co-heiress of Studley, and sister-in-law to George Aislabie of Ripon, attended a ball at the Duke of Buckingham's house in Skeldergate in January 1674, with members of the Aislabie family and her fiance Jonathan Jennings, who were all staying at Treasurer's House. Owing to a misunderstanding she missed the servant sent to escort her back from Skeldergate and Jonathan took her in his own carriage; but when they reached Treasurer's House repeated knocking failed to bring anyone to the gates and, since it was so late, Jonathan took Mary to spend the night with one of his relatives. Next day there was an argument between Jonathan Jennings and George Aislabie about what had actually happened. Words led to blows and very soon a duel had been arranged for dawn the next day. The duel was duly fought and George Aislabie, mortally wounded by a rapier thrust, was carried home to die.

Treasurer's House in York, at the north-east corner of the Minster.

The Tapestry Room in the Treasurer's House which has a unique and forbidding atmosphere.

Jennings, who seems to have acted under provocation and to have done all he could in the circumstances, nevertheless came off badly. Grieved and shocked to hear of the death of his adversary, he hurried to London to seek a pardon from Charles II. Exactly what happened we do not know but although Jennings eventually returned to York, Miss Mallorie — the cause of all the trouble — never married him or anyone else.

George Aislabie and his wife are buried in the Minster Choir but according to my friend John Mitchell, who has extensively researched and written on the subject of the ghosts of York, his ghost continues to this day to haunt Treasurer's House, where he died. It does seem that some aura of the antagonism that resulted in the death of the unfortunate George Aislabie still lingers here. Several people who knew nothing of the Aislabie story have reported feeling an overwhelming sense of the necessity of suddenly protecting themselves as they have passed the door of Treasurer's House; a feeling that is acute and terrifying and very real to those who have experienced it.

A similar feeling has been reported inside Treasurer's House, and especially in the Tapestry Room on the first floor after the new owner Mr Frank Green undertook extensive alterations in 1897, including stripping off several layers of wallpaper to disclose fine seventeenth-century panelling in this room. People continually remarked on an unpleasant atmosphere after the renovations; nobody cared to use the room, complaining of the gloomy and forbidding influences that seemed to permeate the large and important room that always felt much colder than the rest of the building. There is a story that the atmosphere of this room so affected the wife of one occupant that she murdered her cruel husband, and although no one has ever reported seeing a ghost in the room, it is thought that something of the atmosphere lingers on at the scene of this tragedy.

But what is perhaps the most remarkable ghost story to come out of York was related to me by Harry Martindale, now a policeman, as he led the way to one of the cellars of Treasurer's House. Here, in the early 1950s, when he was a plumber's apprentice, Harry was working in this particular cellar, helping to install piping for central heating. At the time still more alterations were being made to the building and a team of archaeologists were preparing a survey. Suddenly, as he was standing on a short ladder, his thoughts those of a lad of seventeen and far removed from ghosts, he thought he heard the sound of a trumpet. He took little notice of this, other than thinking it odd that such a sound should have reached him where he was working; but the sound seemed to come nearer and nearer and then, to his astonishment, he saw the figure of a horse come through the wall, huge and lumbering, bearing a man on its back, a soldier dressed in Roman costume!

Harry fell from the ladder to the earth floor, thoroughly shocked and confused but, wide-eyed, he saw the mounted soldier followed by a group of foot-soldiers, carrying lances and short-bladed swords and wearing Roman helmets ... they were not marching in formation but rather they were shuffling along with their heads down in a dispirited sort of way. They took no notice of Harry, still lying on the floor hardly able to believe his own eyes — but he took in every detail and the remarkable sight is as clear to him today as when he saw it.

He remembers being surprised by their short stature and shabby appearance, the rough, homemade clothes they were wearing, their sandals, cross-gartered to the knees, and the green, kilted skirts. He recalls the round shields they carried but cannot remember seeing any banner or standard — he does remember vividly the helmets (the finest part of their equipment) with the fine plumes of undyed feathers. When the horse first came out of the wall followed by the soldiers, they all appeared to be cut off at the knees. Later excavations revealed that they were in fact appearing at the original level of the Roman road that once traversed this spot. The whole group had an air of utter dejection and he watched them cross the cellar and silently disappear into the opposite wall.

Trembling with shock young Harry rushed out of the cellar as fast as he could and up to the ground floor where he bumped into the Curator who, noticing his agitation, said at once: 'You've seen the Romans, haven't you?' The Curator suggested that Harry immediately write down what he had seen; he did so and then the Curator showed him other accounts, written by two separate people, giving identical details of the appearance of a group of Roman soldiers in the cellar he had so recently left.

Harry Martindale told me he had been questioned by experts in Roman history who were much impressed by the details he disclosed, such as the fact that the foot-soldiers carded round shields, an unusual but not unknown feature. Archaeologists later uncovered evidence suggesting the presence of a Roman headquarters in the vicinity of Treasurer's House and the fact that the ghosts were walking where there had once been a Roman road.

I must say that Harry Martindale impressed me as an honest and responsible man and I do not think there is any doubt that he did have a very strange experience in the cellars of Treasurer's House; nor do I think that at the time he knew anything about other stories of Roman ghosts being seen there years earlier.

Mr Frank Green of Nunthorpe Hall owned Treasurer's House from 1896 until he gave it to the National Trust in 1930. His portrait by Prince Paul Troubetskoi hangs in the gallery.

On one occasion Frank Green held a fancy dress party at Treasurer's House and the guests were invited to explore the historic house. One young lady found her way into the cellars and she was about to proceed along a passage when she saw, as she thought, another guest dressed as a Roman soldier. After a moment she went forward and was very surprised when the figure barred her way by holding his spear across the passage. He said nothing but his action and expression left no doubt in her mind that he did not wish her to proceed. Puzzled and a little annoyed at his dictatorial manner, she turned on her heel and returned upstairs where she asked her host the name of the guest dressed as a Roman soldier. She then learned and subsequently verified for herself that in fact no guest had come to the party so-attired or indeed in any costume remotely resembling what she had seen in the haunted cellars of Treasurer's House. It should be noted that for reasons of safety and convenience the cellars are not part of the house normally open to the public, although occasionally special permission to visit the cellars is granted, but only by prior arrangement.

There do appear to be other ghosts in York: at Holy Trinity Church, Micklegate; All Saint's Church, Pavement; the Yorkshire Museum; York Minster; Holy Trinity, Goodramgate; the Theatre Royal; the King's Manor; a school of dancing; Castlegate House; St Mary's Hospital; the 'York Arms'; the 'Cock and Bottle'; and several old houses.

Trerice, Newquay, Cornwall

Trerice is a manor house rebuilt by Sir John Arundell in 1571 on the site of an earlier house. Sir John inherited Trerice from his father, another Sir John, who served Henry VIII, Edward VI and Queen Mary. The Arundells supported the Crown during the Civil War and showed great gallantry, but their losses were substantial although they recovered something of their position after the Restoration.

In this delightful house surrounded by delightful gardens I talked with the Administrator, Mrs Watts. She was gracious and helpful but she had only been there a matter of months so she gave me the name of the previous Administrator, Dr Walker, who had been known to complain of doors opening and closing by themselves and many other apparently inexplicable disturbances. There are vague stories here, I learned, of unidentified phantom ladies, of quiet footsteps, gentle music, an impression of the presence of invisible, happy, presences, and the unexplained fragrance of perfume.

Dr David Walker tells me that when he was Administrator at Trerice he was fed with a plenitude of stories and, on his first Walpurgis Nacht (one of the two nights of the year when the forces of evil are reputed to hold sway over the earth and when ghosts are most likely to walk) he thought he would set out and see for himself whether any ghosts were abroad at Trerice.

The scene could hardly have been more conducive, he tells me, for it was blowing a gale and the moon was full. He wandered all round the house and garden with a shaking torch but 'apart from the odd twig and a spit from a dying log in the fire in the great hall, I only heard ghostly chuckles!'

He tells me there is little doubt that there was once a chapel across the road from the house, in a meadow still called 'Chapel Field', but no signs of even the foundations of such a building remain today. Legend has it that the family — or was it ghosts — used to visit this chapel at the time of the Reformation, when they were 'busy swapping sides'. This may well have been true; it is equally likely that the place may have become a cache for smuggled rum, to which all Cornish, past and present, are addicted'. 'There is another story, fairly well substantiated, that a stable lad was killed by a stampede of horses just below the courtyard ', but his ghost is reputed to haunt elsewhere. 'All this is not to say that Trerice does not have "atmosphere"; indeed the vast majority of visitors from all walks of life and many countries daily comment upon it and go away in awe.'

Research on the spot suggests that Trerice may still be haunted by a Grey Lady, or rather the feeling or sensation of a Grey Lady, who walks occasionally in the north wing of the house but most often along the gallery, and disappears down the stone circular stairway that is reached through the closed door halfway along the gallery, steps that once formed the main and original entrance to the house. The long gallery has a definite atmosphere, I felt; the low ceiling dome-shaped and decorated with plasterwork.

From time to time visitors have remarked upon the presence of a scent or perfume of lilac in the library where one visitor said she had the vivid impression of a coffin resting there amid the accompanying smell of lilacs. In a house of such long history it is by no means unlikely that at some period a coffin has indeed rested here.

In the hall, with its little musician's gallery at one end, behind the row of small recessed arches set high in the comice, another visitor became so affected by the atmosphere that as she made to enter the library she said she could not do so. This particular lady was a frequent visitor to Trerice and previous to this visit had always found the atmosphere delightful throughout the house; but this time, she said, it was very different, and try as she would, she simply could not bring herself to walk into the library and in fact she immediately left the house.

Two of the guides admitted to me that on certain occasions and especially on dark evenings there is a curious atmosphere or feeling in the gallery, almost as though one has stepped back in time. Although there do not appear to be any coherent stories that might account for any haunting or ghostly appearance at Trerice, there are unsubstantiated [...text continues on page 341]

The gallery at Trerice, which is still haunted by a Grey Lady who walks along the long room and disappears down some steps that once formed the main and original entrance to the house.

The scent of lilacs in the
air has often been
remarked upon in the
library at Trerice.

stories, as indeed there are about many old houses; stories of a long ago head of the house seducing a young servant girl and of her form being seen from time to time after her tragic death; there are stories too of fearful dungeons and a secret tunnel. Silly stories perhaps, yet a certain room in the house was once known as 'the dungeon' and there once was a passage leading to a little chapel nearby; probably both were conveniently used by smugglers in days gone by.

During alterations in the north wing, which had only been open about three years when I was there, a number of unexplained disturbances were reported. On one occasion a workman swore that two doors had opened and 'something' had entered the area where they were working; something that made a 'swishing' sound on the floor, like that made by a person passing by who was wearing a crinoline. And both workmen noticed and remarked upon a pleasant fragrance. The greatest difficulty was experienced, I was told, in getting these hard-headed workmen to return and finish their work in that particular part of the north wing.

Years ago the gallery would have been used for exercise, by the ladies of the house, during the winter months when the menfolk were out shooting or hunting or otherwise engaged and one cannot help wondering whether an echo from the past, for no particular reason, still lingers here. It is certainly interesting that the gentle swishing sound that moves along and also a 'whiff of perfume', both manifestations that are likely to be associated with ladies, have been noticed here, especially in the north wing and the entrance to the gallery and the gallery itself.

One of the guides I talked to, a small, neat, practical and sensible person, had herself experienced the 'inexplicable fragrance' on two occasions — the first time before she had heard anything about such a thing having happened before at Trerice. When she said she thought she had noticed the fragrance of perfume when there was no obvious explanation, she learned that such a harmless and infrequent echo from the past had indeed been part of the accepted ghostly' associations of the house for many years. She is among several people at the house who have on occasions had a distinct feeling that something or someone has passed by or is in the vicinity when clearly there is no human being present. Not an easy impression to describe but a very real one to those who have experienced it. On the other hand, another guide will tell you that there are no ghosts at Trerice and never have been; it is all imagination. So you pay your money and you take your choice, as you wander through this delightful Elizabethan house so full of memories.

U

Uppark, South Harting, West Sussex

From outside Uppark is a charming Wren-style country house — it was built about 1690 with William Talman as architect — but inside it is all eighteenth century for the house was completely re-decorated and re-furnished in 1750 and today it presents an unusually complete preservation of an eighteenth-century interior.

The builder of the present house, Forde, Lord Grey of Werke, later Earl of Tankerville, had an adventurous career, becoming involved in major social and political scandals. When married to Mary Berkeley, he ran off in 1682 with her sister Lady Henrietta, who was only eighteen years of age. Lord Berkeley sued for her return and at the trial Lord Grey was found guilty 'of the most odious abuse of confidence, the meanest duplicity, the basest falsehood, the most ungenerous, most ungrateful and most unfeeling selfishness'. Yet Lady Henrietta did not return to her family: she maintained that she was really married to a Mr Turner whom no one had heard of before and hardly heard of again.

A few months later Lord Grey faced a charge of high treason arising out of his close association with the Duke of Monmouth; indeed Grey has been described as Monmouth's evil genius. The same year, when the Rye House Plot was uncovered. Lord Grey was arrested, brought before the Council, and committed to the Tower. 'But the gates were shut: so he stayed in the messenger's hands all night, whom he furnished so liberally with wine that he was dead drunk. Next morning Lord Grey called for a pair of oaks and went away, leaving the drunken messenger fast asleep.' He rode straight to Uppark where he met Lady Henrietta and after supper in the woods they rode to Chichester and together took ship to the Low Countries.

Nor was this the end of his adventurers for he rejoined Monmouth and together they landed in England to form part of Monmouth's Rebellion. Taken prisoner by James II he may have turned King's Evidence for he was treated with remarkable leniency, being released with a fine when many minor rebels were treated very harshly. Certainly he made a very full confession to the King but still, surprisingly, he was allowed to return to Uppark where he enjoyed his diminished estate until his death in 1701, the estate then passing to his only child, a daughter who married Charles Bennett. In 1747 their grandson sold the estate to Matthew Fetherstonhaugh and it is a member of this family whose ghost may haunt the house to this day.

In 1780 the then Sir Harry Fetherstonhaugh brought to Uppark a fifteen-year-old country girl from Cheshire, 'a beauty who distracted all beholders', a showgirl' he had met at the so-called Temple of Aesculapius in the Adelphi, an establishment that might be called an unsavoury night club. True, she already had a baby on her hands and during the year that she was at Uppark conceived another, but she went on to be painted by Romney, married to Sir William Hamilton and loved by Nelson. She was Emma, and for all her charm and 'giddy' ways Sir Harry sent her away from Uppark with barely enough to get to her grandmother in Hawarden. But there is one print of her in the house to show that Sir Harry cherished the memory of her, and long after Nelson was dead and Sir William too, Sir Harry helped Emma to pay her debts. There is no record, however, that she ever visited Uppark again. What a pity it is not her ghost that haunts Uppark!

In fact it is a wonder her ghost has not returned, for after Nelson's death at Trafalgar the government ignored his last request that the country should look after Emma and their surviving daughter Horatia, and eventually poor Emma died in drink-ridden squalor.

Other interesting people who knew Uppark but also spurn to haunt this happy house include the Prince Regent who was often here between 1785 and 1810 and always before a visit he would request that he be put in 'my old room' ... H.G. Wells knew the place for his mother was housekeeper here for thirteen years; indeed he admitted in his autobiography that the place had a great effect upon me'; but sadly neither 'Prinny' nor the visionary and great imaginative writer deign to haunt the rooms at Uppark.

In 1825 Sir Harry, then over seventy, decided to marry Mary Ann Bullock, his head dairymaid. He sent her to Paris to be educated and as far as is known she made him an excellent wife until his death twenty-one years later. And it is the ghost of Sir Harry Fetherstonhaugh, who died here at the age of ninety-two, that is reputed to haunt the Red Room.

Here, the benign ghost of Sir Harry is said to have made his presence known, beneath his portrait by Pompeo Batoni that was painted in Rome in 1776 and now hangs over the fireplace. It has been noticed that whenever an antique firescreen is placed in front of the fireplace the wrong way round, the ghost turns it round the right way! This has happened, I was told when I was there in 1981, times without number. There have been other disturbances in this room too, the unexplained opening and closing of windows and various strange noises and inexplicable sounds.

The Administrator, Mr John Eyre, told me that he was very interested in the story of the firescreen that moved by itself or was moved by a ghost, and when the firescreen had to go away to be repaired he thought he would try a little experiment. He placed an antique desk that incorporated a sliding firescreen in front of the fireplace, and beneath the portrait of Sir Harry, with the screen carefully raised and fixed at an appropriate height. Each morning the screen would be found to have been lowered. Thinking that the answer must lie in simple gravity, Mr Eyre arranged for the screen to be wedged open at a certain height; still the screen was found lowered next morning.

Eventually the carpenter fixed the wedges so that it was quite impossible to move the screen at all and so the ghost was balked! Mr Eyre told me that he was looking forward to the return of the original screen when he planned to carry out some scientific experiments to establish just why the screen 'moved by itself. I wish him luck but have my doubts as to whether he will solve the matter without disturbing the ghost (if ghost there is) — which would be a great pity for this lovely home deserves a gentle and harmless ghost.

W

Wallington Hall, Cambo, Northumberland

'At Wallington are endless suites of huge rooms, only partly carpeted and thinly covered with eighteenth-century furniture, partly covered with faded tapestry. The last of these is the Ghost Room, and Wallington is still a haunted house: awful noises are heard through the night; footsteps rush up and down the untrodden passages; wings flap and beat against the windows; bodiless people unpack and put away their things all night long, and invisible beings are felt to breathe over you as you lie in bed.' So wrote Augustus Hare, the diarist and inveterate collector of ghost stories associated with great houses, following a visit to Wallington in 1862; a house built in 1688 on the site of two previous properties, a house that passed into the ownership of the Trevelyan family in 1777 and with whom it remained until given, with many of the contents, to the National Trust by Sir Charles Trevelyan, in 1942.

Hare certainly found the bedroom allocated to him, 'quite horrid'. It opened into a long suite of desolate rooms by a door without a fastening, so he pushed a heavy dressing-table complete with weighty mirror against the door to keep out whatever might try to get in. Hare's host, Sir Walter Trevelyan, was the son of old Lady Trevelyan, 'a very wicked woman', and Sir Walter himself was never known to laugh. He was, says Hare, 'a strange-looking being with long hair and moustache and an odd, careless dress, and he enjoyed or endured the reputation of being a miser, like his mother'. Another 'strange being' in the house at that time was a certain Mr Wooster, who had come to the house four years earlier to arrange a collection of shells and had never gone away. He, it seems, looked like a 'church monument incarnated' and 'turned up his eyes when he spoke to you till you saw nothing but the white. He also had a long, trailing moustache, and in all things imitated, but caricatured, Sir Walter'.

Here, where Eric Maple describes the haunting as being 'an as yet unidentified monster which flaps its wings against window-panes and awakens sleepers with its heavy asthmatic breathing', Marc Alexander writes of Wallington being 'one of the most pleasant haunted houses' he has visited.

When Marc Alexander was there he was told about the invisible birds' wings beating against the window-panes and the sound of heavy breathing, but no one seemed to know any story that might account for these disturbances. He wonders whether it may be connected in some way with Sir John Fenwick, the last of his line, who was executed in 1697 for planning an assassination attempt on William III. The Fenwick family had added the Tudor house to an existing medieval pele tower, long before the erection of the present house.

After Sir John had been executed, his famous horse White Sorrel was confiscated and used by the King until one day the horse is said to have stumbled over a molehill, throwing the King, who died of his injuries. Thus, it has been suggested, White Sorrel avenged his master. The incident was to be recalled many times by the Jacobite toast: To the little gentleman in black velvet.' In spite of being a pleasant house Wallington has, according to all accounts, an indescribable atmosphere in keeping with the best traditions of haunted houses.

Washington Old Hall, Washington, Tyne and Wear

A small seventeenth-century manor house in which were incorporated parts of an earlier house built in the twelfth century (when the name was spelt Wessington), Washington

Old Hall is a mecca for visitors from America and students of American history for, from 1183 until 1613, it was the home of the ancestors of George Washington, first president of the USA.

Having become dilapidated by 1936 the property was rescued from further deterioration by the Washington Old Hall Preservation Committee. With help from both sides of the Atlantic the house was restored and furnished with a wealth of Jacobean furniture and in 1956 transferred to the National Trust who in 1975 gave the people of the United States of America a titular twenty-five year lease as a Bicentennial gift.

The unidentified ghost here is that of 'a lady in a long grey dress', a figure that has been seen quietly gliding along an upstairs corridor. Over the years there have been increasing numbers of visitors to Washington Old Hall and interestingly enough a proportionately increasing number of sightings of the ghost. Some of the witnesses have claimed that there is a likeness between the ghost and one of the family portraits that hang in the hall.

West Wycombe, Buckinghamshire

West Wycombe has a haunted manor, a haunted park and a haunted inn. In the eighteenth century Sir Francis Dashwood inherited his title and West Wycombe Park from his father — who married four times — but the name of Sir Francis Dashwood has become associated with blasphemy and lechery; for he founded the infamous Friars of St Francis, better known as the Hell Fire Club or the Brotherhood of Medmenham, who met in the constructed ruined' chapel of Medmenham Abbey, about six miles from West Wycombe Park.

After some ten years, when some of the leading members died and highly scandalous tales of the activities began to become public knowledge. Sir Francis disbanded the club before there was open scandal. He returned to his estate at West Wycombe but he did not give up his love of the exotic and in fact he sought new ways of pandering to his pulsing sensuality.

Years before he had provided work for his villagers by paying for a road to West Wycombe, the chalk coming from some prehistoric caves that had been discovered by tunnelling into a hill; and by the time the work was finished the caves had become a labyrinth of passages and caverns. Their eerie atmosphere fascinated Sir Francis and he decided they would make an ideal new meeting place for his 'Franciscan brothers' and their female companions. The caverns and corridors and caves were suitably furnished and Lord Sandwich, First Lord of the Admiralty, among many other members, came down from London to continue their revels — with local girls and London prostitutes to provide the entertainment. But it was not to last. Some of the members became old men before their time and even Sir Francis's unusual powers began to fail.

In 1774, Paul Whitehead, one of the faithful stewards of both clubs, fell ill and died. He had asked that his heart should be embalmed and given to his old friend Sir Francis Dashwood to be preserved in a silver casket in the mausoleum beside the caves. This was done, amid great pomp and ceremony, but in 1839 some soldiers stole the gruesome relic.

After Lady Dashwood's death, Francis took a mistress, a Mrs Barry, by whom he had a daughter, Rachel Antonina Lee, who grew up to be almost as great an eccentric as her father. Gradually the rumbustious Sir Francis Dashwood lapsed into domesticity and there are reports of the old rake sitting dreaming by the fire, being read to by his mistress.

These quiet days in the autumn of his life were disturbed in 1781 when the ghost of Paul Whitehead was reportedly seen, time and time again, among the trees and bushes in the ground of West Wycombe Park, perhaps seeking the company of his old friend for sometimes he seemed to beckon before disappearing.

One witness, Lady Austen, told William Cowper, the poet, that the ghost had been seen more than once by every member of the household, both during the daytime and at night. Occasionally the spectre appeared within the home of his former friend, as if anxious to lead him towards death or whatever lay beyond this life. Other signs and omens worried the ailing and ageing Sir Francis. A stain resembling five red fingers appeared on the marble table erected in the church to the memory of the first Sir Francis Dashwood. The frightened and superstitious villagers tried every means they could think of to wash the marks away, but next day they always returned. Even as he lay dying, the optimistic Sir Francis was planning another trip to Italy, to revisit the scenes of some of his old revels.

The ghost of Paul Whitehead, seen so frequently 200 years ago, disappeared after the death of Sir Francis, so perhaps he was only waiting for the company of his old friend before leaving forever the haunts of earlier days. The nearby caves have been restored as far as possible as they were during the 'Franciscan Friars' days of revelry and they attract thousands of visitors every year, but there are no reliable reports of the caves being haunted.

Perhaps there are only minor ghostly disturbances these days in the great Palladian house that passed into the Dashwood family in 1670 and was rebuilt in 1745-71, although the present Sir Francis Dashwood and his family will tell you that some of the rooms have a distinct and very odd atmosphere that is remarked upon by many visitors, and there

The beautiful Palladian house
at West Wycombe in
Buckinghamshire.

The Music Saloon at West
Wycombe Park, where Nole
Coward suddenly became aware
of the presence of someone
leaning against the piano.

have certainly been strange incidents in the past that suggest the house is haunted.

In the 1930s a guest who was staying at West Wycombe lingered over his port and found himself alone in the dining-room. He is reported to have suddenly left the table and rushed out of the room, refusing ever to be left alone there again. As he had sat, looking round the empty room, he had noticed a sudden chill in the air and an unearthly silence, almost as though time had stopped, and he had found himself joined at the table by eleven ghostly figures. He knew that the infamous Sir Francis had a predilection for twelve diners, and not waiting to finish his port, he summoned every ounce of will-power and fled from the silent room.

There was the time too when Noel Coward visited the house and he often spoke afterwards of the occasion when he had been sitting in the saloon, quietly playing the piano, and had suddenly become aware of the presence of someone leaning against the piano, looking down at him. When he glanced up, he found himself looking into the amiable and smiling face of a man dressed in a monk's habit and hood. Before he had time to recover from his surprise at encountering such a figure, the form had completely and quite inexplicably disappeared.

Another time, an old school friend of Mr Francis Dashwood, while staying at West Wycombe Park, suddenly came face to face with the figure of an old monk in one of the rooms; a figure that also quietly disappeared, but this witness spent the rest of his stay highly apprehensive of what he might experience in the history-laden house where figures from the past seemingly still appear from time to time.

When my old friend and clairvoyant Tom Corbett visited West Wycombe Park in 1962 he distinctly saw a ghost in the Music Room. He described her to me as 'a very beautiful woman, her greying hair drawn softly back from her face and parted in the middle, and dressed in blue; a ghost who returned to the house because she had been happy there; a fairly recent ghost who seemed to wish to express her approval at recent innovations and alterations carried out at West Wycombe Park'.

When Tom Corbett described the figure he had seen to Sir John Dashwood, his response was immediate; Oh, you've seen my mother. The description fits her exactly.' Perhaps she returns to a house that is familiar to her since the pictures, the tapestries and the furniture remain in the ownership of the Dashwood family who still live at West Wycombe Park.

In the National Trust village of West Wycombe there is an inn which has long been haunted by a White Lady' and perhaps by two other ghosts. When I was at the George and Dragon a few years ago the landlord, Barry James, regaled me with stories of ghostly manifestations regularly reported by staff and visitors to the eighteenth-century inn that replaced an older hostelry that may well have gone back to the fourteenth century. The yard, where so many stagecoaches have rattled in and come to stop beside the ancient mounting-stone, leads into a garden, a garden — pleasant enough in daylight — but which on dark nights becomes one of the haunting-places of the White Lady ghost.

The origin of this ghostly figure seems to be a sixteen-year-old servant girl who worked at the George and Dragon 200 years ago. A buxom, good-looking girl, with long golden hair, she was known as Sukie, although her real name was Susan. Young as she was, Sukie had no illusions when male heads turned as she passed; she was aware of her charms, some say she flaunted herself and certainly it amused her to play off one admirer against another. In particular three local lads all told her they were in love with her, but she thought she could do better and she enjoyed encouraging first one and then another of these ardent, lusty lads.

One day, according to tradition, a young gentleman came to the inn, an elegant and handsome stranger whose clothes and bearing told the serving girl that he was rich, and she quickly set out to catch his eye. Before long an expectant air of teasing and familiarity existed between the two, a form of banter that continued and grew each time the handsome stranger came to the inn for a meal.

Sukie never learned the name of the young gentleman who set her heart fluttering but she heard stories that he was a nobleman and this she seems to have believed, ignoring the dark hints that he might be a highwayman — a story perhaps originating in the imagination of her three local admirers who watched Sukie and the good-looking stranger become more and more friendly. Once the three local lads had been rivals; now they were comrades in a common cause and they hatched a plan that would humiliate the impressionable girl and remind her of her place in life.

They settled on their plan, and a few days later sent a message to Sukie, purporting to come from the mysterious stranger, asking her to meet him secretly in the caves nearby on a certain night when everyone was asleep. With beating heart Sukie read a postscript to the note: it asked her to wear a wedding dress! Hastily the eager Sukie altered a white dress, romantically dreaming of herself as a bride married to the son of some famous family. On the appointed night she waited until all was quiet and then slipped out of the inn and hastened to keep her rendezvous, dressed becomingly in a long, white dress.

She hurried along the tunnel and reached the cave, in accordance with the instructions she had received, expecting to run into the arms of her handsome young gentleman;

imagine her horror at finding instead the three local lads who were always pestering her. Now they stood there, grinning and laughing at her discomfort and disappointment, full of ale and nasty words and ugly taunts.

In her sudden anger and frustration Sukie, tears of unhappiness pouring down her cheeks, picked up the nearest lump of chalk and threw it at her tormentors. Still they only laughed and Sukie tried again, becoming more and more angry and occasionally more accurate with her missiles. After several had found their mark the laughter died away and the lads began to fight back. They pushed and pulled at Sukie, tearing her dress and eventually causing her to fall: as she did so she cracked her head against the jagged wall and fractured her skull.

The limp, crumpled and bleeding form sobered the three jokers, and, hoping she was merely stunned, they picked her up and carried her back to the inn. One version of the story says they used a secret passage, emerging inside the George and Dragon (some say in the vicinity of the priests' hiding-place), but at all events they apparently succeeded in laying her on her bed and sneaking home without being seen. Next morning Sukie s dead body was found in her room. Before long the ghost of Sukie in a white dress was seen in the George and Dragon and she is reported to have haunted the inn ever since.

In 1967 an American author described his experiences during a night he spent at the George and Dragon. He stopped on his way to Oxford where he was going to consult a college library. During the night he felt cold fingers touch his cheek. He switched on the light and the sensation disappeared, but when he turned the light off, the cold hand resumed its exploration of his face. After this had happened several times he saw an 'opaque and pearly white' shape near the bedroom door, a shape that seemed to grow into the shape of a female form that approached his bed. The room felt icy cold as he leapt out of bed and switched on the main bedroom light; it ws 3.15 in the morning and his room was utterly deserted.

The wife of a former landlord, Mrs Dorothy Boon, who did supervisory work at the inn following the death of her husband, saw the ghost in the haunted bedroom and at first she did not realize it was a ghost that she was looking at. Mrs Boon went to look for a young member of the staff who was supposed to be working in the kitchen.

Thinking that something must be wrong with the girl who slept in the staff quarters, Mrs Boon went to find her. As she reached the servant's room Mrs Boon opened the door and saw the figure of a young girl sitting on a stool gazing into the fireplace, her long golden hair falling down her back. She seemed utterly miserable but, before Mrs Boon could approach and ask her what the trouble was, the form simply disappeared.

During the course of a visit to the George and Dragon by members of the Ghost Club, a ghostly presence was distinctly felt by one member and another believed he caught a glimpse of the ghostly Sukie when he popped back into the room by himself. She may be a shy and elusive ghost but there seems little doubt that Sukie's ghost is still seen on occasions at this delightful inn.

There may be another murder connected with the George and Dragon. A somewhat vague story tells of a guest being murdered in one of the upstairs rooms many years ago, and in 1933 an article over the name of H. Harman appeared in the Journal of the Royal Society of Arts stating: 'It is the age-old staircase that is supposed to be haunted ... distinct footsteps have been heard coming down the stairs at night, reputed to be those of a man who, by tradition, was murdered in one of the rooms in the dim past.' Although no record of a murder has ever been discovered there is no doubt that ghostly footsteps are heard on the stairway, as loud and distinct as ever, and without anyone ever being found to be responsible.

A few years ago a guest at the inn who professed to have psychic powers said she had the overwhelming impression that the place was haunted, especially in the vicinity of the staircase. She said she had the feeling that there had been a terrible quarrel on the stairs, with tragic results. She was unaware of the story of a reputed murder at the time.

Finally the ghost of Sukie or that of the murdered man or possibly some other prankish spectre seems to delight in annoying the staff by moving articles and objects from their accustomed places. Nothing completely disappears but articles are repeatedly found to be missing and later found elsewhere, often in some unlikely place. But perhaps we are moving out of the realm of ghosts into that of misplaced humour or possibly the presence of a poltergeist or elemental personality.

Westwood Manor, Bradford-on-Avon, Wiltshire

A mellowed stone house in the beautifully situated village of Westwood, Westwood Manor dates from the fifteenth century and retains some Gothic windows. In the Middle Ages it belonged to the priory at Winchester and was eventually sold in 1861. Thereafter the house was altered by a succession of tenants and owners until it was bought by Mr E.G. Lister who restored it with knowledge and discretion to its earlier state. On his death he left the house and his collection of furniture to the National Trust.

My good friend and fellow Ghost-Clubber, Air Commodore R.C. Jonas, knew Mr Lister and visited Westwood Manor when he lived there. Lister said that there was one bedroom in the house that was undoubtedly haunted. On several occasions he had seen the ghostly form of a woman in that particular room. He had also heard unexplained footsteps.

He seemed to take the haunting very much for granted and simply a part of the house in which he lived.

I have talked with the present occupant, Mr Denys Sutton, editor of Apollo, 'the monthly magazine of the arts for connoisseurs and collectors', and he tells me that Westwood has two ghosts.

One upstairs bedroom is certainly haunted and the disturbances are believed to be connected with some rather fine hangings that came from haunted Littlecote. One of the ghost stories there concerns 'Wild' or 'Wicked' Will Darrell who is said to have murdered a new-born child. A midwife was bribed to deliver a young woman of a child in secret at Littlecote behind closed curtains; as soon as it was bom, the child was snatched away by Darrell and thrown into the fire where he held the infant down with his boot until it was quite dead. The midwife was blindfolded on her journey to and from the house and although she never saw the face of the man concerned, she managed to take a snippet of the curtain and to count the steps on the stairway.

On her deathbed the midwife told a magistrate the whole story and showed him the piece of material she had snipped from the curtains, and suspicion fell on Wild Will Darrell and Littlecote as the house. Darrell was arrested but the account of the trial is confused. What is certain is that Darrell had several mistresses, including his own sister, and any one may have been the unfortunate young mother of a few minutes only. The original bed went to America, I was told when I was there with a party of Ghost Club members, and the bed-hangings now at Littlecote are comparatively recent. It is part of the original bed-hangings that shielded the secret birth and the shocking murder that may now hang at Westwood.

Denys Sutton tells me that he sleeps in this bedroom and sometimes it is very eerie and sometimes he sleeps very badly.

There is little doubt that the room is haunted; two successive occupants to my certain knowledge having asserted that such is their considered opinion.

Some thirty years ago Denys Sutton entertained to luncheon at Westwood a Danish ballet company and the large party included the Danish Ambassador and his wife. As soon as the wife of the Ambassador entered the haunted bedroom she stopped short and said she knew there was a ghost in the room. This was just one instance of a psychically sensitive person being immediately aware of the unusual atmosphere in this one bedroom at Westwood without knowing anything about what had been experienced there or any of the stories connected with the place.

Denys Sutton also tells me there is reputed to be a headless ghost at the house; a fearsome, silent figure that wanders round the house and was certainly seen during the time of Mr Sutton's predecessor; perhaps the presence of such a figure, either visible or invisible, has resulted in the heightened expectant feeling that sometimes pervades Westwood, an atmosphere that at times is almost unbearable to some people. Denys Sutton tells me that when his children were at Westwood they were sometimes scared stiff.

Westwood Manor is a treasure of a house, full of the past, and sometimes positively pulsating with psychic activity.

Wicken Fen, Cambridgeshire

The 700 acres that comprise Wicken Fen are almost all that remains undrained of the once extensive fens of the Great Level; a vast and untamed area that is almost unchanged since the days of Hereward the Wake; primitive and mysterious, where night-winds whisper through the tall reeds and the bittern booms his ghostly love song under the cold stars of spring.

In this strangely quiet atmosphere it is easy to imagine that the place is haunted; that the sounds that come from all sides in the gathering dusk may not be made by some mammal or water bird scampering among the rare plants and flowers. It is a place where the past has been preserved to such an extent that those who are sensitive to such things have no doubt that something of those who once roamed these hidden stretches of land returns from time to time. All around there are stories of ghostly Roman soldiers; of sounds of long-forgotten battles; of witchcraft and strange forms, some lifesize and some diminutive, that disappear when they are approached; of black dogs that vanish equally inexplicably....

Old Tom Fuller, whose family have lived at Wicken for centuries, has told me of incidents when his dogs have suddenly attacked 'something' invisible; the dogs, their hackles rising, springing into the air again and again to drive off some unseen adversary. Perhaps these notoriously sensitive creatures sense or see something or someone connected with some of the last fighting stands of the native Britons in this area.

Once, Tom s grandfather, Joseph Fuller, encountered a vague ghostly form one evening as he was driving home at dusk. He struck at it with his whip which went clean through the strange form and had no effect whatever! Joseph Fuller hurried on home, leaving whatever it was to disappear into the blackness of Wicken Fen.

Strange lights have been encountered here and while some of them are certainly 'ignis fatuus' or marsh gas, such an explanation is difficult to reconcile with some witnesses' experiences of what have been called 'Jack-o'-Lanterns', 'Will-o'-the-Wisps', 'Hob-o'-Lanterns' or, more ominously, 'The Lantern Man'.

These 'Lantern Men' were commonly supposed to be dangerous to life. The late Lady Cranworth's coachman had no doubt about such things, although he always laughed to scorn stories of ghosts. But 'the Lantern Men' were something different; he claimed to have seen them scores of times and he said they would alway run towards a whistle.

One old fisherman used to tell of a 'Lantern Man' following him after he had whistled and increasing speed as he ran and how he finally threw himself flat on his face and then the 'Lantern Man' passed over him. A common belief was that such lights were evil spirits that would attack a man on sight; another legend has it that the light, instead of attacking, sought to lead one to a watery and ghastly grave, deep in the smelly Fen.

There are many stories of encounters with the ghosts of Roman soldiers hereabouts; silent, ominous figures that loom up out of nowhere and quickly disappear into the dark shadows from which they have emerged; of visitors seeing, across some dark stretch of water, an enormous black dog, padding silently along and disappearing into the mists.

Of the many stories of ghostly witches seen at Wicken perhaps the best known is a witch with a Fen name that dates from Norman times. James Wentworth Day once told me he had spoken to a woman whose husband had been bewitched by such a ghost. The unfortunate man had fallen ill and the doctors didn't know what was wrong with him. When the witch woman called at the house, she was invited to take a seat in a chair where a Bible had been hidden underneath the cushions. She sprang away from the chair as if it were red hot. As she left the brave wife stuck a hat pin into the old woman and when she slammed the door she shouted: You can't do any more harm here — I've drawn your blood.' And, it is said, her husband soon mended and was well again. This ghostly witch is still to be encountered, if reports are to be believed, along the quiet pathways of Wicken Fen.

Windermere, Cumbria

The National Trust owns many acres of land here including the woodland stretching from Wray Castle to near haunted Ferry Nab. Local legends tell of a spectral white horse; a phantom boat 'with terrible sights aboard'; and an unearthly moaning sound that echoes from the lake and may or may not have a paranormal origin. But the best known ghost is said to date from the days of the Reformation and was documented and written up more than a century ago.

It was a dark and stormy night, so goes the story, when a party of travellers who had been making merry at a nearby tavern, looked for a ferryboat to take them across the lake, but the quiet and sober boatman had just heard, he thought, a cry for help from the lake and he had left in his boat, wild and dark as the night was.

Eventually he returned and the merrymakers gathered on the shore to see whom he would bring back but he returned alone, his eyes wild with terror, his lips closed by the unspeakable horror he had seen. They could get no sense out of him and he was put to bed. Next morning he had a fever and in a few days he was dead without ever saying what he had seen out on the lake when he had answered a call.

For many months afterwards there were strange shouts and screams and howling noises in the vicinity of Ferry Nab and it became so widely believed that there was something weird out on the lake at night that no boatman would attend a call after dark.

At last a monk was prevailed upon to visit Nab and exorcise the place and the waters of the lake. He arrived one Christmas morning, assembled all the local people and performed in their presence a service of exorcism and curtailment that would forever confine the ghost to the quarry in the wood behind the ferry, a ghost that became known as the Crier of Claife. Another version of the story says the holy monk blessed the lake and took from it some terrible form that, in the presence of the inhabitants, he conveyed with great difficulty to the quarry and there laid the ghost. Be that as it may, there are few local people who venture there after dark and within living memory it is said that during a fox-hunt the hounds, eagerly on the trail one moment, came to a full stop the next and would not pass the place. And then there is the schoolmaster from Colthouse who laughed at the story of the Ghost Crier and set out one night to balk the ghost. He was never seen again.

Windsor Castle, Berkshire

Windsor Castle is full of ghosts', states one guide to British ghosts, and certainly this royal palace — the largest inhabited castle in the world — originally built by William the Conqueror and today the resting-place of many English sovereigns, is reputed to harbour at least five royal ghosts in addition to a cluster of unrecognized phantoms.

The cloisters near the Deanery are said to be haunted by the ghost of Henry VIII, whose bulky form has been reported hereabouts, and in the passages ghostly groans and the sound of dragging footsteps have been heard, almost like someone shuffling along suffering from gout. This easily recognised ghost was also reportedly seen as recently as 1977 by two soldiers on the battlements; as they watched, the figure faded into a wall. The ghost of Queen Anne Boleyn is said to have been seen at a window in the Dean's Cloister and her ghost has also been seen, according to an American parapsychologist, 'walking along the eastern parapet'.

The Long Walk, Windsor Castle - an eerie place that has been known to cause night sentries to think that some of the marble statuary moves.

The Horseshoe Cloisters, Windsor Castle, scene of the appearance of a ghostly horse and groom.

The Dean's Cloisters
at Windsor Castle,
which are said to be
haunted by the ghost
of Henry VIII.

Ghostly footsteps were heard by Hector Bolitho, the royal biographer, when he lived at the old Deanery. 'I used to hear them at night, walking quickly past my bedroom door,' he told me. Oddly, there were only three steps, but the unseen ghost seemed to take four steps down before resuming his hurried pace but later I discovered that the flooring in this part of the old house had been raised from its early level and in the process one step had been eliminated. Some forty years ago a ghostly little boy was often seen in one of the bedrooms here. 'I don't want to go riding today,' he always seems to say before suddenly vanishing.

The ghost of Charles I is reputed to revisit the Canon's House which stands in the castle grounds. Those who have seen the apparition of this tragic king have all mentioned that the face with its melancholy features is remarkably like the famous Van Dyck portrait of the monarch.

Perhaps the most persistent legend of a ghost at Windsor Castle is that concerning Elizabeth I who is said to haunt the Royal Library (which is not open to the public). In Tudor days this would have been part of the State Apartments. There was considerable discussion of the matter in 1897 when the experience of an officer of the Guard, one Lieutenant Carr Glynn, appeared in print. In the February of that year of Queen Victoria's Diamond Jubilee Lieutenant Glynn availed himself of the privilege of visiting the Royal Library. The story is well-authenticated from contemporary records and tells of Glynn sitting on a chair, reading, on the east side of the library when he became aware of someone passing into the inner library. He heard the tap tap of high heels on bare boards and when he looked up he saw a female figure in black with black lace on her head which fell to her shoulders.

A few steps led up into a gallery built by Elizabeth I as a picture gallery (it is now filled with books) and Glynn saw the lady in black pass him, enter the gallery, and after traversing it a little way, turn sharply to the right and disappear into a bay from which, in former times, the great Queen used to descend by a staircase to the terrace that looked out over the Thames valley. It was four o'clock in the afternoon, just before closing time, and when the attendant came to close the library, Lieutenant Glynn asked about the lady who was at work in the inner room. 'There is no one but yourself here at present,' the attendant replied. 'But I have just seen her walk into the inner room,' insisted Glynn. The attendant then went to see for himself, found no one and returned. 'She must have gone out of a door in the corner,' commented Glynn, pointing to the bay. But there is no door there,' replied the attendant, 'although there was one many years ago.'

Puzzled by the sudden disappearance of the lady in black lace Lieutenant Glynn departed, little thinking that he was perhaps the first man to have seen the ghost of Elizabeth I for many years. The attendant reported the occurrence to the Librarian, Dr Holmes, who at once sent for Glynn and asked for a description of the figure he had seen. When he had been given it, the Librarian said; It is the same. You have seen the apparition of Queen Elizabeth.'

Glynn then learned that the same ghostly figure had been seen many times in the past and the Empress Frederick, Queen Victoria's eldest daughter, is only one who claimed to see the apparition in the same place, as a child. The Librarian had been familiar with the story for twenty-seven years and had sometimes sat late himself waiting to see the ghost but he had never done so.

Another well-authenticated ghost at the castle is that of George III — a story recounted by Sir Owen Morshead, a later Royal Librarian, in his erudite book on Windsor Castle. During his last years the King was confined to a set of rooms below the Royal Library. To all intents and purposes he was mad but today he is thought to have suffered from the obscure disease called porphyria. These gloomy rooms overlooked the north terrace and sometimes the sounds of the approach of the Palace Guards would bring the King back to normality temporarily and he would stand at the window and watch them pass below, raising his hand in acknowledgment of the Guard's command, Eyes Right'.

The King died at the castle on 29 January 1820 and, while his body lay in state in another part of the castle, the routine changing of the Guard took place as usual and as they passed the King's old room, the commander automatically looked up and, to his surprise, saw the bearded figure he knew so well. The well-trained Guards followed his command 'Eyes Right' and the figure at the window made the customary response. The officer concerned was William Knollys, later Comptroller to the young Prince of Wales, later Edward VII. Sir William lived to a great age and related the story to the Prince's second son who was to become George V. There are also stories of the ghostly sounds of George III in other parts of the castle, muttering, 'What, what?' a familiar phrase of the King.

Some of the houses in the Lower Ward have peaceful echoes of former inmates and Angus Macnaghten, the Berkshire historian, told me when he gave a talk at the Ghost Club that his mother once met one of the Military Knights who occupy these houses and he told her of a conversation he had had with an old gentleman soon after he moved into the house. The old man said he had lived there for many years and he wished the new inhabitant similar happiness — then he vanished.

Angus Macnaghten obtained one first-hand account of a ghost at Windsor Castle. This came from a man who as a boy lived in one of the houses in the Horseshoe Cloisters. One day, when he was washing his hands at the kitchen sink, he suddenly saw a man, leading a horse, cross the room and vanish into the wall. A maid, who was in the kitchen at the same time, also saw the man and the horse but neither was believed by the rest of the family when they described what they had seen. Some time later, when repairs were being undertaken in the kitchen area, a large underground stable was found behind the wall into which the horse and groom had disappeared.

The lower ward of the castle has long had a tradition of ghostly footsteps, especially on the stairway in the Mary Tudor Tower, and Miss Kavanagh, who lived there for many years when her father General Sir Charles Kavanagh was Governor of the Military Knights, told Angus Macnaghten that she often heard footsteps coming up the stairs towards her room, situated at the top of the house. She later read an old book about Windsor Castle and there learned that earlier inhabitants of the Tudor Tower had similar experiences. A strange phenomenon in this part of the castle which worried guests from time to time was the distinct impression that a wall between two bedrooms seemed to move in the night.

Sir George Villiers, father of the ambitious Duke of Buckingham and friend of Charles I, apparently appeared to an officer resident at the castle who woke one night to see a man of very venerable aspect' in the room; a figure who drew the curtains and then fixed his eyes upon the startled officer — and disappeared.

The long walk, an eerie place at the best of times, has been known to cause night sentries to think that some of the marble statuary moves and it is here that the ghost of the legendary Herne the Hunter is reputed to walk; but one ghostly manifestation here is worthy of serious consideration. In 1927 a young guardsman shot himself while on duty in the long walk and a few weeks later Sergeant S. Leake was detailed for similar duty. Just after 2.00 a.m. he was surprised to meet a guardsman marching towards him. Looking at the features below the man's bearskin cap, he recognized the guardsman who had shot himself! The next moment the ghostly guardsman had completely vanished. Later, noticing some agitation in the guard who had relieved him, Sergeant Leake asked what had happened and learned that the other guardsman had had an identical experience: both men had seen the same ghost at different times! Talking to my friend Dennis Bardens about the experience, ex-Sergeant Leake said that at the time he could feel his hair standing on end on his neck and added: 'It still does when I think about it more than forty years later.'

The Norman Tower, adjoining the Round Tower, is another part of Windsor Castle that is haunted. A room that in the past was used as a prison seems to be haunted by the harmless ghost of an unknown man. Children playing in the room have seen him but have never been frightened and other people, living in the North Tower, have felt someone invisible brush past them in one particular passage. In 1983 a resident at the castle wrote to me to say she had 'had many very strange experiences at the castle' and in 1984 John Howden of Solihull related to me a couple of experiences that he had at Windsor Castle.

During the early 1970s he was in the Scots Guards and stationed at Windsor Barracks. He took part in ceremonial occasions at Windsor Castle and carried out many other duties there by day and by night. One Saturday in June he had performed his duties at different posts throughout the castle complex and again went on duty at eight o'clock in the evening to a position at the rear of the castle, situated in fact within the private quarters of the castle, facing the gardens and the statues, well away from anywhere frequented by the public. This particular post was known by all the Guardsmen to have a reputation for being haunted or uncanny, inasmuch as the twelve statues standing in the gardens were invariably counted as thirteen at night-time! And this John Howden experienced himself although how it happened he has no idea, but it was a fact and any Guardsman at Windsor at that time would confirm this strange phenomenon.

On this particular evening, after carrying out a number of patrols in front of the castle and finding everything very quiet, he eventually returned to his sentry-box to have a rest. He had by then been on duty perhaps forty-five minutes and it was beginning to get dark, although it was a warm evening with a slight breeze blowing up that caused the leaves around his sentry-box to rustle and blow about.

He was standing and admiring the view of the gardens in the light of dusk on a summer night when he became aware of a movement on the right-hand side of his sentry-box. He looked and saw what appeared to be a tall figure or dark shape about thirty-five yards away from him. He noticed that it walked very slowly and as it came nearer he could make out that the form was wearing a cape which he could see blowing slightly in the breeze. He left his sentry-box and faced the figure, raising his rifle and bayonet and adopting the 'on guard' position. He called: 'Halt! Who goes there?', and when there was no reply, he again challenged the figure. This time it stopped and seemed to acknowledge his challenge by raising a hand in greeting. By now it was quite close and somewhat to his surprise he saw that it was a policeman; he could see the police helmet and although the badge was black he could make out the black chain on the man's cape.

He beckoned the stranger forward and as he came closer the figure spoke, remarking on the pleasant evening, saying it was just the night for a walk and adding that it had been a long time since he had done that particular patrol.

Guardsman Howden replied and asked the policeman whether he was authorized to patrol the private quarters of the castle, meaning the gardens, as he had never seen him there before. The policeman assured the soldier that it used to be one of his regular patrols some time back and added that he had always enjoyed the quiet beauty of the gardens. The sentry then noticed that the policeman wore his P.C. number on the collar of his tunic, which was sticking out above his cape; that seemed rather odd as he knew that present-day policemen wear their numbers on their tunic shoulders. At the same time he noticed that the whole uniform looked old-fashioned and he was on the point of remarking on the subject when the policeman spoke again, asking the soldier whether he would like a cigarette.

Howden replied in the negative and he was then asked whether he had any objection to the policeman smoking; again he replied in the negative. The policeman then lifted his cape up to reach for his cigarettes, taking them out of the breast pocket of his uniform, and the soldier then noticed a black leather belt around the tunic with the buckle shaped like a twisted snake. The policeman lit his cigarette and stood beside the sentry-box, smoking it, allowing the Guardsman to take a good look at the figure. He seemed to be very relaxed, aged perhaps forty-five to fifty, five feet nine inches in height and weighing around thirteen stone. John Howden then said, by way of conversation, that he expected he would see the man again but all the policeman did in reply was to smile and nod his head.

The whole encounter must have lasted several minutes when all of a sudden the policeman said he had to go, mumbled 'goodnight' and disappeared quickly around the corner and out of sight. The Guardsman was rather startled by the sudden departure of the figure; it all happened so quickly, one minute he was there, the next minute he had gone. Then the soldier hurried to the corner and looked for the retreating policeman but there was no sign of him; in a couple of seconds he had completely vanished. John Howden returned to his sentry-box and stood there thinking it was all rather weird and certainly it was odd to suddenly disappear as he had.

He patrolled a few more times along the front of the castle, hoping to catch sight of the policeman again but he did not do so and then he returned to his sentry-box just as a patrol came round. He informed the N.C.O. in charge of what he had encountered, adding that the patrol must have passed the policeman on the battlement pathway that they had just come along; but he was assured that they had not seen anyone or passed anyone, and he was to report the incident at the Guardroom on completing his duty. This Howden did and his report was logged accordingly, but he was then told that what he had seen and spoken to was the ghost of a policeman who died some thirty to forty years previously, after a heart attack on that particular part of the castle grounds; a ghost that had been encountered many times previously.

Windsor Castle has indeed many ghosts and I don't think anybody was particularly impressed by a Buckingham Palace spokesman who has been quoted as saying: 'We have never heard of a ghost at Windsor Castle.'

The Winnats, Castleton, Derbyshire

Towering Mam Tor or Shivering Mountain, so-called because of its sliding strata of grit and shale — overlooks Winnats Pass, with its impressive limestone sides; both 'nestle snugly in the heart of Peakland, in the gentle loveliness of the Hope Valley,' as Arthur Mee puts it. Castleton itself has wonderful caves and one, a magnificent natural arch that used to be known as the Devil's Hole, rises to some twenty metres in the wooded face of the cliff. Winding passages lead into chamber after chamber, gallery after gallery, lofty hall after lofty hall, for a mile or more into the heart of the hill, while the sound of hidden waters add to the indescribable weirdness of the place.

But to return to the Winnats: in this old, old place, where the rocks are riddled with caves and the earth with worn-out mines, where men in the dawn of history had a hill-fort, the ghosts date from a comparatively recent tragedy. The name of this wild, romantic gorge, the Winnats or Wind Gates, aptly describes the fury of the winds that haunt this winding mile. Nor is the wind all that may be encountered here.

For nearly a quarter of a century, in the middle of the eighteenth century, Peak Forest was the Gretna Green of England, where anyone could be married immediately, at any time of day or night, and runaway couples came from far and wide.

Such a couple were Allan and Clara; youngsters who were deeply in love, but Clara was the daughter of a wealthy landlord and Allan a poor lad from a humble family. Clara's father would not hear of such a match and even encouraged Clara's brother to chase Allan away, threatening him with a shotgun if he was seen near Clara again.

The young lovers made their secret plans and one dark night they mounted two horses and set off for Peak Forest and happiness. On the way they stayed at a village inn where Clara had a nightmare: during their journey they had entered an awesome dale and when partly through they had been attacked and robbed and Allan had been murdered before her eyes; when the attackers came towards her, Clara woke up screaming....

Allan tried to comfort and soothe her for the dream had seemed so real and lifelike that she had misgivings about continuing their journey together. Eventually Allan did reassure her and next day they set out for Castleton. Here too they stayed the night at an inn where five miners noticed their neat and apparently comfortable appearance; these men soon became the worse for drink and the landlord turned them out of the inn. Sore at the treatment they had received, full of liquor, and bitter at life in general, they decided to set upon the prosperous pair when they left the inn next day and rob them of any money they possessed.

The miners had overheard the young couple asking for directions and knew their way led through Winnats Pass. They made their own way there and picked the spot for the attack.

As they entered the Pass, Clara became very apprehensive for the setting greatly resembled her dream but Allan laughed her fears away and together they proceeded into Winnats Pass. About halfway through the five men leapt from their hiding-places and within minutes the young couple were dragged from their horses, overpowered, and as Clara muttered between her tears, 'My dream, my dream ...' they were manhandled into a nearby shed and, after repeated threats, Allan handed over all the money in their possession, about £200.

Leaving the frightened couple to comfort themselves as best they could, the rough miners went outside to discuss what to do next, for they could hardly let the young people go and already they had cast lustful eyes at the youthful Clara. When the miners returned both Allan and Clara pleaded for each other's lives but the men stared silently at them and made no attempt to let either of them escape from the hut alive. Allan could stand the tension no longer and he flew into the men with fists flying, frustration and anger lending him the strength of three men, but he was soon overpowered by his five adversaries and one of the miners struck Allan a vicious blow on the head with a pickaxe. Without a sound Allan slumped lifeless to the floor at Clara's feet.

Unable to believe her eyes, Clara sobbed quietly, but was too stunned and full of sorrow to offer much resistance when the husky miners tore the clothes from her body and had their way with her. One by one they abused her and then left her to her sadness. After a hurried conference they came to the only possible decision, returned to the shed and ignoring poor Clara's sobs and pleadings, they struck the defenceless girl time after time until her battered and lifeless body lay beside that of her beloved Allan.

The miners, silent now as they realized the terrible things they had done, left the hut as darkness fell and resolved to return to bury the bodies at dead of night in some secret place. At midnight return they did, but as they approached the hut they were astonished to hear a noise coming from within the shed and, frightened out of their wits, they fled. Next night the same thing happened and after they had again run away, they stood and listened to the sounds of screaming, shouting, dull thuds and sobbing emanating from the empty and dark hut. The following night, fortified by drink and telling themselves no living thing that could harm them could possibly be inside the hut, they did manage to return, wrap the bodies in sacks, and bury them. Dividing the spoils, they separated, glad to see the back of Winnats Pass.

Four days later the horses that the young people had been riding were found wandering some miles away. A search revealed no trace of the couple and the affair would probably have soon been forgotten had it not been for stories of strange happenings that began to filter out of Winnats Pass. Travellers would tell of odd and frightening noises, thuds, faints screams, an ominous dragging sound, that seemed to be in the air around them when they were halfway through the Pass. Some maintained that they had glimpsed a pair of youngsters, desperately trying to scramble up the sheer cliffs bordering the Pass or slipping hurriedly, hand in hand, round a corner where they disappeared.

One Sunday morning one of the murdering miners' daughters appeared at church wearing an expensive dress —

could it have once belonged to Clara? Tongues began to wag, and although the five men were never brought to justice all of them lived in misery for the rest of their lives. One was dead within a year, but he revealed the story of the murders on his deathbed, swearing his confidant to silence. A second man, walking near the scene of the crime, saw something that so terrified him that he climbed up to a buttress to get away from it and fell to his death. A third hanged himself. The fourth found himself in Winnats Pass one day, close to the scene of the murders, and he too saw something that stopped him in his tracks; a boulder rumbled down from high up the cliff-side, hit him squarely on the head and he dropped dead. Finally, the fifth man became almost insane from constantly remembering the murders; more than once he tried to commit suicide but he never managed it and eventually died, of natural causes but miserable, babbling out the whole awful story.

Some ten years passed before some workers, digging in a mine shaft, came across two skeletons which were believed to be those of the young lovers, Man and Clara. But still there are occasional reports of odd and unexplained noises in Winnats Pass; the sounds of crying, screams, heavy panting sounds, dull thuds, shouting and that strangely disturbing dragging noise, while the dark figures of two young people, hand in hand, are still reportedly seen from time to time, scrambling up the cliffs at the side of the Pass or running away into the distance. This awe-inspiring place deserves to be haunted and haunted it assuredly is.

Woburn Abbey, Woburn, Bedfordshire

My first meeting with the thirteenth Duke of Bedford was at Broadcasting House where we had both just broadcast; the second was at an Authors of the Year party at the Martini Terrace overlooking Trafalgar Square; and the third, at his kind invitation, was when I took a party of Ghost Club members to visit his home, Woburn Abbey. He had told me, as he had autographed a copy of his autobiography, A Silver-Plated Spoon, for me, that Woburn had a number of ghosts but some of them were in the private apartments and portions of the grounds not open to the public — but he would gladly show all the haunted areas to Ghost Club members.

At Woburn we were met by the Duke and Duchess and some of the family and in a delightfully informal way they told us of the many unexplained happenings at beautiful and dignified Woburn Abbey, home of the Dukes of Bedford for over three centuries and today housing one of the most important private art collections in the world.

The Duke had told me that his introduction to psychic matters came when he was a young man and had attended a party given by Lord Tredegar, 'a very odd man who was much interested in black magic and the supernatural'. At night, in one of the enormous rooms of his house in Wales, with an owl flying around the room (!), Lord Tredegar would don cabalistic garb and 'tell fortunes and read characters'. The strange thing was that as soon as he began the temperature in the room suddenly dropped; everyone present agreed about this, and although the Duke was situated in front of a huge and roaring fire, he found himself shivering. He never forgot that visit to Wales and he and his family always accepted the possibility of ghosts at Woburn.

One of the most obvious manifestations — witnessed by all the family and a number of other people — was the persistent and inveterate door-opening phenomena that, the Duke told us, had eventually forced him and his family out of what had once been their television room. Times without number a door handle would turn and the door would open and then, after a pause, just long enough it seemed for someone to walk the length of the room, the door at the opposite end of the room would open by itself. New locks were fitted and the doors were kept locked but still they opened by themselves; the doors were re-hung so that they opened differently — but still they opened by themselves. In the end the wing was reconstructed and now there is an open passage where the doors of the television room used to be. 'But the ghost simply turned its attention to other doors,' went on the Duke, and he recounted how his son Francis, his wife, the servants and various visitors, including their friend Paul Getty, had all experienced the opening by themselves of bedroom doors at Woburn Abbey.

Paul Getty often visited Woburn at one period and the Duchess told us that he had slept in practically every bedroom; in three particular ones he had heard footsteps padding round the room although he had seen nothing. Other people had heard the same thing in the same rooms. One morning the Duchess came upon Paul Getty jumping up and down in the east corridor where the main guest bedrooms are situated. Penelope Kitson, the interior designer, was also staying at Woburn at the time and she had complained that the doors of her bedroom had opened by themselves again and again during the night. Practical Paul Getty was trying to see whether the weight of anyone walking along the corridor outside would cause the doors to open; needless to say his experiment was unsuccessful and the door-opening continued.

We were shown the Duke's beautifully proportioned bedroom and he related some of the other unexplained incidents that he and the Duchess had experienced: some very unpleasant and yet not really frightening happenings — except for the occasional touchings on the face, almost like a wet hand, that they had both felt on several occasions. Although nothing was seen here there was almost certainly an atmosphere in this part of the house, a restlessness and not altogether pleasant feeling. A similar atmosphere pervaded the Wood Library and an office and in both the Duke told us he found difficulty in concentrating, yet he continued to use them.

Clairvoyant Tom Corbett had the feeling that, long ago, someone had been shut up against their will in this part of the house, resulting in the persistent door-opening. What happened there, he said, had left an atmosphere so strong that it could influence people and it was an unpleasant atmosphere resulting from an unpleasant happening.

Later we visited the only place in the 3000-acre grounds that is barred to the public; an isolated little summer house on the west side of the park which the Duke said was an overwhelmingly unhappy place and definitely haunted. Its dark and overgrown garden is surrounded by a tall wooden fence and the gate is kept locked. The Duke's grandmother, 'the flying Duchess' as she came to be called, loved the isolation of this summer house, especially toward the end of her increasingly unhappy life and soon she took off in her Gypsy aeroplane from Woburn on the flight from which she never returned .... The Duke told us he felt very strongly that her ghost haunted the summer house: 'I feel her presence very strongly every time I come here,' he said. 'We have a room devoted to her memory at the house, but for me she is here where she used to escape from the unhappiness she felt in the house and nearly every afternoon she would come here and sit and think and be alone and write her diary.'

We saw the fairly recent additions to the house, rooms that have been added in the space along the corridor where there had once been enormous cupboards for storing various items including the collection of fancy clothes that had been used for masquerades and balls in the old days. The Duchess told us that in the time of the seventh Duke a manservant was murdered in the Masquerade Room and his body hidden in one of the cupboards before it was pushed out of a window, dragged to the lake and thrown in. It is the ghost of this murdered manservant who is supposed to haunt this part of Woburn to this day.

More than once the Duchess has felt the presence of ghostly forms in the corridor on the first floor, and her dogs have reacted to something invisible to her; crouching against the wall with their tails tucked between their legs and howling pitifully.

In the north wing we visited a room in the staff quarters that has long had the reputation of being haunted and, when she found that nobody was willing to sleep there, the Duchess used the room for storing some laundry-baskets filled with things she had brought over from France. One day she was sorting through the things when suddenly the dogs began howling and trembling with fear. Suddenly the door opened by itself she felt an overwhelming sense of 'something' having entered the room — then it felt very cold and she left the room.

At one time excavation was taking place under the Abbey to provide an exit staircase for visitors and one evening everyone had left except for one of the cleaning ladies who was sweeping the floor ready for the next day's work. After about ten minutes she came out in a very frightened condition, saying she had seen a monk walking about down there. Everyone laughed and one of the men went down to lock up. Two minutes later he returned, white and shaken, saying he too had distinctly seen the figure of a monk down there. Oddly enough the digging had taken place in what had once been the monks' burial ground and some of the ancient bones were unearthed.

More recently there have been reports of a ghostly gentleman in a top hat in the Antique Centre at Woburn. Several visitors and some members of the staff have reported encountering the figure on the second floor. The figure always

Woburn Abbey, where
the Duke of Bedford
reconstructed a wing to
cure inexplicable door-
opening and closing.
Now other doors open
by themselves.

seems to be seen in the same place, formerly a walled room that was only disclosed when the Centre was opened. The Duchess told us that no one seems to know the story of the room but it was once occupied by the head groom and it seems likely that a top hat would have been part of his uniform.

We visited the beautiful sculpture gallery where at least ten women on different occasions have reported being touched by an invisible hand; and here too several guests at a dinner in this room asked about the monk who seemed to be lurking between the entrance pillars before gliding through a closed door.

Up on the second floor the Duchess showed us her personal bathroom where, according to one 'expert in psychic matters', there were no less than nine ghosts; but the Duchess has yet to see one!

As we left the mellow, brooding house that is Woburn Abbey, the Duke told us that he hated the atmosphere in some parts, but what could he do? 'One day', he said, 'my wife and I are going to get right away from here; somewhere we can live in peace; and leave the ghosts to get on with it.' It's nice to think that before long he did just that. But there is no doubt that the ghosts remain. As the Duchess told us: 'Ghosts are quite frequent and mostly friendly at Woburn ... when I first came I did not believe in them ... now I have to believe in ghosts.'

The carved mermaid in Zennor Church, Cornwall; scene of the best-known mermaid story in Britain.

Z

Zennor, Cornwall

The site of the best-known mermaid story in Britain: at Zennor a mermaid seemingly changed into a handsomely dressed woman. At Pendour Cove (overlooked by National Trust property) a ghost voice was heard singing from the sea, wafting up the rugged headland where granite and bluestone cliffs rise 350 feet out of the Atlantic.

There are several versions of the story, immortalized by a carved mermaid on a bench-end in Zennor Church, but it is said that one day the vicar was strolling along the beach when he came across a mermaid, singing softly to herself. Struck by her beautiful voice and modest bearing he invited her to attend his church next Sunday. She duly appeared and after that first time a strange, gentle and well-dressed woman attended service each Sunday for many years in Zennor Church. She always sat demurely at the back of the church so that her dampness would not inconvenience others (!).

As time passed it was noticed that she never appeared to age and she captivated successive generations of Zennor men with her quiet beauty and exquisite voice. From time to time she would be followed but always she would disappear from view amid the dour grey hills in sight of the sea and no one knew where she lived; in any case there was a mysterious air about her that discouraged curiosity.

One day she was noticed by a handsome young man named Matthew (or Mathey) Trehella (or Trewella). Some say he was the local squire's son, others that he was the son of the churchwarden, others again that he was a chorister, but all agree that his was the finest male voice in the church. At all events they were each enchanted by the other's voice and they met and fell in love.

One Sunday, after service, the couple left the church together, set off towards the beach, and were never seen again although for many years afterwards the sound of sweet singing could be heard in Pendour Cove.

Years later a fishing skipper dropped anchor off Pendour Cove and was surprised to hear a sweet and seductive voice hailing him. When he leaned over the side of the boat he was astonished to see a mermaid who popped her head out of the water to complain that he had dropped anchor across the entrance to her cave and until it was moved she could not reach her lover Matthew. The skipper obligingly weighed anchor and moved his boat.

When the folk of Zennor heard this they knew that the strange damp lady with the beautiful voice had really been a mermaid who had enticed the young man to her home beneath the waters; and to commemorate her they carved her image in holy oak for a pew in their church, albeit somewhat unflatteringly with waist-length hair and a scaly tail, holding a mirror and comb. She is also depicted on the dial of the clock.

Nearby, a rock formation known as Witch's Rock, or Giant's Rock is reputedly endowed with the power of transferring to anyone the powers of a witch; anyone that is who climbs the rock nine times at midnight. Others say that simply touching the stone nine times at midnight on Midsummer Eve will serve as insurance against misfortune. It does seem certain that hereabouts witches met on Midsummer Eve's long ago and it is said that the last true Zennor witch died in the eighteenth century although even today there are casters of spells in the area.

SELECT BIBLIOGRAPHY

ABBOTT, Geoffrey
Ghosts of the Tower of London - Heinemann 1980
ALEXANDER, Marc
Enchanted Britain - Arthur Barker, 1981
Haunted Castles - Frederick Muller, 1973
Haunted Churches and Abbeys of Britain - Arthur Barker, 1978
Haunted Inns - Frederick Muller, 1973
Phantom Britain - Frederick Muller, 1975
ATKINS, Meg Elizabeth
Haunted Warwickshire - Robert Hale, 1981
BROOKS. J.A.
Ghosts and Witches of the Cotswolds - Jarrold, 1981
BROWN, Raymond Lamont
Phantoms of the Sea - Patrick Stephens, 1972
BYRD, Elizabeth
A Strange and Seeing Time - Robert Hale, 1971
CAMPBELL, John L,, and HALL, Trevor, H.
Strange Things - Routledge & Kegan Paul, 1968
CHRISTIAN, Roy
Ghosts and Legends - David & Charles, 1972
COLBOURNE, Maurice
The Real Bernard Shaw - Dent, 1950
COXE, Antony D. Hippisley
Haunted Britain - Hutcheson, 1972
DANIEL, Clarence
Ghosts of Derbyshire - Dalesman, 1977
D'AUVERGNE, Edward B.
The English Castles - T. Werner Laurie, n.d.
DAY, James Wentworth
Essex Ghosts - Spurbooks, 1973
Ghosts and Witches - Batsford, 1954
In Search of Ghosts - Frederick Muller, 1969
DEANE, Tony, and SHAW, Tony
The Folklore of Cornwall - Batsford. 1975
EYRE, Kathleen
Lancashire Ghosts - Dalesman, 1976
FEA, Allan
Rooms of Mystery and Romance - Hutchinson, 1931

FORTESCUE, S.E.D.
People and Places, Great and Little - Bookham published privately 1978
FOWLER, P.J., (editor)
Recent Work in Rural Archaeology - Moonraker, 1975
GRAY, Affleck
The Big Grey Man of Ben MacDhui - Impulse Books 1970
GREEN, Andrew
Ghosts in the South East - David & Charles, 1976
Ghosts of Today - Kaye & Ward, 1980
Our Haunted Kingdom - Wolfe, 1973
Phantom Ladies - Bailey Bros and Swinfen, 1977
GRIGSON, Geoffrey
The Shell Country Book - Pheonix House, 1962
HALLAM, Jack
Ghosts of London - Wolfe, 1975
Ghosts of the North - David & Charles, 1976
The Ghosts' Who's Who - David & Charles. 1977
HARPER, Charles G.
Haunted Houses - Chapman & Hall, 1907
HARRIS, John
The Ghost Hunter's Road Book - Frederick Muller, 1968
HOLE, Christina
Haunted England - Batsford, 1950 HOPKINS. R. Thurston
Ghosts Over England - Meridan Books, 1953
HUNT, Peter, (editor)
The Shell Gardens Book - Phoenix House. 1964
JACKSON, A.W.
The Celtic Church Speaks Today - World Fellowship Press, 1968
JONES, Sally
Legends of Devon - Bossiney Books, 1981
MACNAGHTEN, Angus
Windsor Ghosts and other Berkshire Hauntings - Published privately 1976
MAIS, S.P.B.
Glorious Devon - Great Western Railway Co., 1928
MAPLE, Eric
The Realm of Ghosts - Robert Hale, 1964
Supernatural England - Robert Hale, 1977
MEE, Arthur, (editor)
Derbyshire, The King's England - Hodder & Stoughton, 1937

Surrey, The King's England - Hodder & Stoughton, 1938
MERRILL, John N.
Legends of Derbyshire - Dalesman, 1972
METCALFE, Leon
Discovering Ghosts - Shire Publications, 1972
MITCHELL, John V.
Ghosts of an Ancient City - Cerialis Press, n.d.
O'DONNELL, Elliott
Family Ghosts and Ghostly Phenomena - Philip Allan. 1933
Haunted Britain - Rider, 1949
Haunted Churches - Quality Press, 1939
OXLEY, C.T.
The Haunted North Country - published privately, n.d.
PEARSON. Margaret M.
Bright Tapestry - Harrap, 1956
REEVE. F.A.
Cambridge - Batsford, 1964
SQUIERS, Granville
Secret Hiding Places - Stanley Paul, 1934
STEPHENSON, Tom. (editor)
Romantic Britain - Odhams, n.d.
SUTTON Harry T.
Ghosts Hunters - Batsford, 1978
THOMPSON, Francis
The Ghosts, Spirits and Spectres of Scotland - Impulse, 1973
UNDERWOOD, Peter
Gazetteer of British Ghosts - Souvenir Press, 1971
Gazetteer of Scottish & Irish Ghosts - Souvenir Press, 1973
Hauntings - Dent. 1977
Ghosts of the North West - Collins/Fontana, 1978
Ghosts of Wales - Christopher Davies, 1978
The Vampire's Bedside Companion - Leslie Frewin, 1975
Ghosts of Devon - Bossiney Books, 1982
Ghosts of Cornwall - Bossiney Books, 1983
Ghosts of Hampshire and the Isle of Wight - St Michael's Abbey Press, 1983
WILLIAMS, Michael
Supernatural in Cornwall - Bossiney Books, n.d.
WILSON, Colin
Poltergeist! - New English Library, 1981
WHITAKER, Terrence, W.

Lancashire's Ghosts and Legends - Robert Hale, 1980
Also Peter Ryan's *The National Trust and the National Trust for Scotland* - Dent, 1969, and numerous booklets and guides to individual houses and properties.

Printed in Poland
by Amazon Fulfillment
Poland Sp. z o.o., Wrocław